# The Two Horizons Old Testament Commentary

J. Gordon McConville and Craig Bartholomew, *General Editors*

Two features distinguish The Two Horizons Old Testament Commentary series: theological exegesis and theological reflection.

Exegesis since the Reformation era and especially in the past two hundred years emphasized careful attention to philology, grammar, syntax, and concerns of a historical nature. More recently, commentary has expanded to include social-scientific, political, or canonical questions and more.

Without slighting the significance of those sorts of questions, scholars in The Two Horizons Old Testament Commentary locate their primary interests on theological readings of texts, past and present. The result is a paragraph-by-paragraph engagement with the text that is deliberately theological in focus.

Theological reflection in The Two Horizons Old Testament Commentary takes many forms, including locating each Old Testament book in relation to the whole of Scripture—asking what the biblical book contributes to biblical theology—and in conversation with constructive theology of today. How commentators engage in the work of theological reflection will differ from book to book, depending on their particular theological tradition and how they perceive the work of biblical theology and theological hermeneutics. This heterogeneity derives as well from the relative infancy of the project of theological interpretation of Scripture in modern times and from the challenge of grappling with a book's message in Greco-Roman antiquity, in the canon of Scripture and history of interpretation, and for life in the admittedly diverse Western world at the beginning of the twenty-first century.

The Two Horizons Old Testament Commentary is written primarily for students, pastors, and other Christian leaders seeking to engage in theological interpretation of Scripture.

# Habakkuk

Heath A. Thomas

WILLIAM B. EERDMANS PUBLISHING COMPANY
GRAND RAPIDS, MICHIGAN

Wm. B. Eerdmans Publishing Co.
2140 Oak Industrial Drive N.E., Grand Rapids, Michigan 49505
www.eerdmans.com

ISBN 978-0-8028-6870-1

**Library of Congress Cataloging-in-Publication Data**

Names: Thomas, Heath, author.
Title: Habakkuk / Heath A. Thomas.
Description: Grand Rapids : Eerdmans Publishing Co., 2018. | Series: The two
    horizons Old Testament commentary | Includes bibliographical references
    and index.
Identifiers: LCCN 2018006911 | ISBN 9780802868701 (pbk. : alk. paper)
Subjects: LCSH: Bible. Habakkuk—Commentaries.
Classification: LCC BS1635.53 .T46 2018 | DDC 224/.95077—dc23
    LC record available at https://lccn.loc.gov/2018006911

*To Jill*

*We are ready to be amazed (Hab 1:5)*

# Contents

# Acknowledgments

I count it a distinct privilege to have been a traveling companion of Habakkuk during the past decade. At times its poetry and vision has carried me forward, stimulating and inspiring me. At other moments it has reduced me to tears. Whether in highs or lows, the book has evoked a deeper, richer faithfulness to God.

This experience with the book is a grace from God, no doubt. I must also recognize those that enabled and supported it. First I must express gratitude to Craig G. Bartholomew and J. Gordon McConville, who invited me to participate in this series. The vision of the Two Horizons series comes from them and I am grateful to have been a part. They have been extraordinarily kind and patient as I developed the manuscript. Their comments have made the work better. Any infelicities in the volume are due to my inadequacies and not theirs. Their scholarship and friendship generate the kind of community that inspires good work. I hope this volume qualifies as such. Thanks to the good people at Eerdmans, especially Andrew Knapp. The team has been exemplary. It is a joy to work with a publisher that supports this kind of endeavor. My doctoral students Justin Orr, Benji Davis, and Chris Hlavacek have heard about or helped with this project in one way or another, and I thank them. Colleagues and friends far and wide have helped me to work patiently through the text. Many are participants in the Scripture and Hermeneutics Seminar (which now convenes in association with the Institute of Biblical Research), but some are not: Chip Hardy, Matt Mullins, Dave Beldman, Matthew Emerson, Luke Wisley, A. J. Culp, Sandy Richter, Bruce Ashford, Danny Carroll, Mark Boda, Nigussie Denano, Federico Villanueva, Dennae and Vermon Pierre. Countless other conversations enriched my thoughts on Habakkuk. I pray that it comes through in the commentary.

Finally, my family has traveled with me on this road for a decade. I am so honored to walk with my wife and partner, Jill. As my closest friend, she challenges me to be a better human being. For that, and countless other reasons, I express joy and gratitude to her. And to my children, thank you for your love and support. I hope this work in some way inspires you to great things and greater faithfulness. After all, we are the same people five years from now that we are today . . . except for the books we read, the people we meet, and the places we go. Maybe this book could be a launching pad for what God desires in your life. I pray that it might be the case.

HEATH A. THOMAS
*Epiphany, 2018*

# Abbreviations

| | |
|---|---|
| AB | Anchor Bible |
| abs. | absolute |
| ACCS | Ancient Christian Commentary on Scripture |
| ACW | Ancient Christian Writers |
| ApOTC | Apollos Old Testament Commentary |
| ATD | Das Alte Testament Deutsch |
| BBB | Bonner biblische Beiträge |
| BBC | Blackwell Bible Commentaries |
| BBRS | Bulletin for Biblical Research Supplements |
| *BHQ* | *Biblia Hebraica Quinta*. Edited by Adrian Schenker et al. Stuttgart: Deutsche Bibelgesellschaft, 2004– |
| BHSCA | Broadman & Holman Studies in Christian Apologetics |
| b. Mak | Babylonian Talmud Makkot tractate |
| *BN* | *Biblische Notizen* |
| BWANT | Beiträge zur Wissenschaft vom Alten und Neuen Testament |
| BZAW | Beihefte zur Zeitschrift für die alttestamentliche Wissenschaft |
| CCCM | Corpus Christianorum Continuatio Mediaevalis |
| CCSL | Corpus Christianorum: Series Latina |
| CCTh | Challenges in Contemporary Theology |
| *CD* II.1 | Karl Barth. *Church Dogmatics: Volume 2: The Doctrine of God. Part 1, The Knowledge of God*. Translated by G. W. Bromiley and T. F. Torrance. London: T&T Clark, 1997 |
| *CD* III | Karl Barth. *Church Dogmatics: Volume 3: The Doctrine of Creation*. Translated by G. W. Bromiley and T. F. Torrance. London: T&T Clark, 1960 |
| COQG | Christian Origins and the Question of God |

| | |
|---|---|
| *COS* | *The Context of Scripture*. Edited by William W. Hallo. 3 vols. Leiden: Brill, 1997–2002 |
| CRINT | Compendia Rerum Iudaicarum ad Novum Testamentum |
| CSB | Christian Standard Bible |
| CSCO.S | Corpus scriptorum christianorum orientalium, Scriptores syri |
| *CurBS* | *Currents in Research: Biblical Studies* |
| DBWE | Dietrich Bonhoeffer Works English Edition |
| ed. | editor, edited by, edition |
| EJL | Early Judaism and Its Literature |
| esp. | especially |
| *ExAud* | *Ex Auditu* |
| FC | Fathers of The Church |
| fig. | figure |
| fol. | folio |
| FOTL | Forms of the Old Testament Literature |
| FRLANT | Forschungen zur Religion und Literatur des Alten und Neuen Testaments |
| *GTJ* | *Grace Theological Journal* |
| H | Hebrew |
| HBM | Hebrew Bible Monographs |
| HCOT | Historical Commentary on the Old Testament |
| HSM | Harvard Semitic Monographs |
| IBC | Interpretation: A Bible Commentary for Teaching and Preaching |
| impf. | imperfect |
| inf. | infinitive |
| ITC | International Theological Commentary |
| *JBL* | *Journal of Biblical Literature* |
| *JBQ* | *Jewish Bible Quarterly* |
| JBTh | Jahrbuch für biblische Theologie |
| JCC | Jewish Culture and Contexts |
| *JETS* | *Journal of the Evangelical Theological Society* |
| *JHS* | *Journal of Hebrew Scriptures* |
| *JOTT* | *Journal of Translation and Textlinguistics* |
| *JRHe* | *Journal of Religion and Health* |
| JSNTSup | Journal for the Study of the New Testament Supplement Series |
| *JSOT* | *Journal for the Study of the Old Testament* |
| JSOTSup | Journal for the Study of the Old Testament Supplement Series |
| *JTS* | *Journal of Theological Studies* |
| KAT | Kommentar zum Alten Testament |

| | |
|---|---|
| LCC | Library of Christian Classics |
| LHBOTS | Library of Hebrew Bible/Old Testament Studies |
| LXX | Septuagint |
| m/masc. | masculine |
| Midr. | Midrash |
| MLBS | Mercer Library of Biblical Studies |
| NICOT | New International Commentary on the Old Testament |
| NIVAC | New International Version Application Commentary |
| *NovT* | *Novum Testamentum* |
| *NPNF* | *A Select Library of Nicene and Post-Nicene Fathers of the Christian Church.* Edited by Philip Schaff and Henry Wace. 28 vols. in 2 series. 1886–1889 |
| NSBT | New Studies in Biblical Theology |
| OBO | Orbis Biblicus et Orientalis |
| OBS | Oxford Bible Series |
| OBT | Overtures to Biblical Theology |
| OTG | Old Testament Guides |
| OTL | Old Testament Library |
| p | plural |
| PBM | Paternoster Biblical Monographs |
| PG | Patrologia Graeca [= Patrologiae Cursus Completus: Series Graeca]. Edited by Jacques-Paul Migne. 162 volumes. Paris, 1857–1886 |
| PL | Patrologia Latina [= Patrologiae Cursus Completus: Series Latina]. Edited by Jacques-Paul Migne. 217 volumes. Paris, 1844–1864 |
| PNTCS | Pillar New Testament Commentary Series |
| PPS | Popular Patristics Series |
| s | singular |
| SCHT | Studies in the History of Christian Thought |
| sg. | singular |
| SHBC | Smyth & Helwys Bible Commentary |
| *SJOT* | *Scandinavian Journal of the Old Testament* |
| *SK* | *Skrif en Kerk* |
| SNTSMS | Society for New Testament Studies Monograph Series |
| SRTh | Studies in Reformed Theology |
| StBibLit | Studies in Biblical Literature |
| STI | Studies in Theological Interpretation |
| StOri | Studia Originalia |
| *STR* | *Southeastern Theological Review* |

| | |
|---|---|
| SubBi | Subsidia Biblica |
| suff. | suffix |
| SymS | Symposium Series |
| TBC | Torch Bible Commentaries |
| *TDOT* | *Theological Dictionary of the Old Testament*. Edited by G. Johannes Botterweck and Helmer Ringgren. Translated by John T. Willis et al. 15 vols. Grand Rapids: Eerdmans, 1974– |
| THOTC | Two Horizons Old Testament Commentary |
| trans. | translated by |
| *TSK* | *Theologische Studien und Kritiken* |
| TTCSST | T&T Clark Studies in Systematic Theology |
| *TynBul* | *Tyndale* Bulletin |
| vol. | volume |
| *VT* | *Vetus Testamentum* |
| VTSup | Supplements to Vetus Testamentum |
| *ZAW* | *Zeitschrift für die alttestamentliche Wissenschaft* |
| ZBK | Zürcher Bibelkommentare |

PART I

# INTRODUCTION AND COMMENTARY

# Introduction

The French philosopher Voltaire liked to make jokes about the prophet Habakkuk. With biting wit, Voltaire teased that the prophet "smelt too strongly of brimstone" to be tolerated by pious Protestants.[1] Evidently, it got so bad that he fabricated the events of Habakkuk's life in various lectures. While in Germany a scholar confronted the philosopher about the infelicities in his narrative about the prophet, all jokes aside. Voltaire defiantly refused to back down, retorting: "Sir, you do not know much about this Habakkuk. This rogue is capable of anything!"[2]

Why did Voltaire think Habakkuk more hellish than holy? What was the grudge? It is not entirely clear. Perhaps Voltaire did not like the fact that "this rogue" asked forceful questions that might be construed as faithless, especially in Hab 1:2–4. If this is the case, then Voltaire is not alone. Jewish and Christian interpreters throughout the history of the book's reception have held similar positions on Habakkuk, as will be revealed in this commentary. Whatever Voltaire's issue may have been, this commentary hopes to demonstrate the book that bears Habakkuk's name is theologically rich and extraordinarily pertinent in the way that it negotiates human suffering and the confusion that arises from it.

This volume reads the book of Habakkuk theologically. That statement may not help as much as one would hope, however, because a "theological" commentary can mean many things. Despite the range of perspectives on theo-

---

1. Bernard Shaw, *John Bull's Other Island and Major Barbara* (New York: Brentano's, 1911), xxxii.

2. The translation from the French is mine. The original reads: "Monsieur, vous ne connoissez guères ce Habacouc; ce coquin est capable de tout!" French quotation from Friedrich August Gottreu Tholuck, "On the Hypothesis of the Egyptian or Indian Origin of the Name Jehovah," *Biblical Repository* 4 (1834): 92–93 n. 3. Unless otherwise noted, all translations of ancient and modern languages, as well as biblical texts, are by the author.

logical commentaries, the goal here is to explore the book in such a way that it helps readers of Habakkuk hear God's address. The specifics of this approach are elucidated more fully in *A Manifesto for Theological Interpretation*.[3] As indicated in the *Manifesto*, this goal does not for one moment avoid academic rigor regarding philological, historical, sociological, or literary dimensions of Habakkuk, which have generally been set under the rubric of "biblical criticism." Nor does it mean that this is an ecclesial commentary that lies outside the purview of academic and critical exploration of Habakkuk. Rather, here biblical criticism is recalibrated within the larger aim of hearing God's address through the prophetic book.

Another way of saying this is that biblical criticism is not an end in and of itself in this theological commentary. With its emphasis on seeing the Scriptures against a historical canvas, biblical criticism is salutary, but alone it remains insufficient for theological interpretation. It is insufficient because it is an effort, for many today, to bracket out either the truth of what the Bible claims or to negate the possibility of divine agency within its field of study. Biblical criticism proceeds on purely naturalistic or humanistic grounds. Because the primary object and agent of Scripture is God and his agency in the world, biblical criticism alone cannot sustain theological interpretation. In a long but fertile quote, Murray Rae puts his finger on the inbuilt limitations of biblical criticism, traditionally defined. The principal reason for its limitation is

> that naturalistic approaches, whether ontological or methodological, preclude the historian from engaging with the subject matter of the Bible, which is precisely the engagement of God with his creation through the course of human history. The Bible tells of the divine economy. It makes no sense, therefore, to suppose that we can study the Bible well by setting aside the category of divine agency.[4]

Theological interpretation understands that the Scriptures testify about God, who has spoken to various peoples at various times in history through various peoples (prophets, apostles, etc.), a claim attested in Heb 1:1. But the word of God, spoken in the past, has been received and written for reception by later generations. In both the former revelation of God to people in history and the way that revelation has been inscribed in the word of God, Scripture is

---

3. Craig G. Bartholomew and Heath A. Thomas, eds., *A Manifesto for Theological Interpretation* (Grand Rapids: Baker Academic, 2016).

4. Murray Rae, "Theological Interpretation and Historical Criticism," in Bartholomew and Thomas, *Manifesto*, 100.

the record and canonical deposit of God's revelation.[5] The *record of revelation* is the reality that God has, in fact, spoken and worked with and through his people in the past and Scripture testifies to God's former speech and action. As it relates to the book of Habakkuk, God spoke to the prophet in the past, and the book of Habakkuk records that past revelation which apparently was for the prophet and his immediate audience. And yet Scripture is also the *deposit of revelation* as well. God's revelation of himself disseminates far and wide by the deposit of former revelation into written and canonical Scripture. Theologian Herman Bavinck describes the relationship between the record and deposit of revelation in this way:

> The written word differs from the spoken in these respects that it does not die upon the air but lives on; it is not, like oral traditions, subject to falsification; and that it is not limited in scope to the few people who hear it but is the kind of thing, rather, which can spread out to all peoples and to all lands. Writing makes permanent the spoken word, protects it against falsification, and disseminates it far and wide. . . . True, Scripture is to be distinguished from the revelation that precedes it, but it is not to be separated from that revelation. Scripture [as a "deposit" of revelation] is not a human, incidental, arbitrary, and defective supplement to [the record of] revelation but is itself a component part of revelation. In fact Scripture [as the deposit] is the rounding out and the fulfillment, the cornerstone and capstone of revelation.[6]

Bavinck's words above indicate the fundamental reality that God speaks, communicating himself to a needful humanity.

Attuning our reading to an attentive "listening for God's address" arises from the Christian affirmation of the Triune God. Scripture in its full testimony speaks to the redemption and comprehensive rule of Jesus, the only begotten of the Father. Transformation through reading the Scriptures occurs with the initiative of God the Father, through Christ, by the illumination of the Holy Spirit. It is the Father who offers the book of Habakkuk, from which he speaks and then leads us to the Son, whom we see and to whom we respond by the prompting of the Spirit. This movement of the Triune God toward a needful humanity is missional and rooted in God's eternal love.

---

5. So the language of Michael Goheen and Michael Williams in "Doctrine of Scripture and Theological Interpretation," in Bartholomew and Thomas, *Manifesto*, 53.

6. Herman Bavinck, *Our Reasonable Faith: A Survey of Christian Doctrine*, trans. Henry Zylstra (Grand Rapids: Eerdmans, 1956), 96.

Reading for transformation, then, is a Trinitarian movement into which we are drawn. As we read for transformation, the Lord ushers readers to a richer understanding and love of both God and the world. Such reading will be alert to (at least) four interweaving threads throughout the tapestry of this commentary:

1. *Attention to the historical, philological, literary, and theological context of Habakkuk enables one to hear God's address.* Yahweh, who is revealed as Israel's God and pictured as Israel's Father (Exod 4:22), provided the oracles of Habakkuk to his people in the past. Its historical context (language, background, social world, etc.) reveals Israel's God, his ways, his message, and his testimony that he wants to give to his people. Especially in Habakkuk, God's message is one of judgment and yet hope, which his people may embrace in faith. Neglecting the discrete witness that God has given to the prophet and his people leads to a denial of the Father's work with Israel and the importance of his word. It also neglects the context in which we understand God, his ways, his world, and his purpose with creation. Without the context, our understanding of the culmination of God's work in Christ suffers. Second, Scripture is written with literary beauty and artistic verve. Attending to the literary components of the text is vital to understanding its meaning. Its literary quality exhibits its placement within the culture of Israel and the ancient Near East. Habakkuk as a cultural phenomenon from the ancient world needs to be understood in all its particularity. Essential to this particularity is the linguistic context from which the prophetic book emerges. As such, attending to philological questions, grammar, syntax, and comparative Semitics opens up Habakkuk meaningfully.

2. *The historical contexts of Habakkuk fit within the dramatic narrative of Scripture.* The Old Testament repeats the events it describes with Israel over and again, and we see this iteration as a wrestling on the part of Israel in their relationship with God. The classic example is the exodus experience, including Egyptian slavery, plagues, deliverance, the miraculous crossing of the sea, worship at Sinai, and provision in the wilderness. This overarching narrative echoes throughout the Old Testament, as Cornelius Houtman has shown in his multivolume commentary and Brent Strawn confirms.[7] Only a brief survey of texts reveals its pertinence in the corpus: in the second generation of Joshua and Caleb in the entrance and conquest of Palestine (Josh 1–12), in the Elijah

---

7. Cornelius Houtman, *Exodus*, 4 vols., HCOT (Leuven: Peeters, 1993–2002); Brent A. Strawn, "With a Strong Hand and an Outstretched Arm: On the Meaning(s) of the Exodus Tradition(s)," in *Iconographic Exegesis of the Hebrew Bible/Old Testament: An Introduction to Its Method and Practice*, ed. Izaak J. de Hulster, Brent A. Strawn, and Ryan P. Bonfiglio (Göttingen: Vandenhoeck & Ruprecht, 2015), 103–16.

narrative at Sinai (see esp. 1 Kgs 18), in the exile and wilderness imagery of Isa 40–55, and in the recitals of the Psalter (Pss 18; 29; 77; 78; 105), among other texts. Exodus tradition is drawn upon in Hab 1 and especially Hab 3. Yet for all its diverse reception and repetition in the Old Testament, the moments of Israel's history enfold within God's larger purposes of redemption of the entire world as testified by the Old Testament *en toto*. God's destiny for Zion as the picture of a broken and battered city, yet ultimately the picture of new heavens and new earth, is a classic example from the book of Isaiah, and a similar picture emerges for Zion in the Minor Prophets. God's activities with Israel in historical moments are not divorced from one another nor are they divorced from God's plan of redemption. Rather, each historical moment is related to God's redemption, and ultimately his redemption that comes in Jesus Christ the Son.

The Scriptures, then, disclose Christ. But this disclosure is not monochromatic. The Old Testament provides the context by which to understand Christ in his fullness: he is the Davidic messiah and suffering servant; he is the firstborn of creation; he is the fulfillment of Israel's story; he is the prophet, priest, judge, and king; he is the second Adam; he is the second Moses; he is the faithful Israelite; he is the Son of God.

So, the Old Testament provides the matrix out of which the Scriptures disclose the fullness of Jesus. From it we understand Christ's identity and mission. By it we come to understand God, the world, and Christ.[8] Trinitarian Christian faith accepts Christ as the clue that leads us to fully understand God's work that brings the discrete historical moments of Israel together in God's economy. As we look to Christ, we see the goal of Israel's history, indeed, the whole of creation's history. Practically, this means that Habakkuk's message and historical moment must be integrated into the full biblical story so that we hear it aright. This is attending to the *deposit* of the scriptural revelation of God.

3. *Attending to God's address means gaining information that leads to transformation.* Theological reading assesses information about the text such as history, context, social location, theological outlooks, and so on. But for theological reading, these bits of information are instrumental toward the transformation of the reader in a spiritual dynamic: to be *captured* by the word. "No one can stand before the Word as a spectator."[9] Theological reading opens the interpreter to participate in the drama of Scripture, to find oneself in its story, to

8. Francis Watson, *Text and Truth: Redefining Biblical Theology* (Grand Rapids: Eerdmans, 1997), 184–85.

9. Mariano Magrassi, *Praying the Bible: An Introduction to Lectio Divina* (Collegeville, MN: Liturgical Press, 1998), 31.

discover one's place in God's economy established therein. Theological interpretation is the kind of reading that opens the reader to Scripture's transformative potential. Interpreters are drawn into Scripture to hear God's word of rebuke, correction, instruction, and change. Theological readers are drawn to Scripture to be transformed into the image of Christ. This is not an informational process alone, but rather a transformational process, a true metamorphosis into a new creation in Jesus.

4. *The Spirit of God illumines hearts and minds so that readers can be transformed by the reading of Habakkuk.* The theological reading envisioned here is Trinitarian and therefore "spiritual." This does not mean "mystical" in the sense that the Holy Spirit gives secret or "gnostic" knowledge apart from either the record or deposit of divine revelation. Rather, by spiritual I mean that the Spirit gives readers the eyes to see both the historical context of Habakkuk and the connections of this book within the economy of God's salvation in Christ, so that readers are transformed into Jesus's disciples. Not all will see or embrace connections or the notion of reading for discipleship because such practice requires spiritual vision. It is entirely possible to gain access to the historical context and linguistic understanding of Habakkuk's time and book, and that is good. But this is but one step toward becoming a fully formed reader of Habakkuk and of Scripture. It is one's responsibility and great joy to be open to the Spirit's work, so that Christ is formed in the receptive reader. Christian reading is, then, a work of the Spirit that attunes our eyes and ears to the work of God in Christ, his church, for the sake of the world. Of course, this is what it means to be spiritually formed, as Augustine knew. This form of spiritual reading complements Augustine's interpretative virtue of charity: reading Scripture for a deeper love for God and neighbor, which should be extended outward to a proper love for God's created world.[10]

These interweaving features are part and parcel of a robust theological interpretation of Scripture.[11] Such an interpretative approach helps us hear what the text of Habakkuk says in its immediate horizons and extended horizons in the canon of Scripture. To help us hear God's address well, this commentary will draw on the canon of Scripture as well as the insights of Christian thinkers and theologians, past and present.

---

10. Saint Augustine, *On Christian Teaching*, trans. R. P. H. Green (Oxford: Oxford University Press, 1999), 17–35.

11. For a fuller exposition of theological interpretation, see Bartholomew and Thomas, *Manifesto*, esp. 197–217, 237–56.

## Hearing Habakkuk

### *God and Faithfulness amid Pain*

Habakkuk presents a robust vision of God and faithfulness, especially amid human prayer and pain. Early Christian reception of the book of Habakkuk understood the book as a source of hope and inspiration for faithfulness to God *in the light of* the faithfulness of God, as Theodoret of Cyrus finds in his notes on Hab 2:4. In his commentary on Habakkuk, Theodoret rightly reckons that God speaks in the verse, and he uses first-person singular personal pronouns to identify God's voice. The "me" and "my" in the quotation below is how Theodoret envisioned God's voice in Hab 2:4: "the victim of a wavering attitude to the promises made by me is unworthy of my care, whereas the one who believes in what is said by me and lives a life in keeping with that faith will reap the fruit of life."[12] Faithfulness to God's revelation, to the promises that he has made to his people, is the indicator of true faith. From this quotation in his reading of Habakkuk, Theodoret believes that true faith is refined in fires of challenge and deep struggle.

Theodoret's insight proves correct. Indeed, Habakkuk serves as a resource for a robust spirituality in the face of pain. The book's relevance stems from its central focus—justice, faith, and God's salvation—and how these relate in the real world. These indeed are large issues that face the people of God from whatever generation. But for the book of Habakkuk, imminent punishment of God's people loomed dark on the horizon. God's people would suffer violence at the hands of the idolatrous Neo-Babylonian Empire. In the book's poems, the prophet confronts God over a shocking discovery: that this very idolatrous nation will thrive, while God's people will flag and die under its greedy policies. Why would God allow this to happen? How could God's people relate to him in the face of this horror? How could they possibly survive? A brooding theological question emerged as well: How could God's people affirm him to be just, considering this disaster? These are the questions the book engages.

Habakkuk reveals that while violence and oppression *may* occur in his world, nonetheless violence and oppression are not ultimate in God's good design for his creation. The book refuses to ignore the problems associated with Babylon's ascendancy and Israel's subjugation. It does not gloss over the challenges of evil in the world and the justice of God with a naive piety that idealistically affirms, "No worries. All shall be well in the end because the sov-

---

12. Theodoret of Cyrus, *Commentaries on the Prophets*, trans. and introduction by Robert Charles Hill, Commentary on the Prophets 3 (Brookline, MA: Holy Cross Orthodox Press, 2006), 197.

ereign God is in control." Nor does the book simply suggest that sinful humans (even God's people) get what they deserve because of their wickedness. Even if the poetry acknowledges this latter point, still the prophet interrogates God with focused appeals: "How long?" and "Why?" (Hab 1:2, 3, 13). These are not idle questions but textual clues that expose the prophet's deep and abiding faith.

But what can be called "faith" in Habakkuk? Some tend to view the book as a traverse from doubt to faith, especially in the popular imagination. In this way of seeing the book, Habakkuk traverses from *fear* (Hab 1:2–2:3) to *faith* (Hab 2:4–3:19) and it teaches that *faith* overcomes *fear*. True spirituality learns that doubt/complaint must be overcome by faith/praise. More will be said on this point throughout the commentary, but I will simply note here that this conception of spirituality, of faith, can be skewed in profoundly unhelpful ways. It is more faithful to the poetry of Habakkuk to see that the prophet's speech is *faithfull* throughout the book. Most commentaries on the book in the early church believed this as well. Jerome was an exception, however, and a significant one.

Jerome thought the complaints of Habakkuk, though honest, were too brash to be faithful. He writes: "For no one has dared with so bold a voice to challenge God to debate about justice and say to him: Why is such great iniquity involved in the realities of human affairs and in the [administration] of the world?"[13] He goes on to say that Habakkuk has a "rash voice" which belongs "in a certain way to one who is blaspheming."[14] Jerome thinks the prophet speaks this way because he is in anguish and has forgotten that "gold is refined by fire."[15] Facing hardship and pain, embracing it, represents a faithful move for Jerome.

While Jerome's comments are understandable, I argue that the complaints of chapter 1 are no less faith-filled than other bits in the book, especially the central affirmation of Hab 3:17–19. However, the complaints of chapter 1 present faith of a different order. As complaints, they anticipate God's salvation in the face of hardship and an unknown future, while expecting that his divine care and justice will be made present in the real world. Praise, as we have in Hab 3:17–19, reflects upon God's salvation, thanks him for divine intervention, and reaffirms his justice and divine care for the future. So, a view that regards Habakkuk as a simple traverse from faith-less doubt to faith-full praise neglects the reality that the questioning bits in the book still reveal a faith-filled spirituality. The praise evinced in the third chapter is not so much faith *overcoming* doubt but rather faith *recognizing* the power and work of God and rejoicing in him for it.

---

13. Jerome, *Commentaries on the Twelve Prophets: Volume 1*, ed. Thomas P. Scheck, Ancient Christian Texts (Downers Grove, IL: InterVarsity Press, 2016), 185.

14. Jerome, *Commentaries on the Twelve Prophets*, 186.

15. Jerome, *Commentaries on the Twelve Prophets*, 186.

Indeed, the questions that Habakkuk raises reveal his deep dependence on God. Many times, when faced with the trials of life, the temptation is to set the world to rights by our own power and sense of justice. Hamlet's words become the picture of such human striving:

> The time is out of joint—O cursèd spite,
> That ever I was born to set it right! (*Hamlet*, act 1, scene 5, lines 197–198)[16]

Hamlet's *egocentrism* represents the antithesis of Habakkuk's *theocentrism*. The prophet understands his humanity: he was not born to heal the brokenness of his day! Only Israel's God can do such grand things. He sets the onus upon God to reorder the world in his divine order. Is time "out of joint"? Then, it is to God he (and we!) must go, for he, and he alone, can put the world to rights.

In this way, Habakkuk exposes how faith shapes human response to God in the travails of life. This process of shaping represents a deep form of spiritual formation that cannot be taught only through praise. *Such deep spiritual formation must be lived, and borne, in and through suffering.* This will become clearer as we move through this commentary in detail.

But before delving into the text of Habakkuk, we turn to several issues that impinge upon reading this book. The first is hermeneutical and revolves around the relationship between the life of the prophet and the book that bears his name. Other questions include how this book fits within the Twelve and how it fits within Christian Scripture.

### Habakkuk the Priest?

Very little is known about the prophet or the specific details of his life. In contrast to other prophets like Isaiah, Ezekiel, Jeremiah, or other prophets in the Minor Prophets, our prophet simply is known by his name as opposed to superscriptions or descriptions of his ministry. The apocryphal Bel and the Dragon (ca. 150–50 BCE) identifies Habakkuk as "the son of Jesus, of the tribe of Levi" (Bel 1:1), which is of course a priestly tribe. This would indicate that he was a priest. In this apocryphal tale, Habakkuk brings food to Daniel in the lions' den. The pseudepigraphal Lives of the Prophets (ca. first century CE) retells the story of Bel and the Dragon but describes Habakkuk as an exile in the tribe of Simeon rather than a Levite. The midrashic historical work Seder 'Olam (perhaps a second century CE

---

16. William Shakespeare, "Hamlet, Prince of Denmark," in *The Complete Works of Shakespeare*, ed. David Bevington, 4th ed. (New York: HarperCollins, 1992).

work, but the first versions in print appear in the fifteenth century CE) perceives the prophet to operate in the reign of Manasseh.[17] The medieval Kabbalistic text Sefer ha-Zohar (ca. 1300 CE) presents Habakkuk as the son of the Shunammite woman raised by Elisha in 2 Kgs 4:16 (Zohar 1:7; 2:44–45), likely due to the similarities between the word "embrace" there and Habakkuk's name in Hab 1:1.[18] Each of these traditions, however, bears no parallel in the remainder of the Old Testament. So this information does little to illumine the life of the prophet.

Another way to ascertain something about the life of the prophet is to scrutinize his name. After all, names of Old Testament prophets sometimes are related to their messages, like Elijah ("Yah is my God"), Samuel ("God hears"), or Isaiah ("Yah saves"). Each of their names has something to do with their prophetic ministry. This is not the case with Habakkuk. His name may be related to the Hebrew word for "embrace" (e.g., Job 24:8; 2 Kgs 4:16), as indicated above. Or it may derive from an Akkadian loanword referencing a kind of garden plant.[19] Neither hypothesis is convincing. It is best to remain ambivalent about the meaning of Habakkuk's name, as it carries neither interpretative significance for the book nor a clue to the life and ministry of the prophet.

To determine the prophet's historical profile, scholars in the past century associated Habakkuk with the cult in Jerusalem, primarily based on internal evidence in the book.[20] Significant among this internal evidence is:

a. The psalmic language of Hab 3:1, "A Prayer of Habakkuk the Prophet, according to the Shigionoth" (cf. Ps 7:1), which may indicate cultic and liturgical use.

b. Likewise, the "watchtower" and "watchpost" of Hab 2:1 may be *termini technici* for cultic prophecy (cf. Neh 13:30; 2 Chr 7:6; 8:14; 35:2).

c. John Sawyer argues that the structure of lament + oracle (Hab 1:2–11) belongs to temple ritual and indicates as well that Habakkuk was a cultic prophet.[21]

17. Chaim Milikowsky, "Seder Olam," in *The Literature of the Sages: Second Part*, ed. S. Safrai et .al., CRINT 3b (Assen: Van Gorcum, 2006), 231–37.

18. Marvin Sweeney, *The Twelve Prophets*, Berit Olam (Collegeville, MN: Liturgical Press, 2000), 2:454; F. F. Bruce, "Habakkuk," in *The Minor Prophets: An Exegetical and Expository Commentary*, ed. Thomas E. McComiskey (Grand Rapids: Baker, 1993), 2:831.

19. James Bruckner takes the former view (*Jonah, Nahum, Habakkuk, Zephaniah*, NIVAC [Grand Rapids: Zondervan, 2004], 199) while J. J. M. Roberts adopts the latter view: *Nahum, Habakkuk, and Zephaniah*, OTL (Louisville: Westminster John Knox, 1991), 86.

20. For the classic formulation of the role of the cultic prophet, see Aubrey R. Johnson, *The Cultic Prophet in Ancient Israel* (Cardiff: University of Wales Press, 1962).

21. John F. A. Sawyer, *Prophecy and Prophets of the Old Testament*, OBS (Oxford: Oxford University Press, 1987), 119. He is speaking of the supposed oracle of hearing that is given by the

Additionally, tradition is brought to bear on the cultic profile of the prophet. The Jewish tradition of Habakkuk being a Levite (as evidenced in Bel and the Dragon) further links the prophet with the cult. It is supposed that Habakkuk was a professional prophet in the service of the temple as opposed to a country prophet like Amos (e.g., Amos 7:14). Donald Gowan follows Sigmund Mowinckel and John Eaton, arguing that because the prophet belongs to the temple cult in Jerusalem, by extension, his book is in some way part of cultic liturgy for God's people there.[22] Perhaps Habakkuk did offer guidance to those coming to the temple with specific life-questions particularly dealing with theodicy, and perhaps he wrote liturgical compositions to deal with these questions (like the book that bears his name). On this view, the cultic flavor of the book addresses theodicy and provides a way forward with God.

Although plausible, these internal and traditional associations are not as firm as one might wish. Wilhelm Rudolph and Peter Jöcken reject the cultic connection completely, while Lothar Perlitt is right to remain cautious about ascribing a specific role to Habakkuk beyond prophet even if cultic language resonates in his prophecy.[23] Francis Andersen is surely correct to note that one employs circular logic to argue for Habakkuk's supposed cultic-prophetic office as informing the supposed cultic-liturgical purpose of the book.[24] Finally, it must be borne in mind that if the prophet and his book originated or was employed in a cultic or liturgical setting, it is suggestive that these originating marks have been obscured to a degree in the book. Unlike the picturesque association between Isaiah or Ezekiel and the cultus, Habakkuk's association remains oblique at best in the final form of the book.

Further distancing Habakkuk from his originating life-setting, his book has been recontextualized within the edited and arranged collection of the Book of the Twelve, also known as the Minor Prophets. This larger literary setting hermeneutically reframes originating settings (liturgical or otherwise), and

---

cultic prophet after a lament or complaint has been uttered, originally advocated by Joachim Begrich, "Das priesterliche Heilsorakel," *ZAW* 52 (1934): 81–92.

22. Donald E. Gowan, *The Triumph of Faith in Habakkuk* (Atlanta: John Knox, 1976), 14–17; Sigmund Mowinckel, *The Psalms in Israel's Worship*, trans. D. R. Ap-Thomas (Nashville: Abingdon, 1962), 2:93, 147; John Eaton, *Obadiah, Nahum, Habakkuk, and Zephaniah*, TBC (London: SCM, 1961), 81–84.

23. Wilhelm Rudolph, *Micah, Nahum, Habakuk, Zephanja*, KAT 13/3 (Gütersloh: Mohn, 1975); Peter Jöcken, *Das Buch Habakuk: Darstellung der Geschichte seiner kritischen Erforschung mit einer eigenen Beurteilung*, BBB 48 (Bonn: Hanstein, 1977); Lothar Perlitt, *Die Propheten Nahum, Habakuk, Zephanja*, ATD 25/1 (Göttingen: Vandenhoeck & Ruprecht, 2004), 41.

24. Francis I. Andersen, *Habakkuk*, AB 25 (New York: Doubleday, 2001), 19.

shapes the message(s) of the book within the broader context of the meaning of the Minor Prophets.[25] We will explore this further, below.

Whether heard on its own or within the Twelve, the book of Habakkuk is not designed to provide a biography of the prophet and his times per se but rather to proclaim the message of the Lord. This does not mean either the background or specific vocation of the prophet remains unimportant. Rather Habakkuk serves as a distinctive character in each of the three poems, and as such plays a distinctive role in the construction of the book's theological message.[26] Whatever information garnered about his real-life vocation and his historical era is useful to help rightly configure him within the book; this will be explored below. Just as the sun illuminates a stained glass window to reveal the message crafted therein, the life of the prophet is a window through which shines the message of the Lord, inscribed in the book that bears the prophet's name. In this way both the prophet *and* his book disclose the message of God's dealings with the world. The prophet's engagement with the divine throughout the book provides the framework through which one grasps the book's overall message or kerygma.

### A Prophetic Book

Our last statement draws us to reflect upon the *book* of Habakkuk. How one understands the book that bears the prophet's name is influenced to a degree by prior commitments in terms of its possible growth and literary unity. Literary approaches to the book generally read it with integrity, with a good number of commentators viewing the book as maximally deriving from the prophet Habakkuk and viewing the message(s) of the book from the perspective of the coherent whole.[27] Richard Patterson, for instance, argues for a coherent literary structure for Habakkuk that displays a coherent argument that derives from the prophet of the seventh century BCE.[28] Likewise, Michael Thompson recognizes

---

25. Heath A. Thomas, "Hearing the Minor Prophets: The Book of the Twelve and God's Address," in *Hearing the Old Testament: Listening for God's Address*, ed. Craig G. Bartholomew and David H. Beldman (Grand Rapids: Eerdmans, 2012), 356–79; Francis Watson, *Paul and the Hermeneutics of Faith* (London: T&T Clark, 2004), 78–163.

26. Sweeney rightly notes his importance as the major character identified in Hab 1:1 and 3:1. His role as a distinctive figure in these verses helps to structure the book. Marvin Sweeney, "Structure, Genre, and Intent in the Book of Habakkuk," *VT* 41 (1991): 63–83.

27. Otto Eissfeldt, *The Old Testament: An Introduction*, trans. Peter Ackroyd (San Francisco: Harper & Row, 1965), 420; O. Palmer Robertson, *The Books of Nahum, Habakkuk, and Zephaniah*, NICOT (Grand Rapids: Eerdmans, 1990), 29–40.

28. Richard Patterson, "A Literary Look at Nahum, Habakkuk, and Zephaniah," *GTJ* 11

the formal diversity within the book (laments, woe oracles, theophany, etc.) but argues these are brought together by one author (the prophet Habakkuk) intentionally and creatively to highlight theodicy.[29] Loren Bliese assesses the poetics of Habakkuk and discovers a unified book with a macrostructure of three tightly constructed poems that contain seven minipoems within each of them.[30] As Patterson and Thompson imply, however, literary approaches do not deny the possibility that distinctive sections of the book may derive from different periods of the prophet's life, but this concession does not then eventuate viewing the book as a random "ragbag" of unintelligibly arranged material.[31]

When it is thought that the book displays unevenness, growth, and development, historical methods naturally come into play to sort out the material and arrange it chronologically to get a better understanding of why the book is the way that it is. The impulse derives in part from unevenness present in the book. A rather abrupt change of perspective occurs between 1:2–4 and 1:5–11, signified by a shift from singular to plural forms. This shift causes one to consider that these sections address two different groups. It has been thought that vv. 5–11 are an intrusion to the order of vv. 2–4 and 12–17, so that vv. 5–11 belong to a different period than the other verses, which are of a piece. It is most common to understand the first two chapters as deriving from Habakkuk the prophet in the latter third of the seventh century BCE, while the third chapter represents a later addition from another hand (or other hands) that serves to reinterpret the earlier chapters. This view primarily arises out of form-critical considerations. Theodore Hiebert, however, reverses this line of thought, arguing that the third chapter is earlier than the other two chapters, even if it was incorporated later.[32]

Others assessed the growth of the book on the basis of redaction criticism. James D. Nogalski argues that the book of Habakkuk is a composite collection that was added (with Nahum) to an earlier version of the Minor Prophets. The reason for this Persian addition is to remind God's people that their Lord is in

---

(1991): 17–27. Patterson argues that the coherent arrangement argues for a unitary author (the prophet Habakkuk).

29. Michael E. W. Thompson, "Prayer, Oracle, and Theophany: The Book of Habakkuk,'" *TynBul* 44 (1993): 33–53.

30. Loren F. Bliese, "The Poetics of Habakkuk," *JOTT* 12 (1999): 47–75. Bliese overdevelops the evidence, in my estimation.

31. So the language of Robert P. Carroll describing the assemblage of the diverse literary elements in Habakkuk, "Habakkuk," in *A Dictionary of Biblical Interpretation,* ed. R. J. Coggins and J. L. Houlden (London: SCM, 1990), 269. Thompson cites this view and argues against it in his "Prayer, Oracle, and Theophany."

32. Theodore Hiebert, *God of My Victory: The Ancient Hymn in Habakkuk 3,* HSM 38 (Atlanta: Scholars Press, 1986), 129–50.

control even if it seems as though the Assyrians or the Babylonians (or the Persians!) have ultimate authority over them.[33] Klaus Seybold suggests the earliest prophetic strata in the book is found in Hab 1:1, 5–11, 14–17; 2:1–3, 5–19 and that a later hand added to this hymnic elements (Hab 3:1, 3–7, 15, 8–13a). Finally, he thinks another hand in the postexilic era added a lamentation that brings the book together (Hab 1:2–4, 12–13; 2:4, 20; 3:13b, 14, 17–19a).[34] Theodore Lescow recognizes a three-step process of redaction as well, but nonetheless views Hab 2:1–4 as part of the earliest strata rather than the latest, among other differences.[35] Recently, David Cleaver-Bartholomew argued that Hab 1:5–11 constitutes part of the original oracle by God depicting judgment against Judah's sin. His instrument of judgment is Babylon (Hab 1:7). Once Babylon is unleashed against Judah, however, the prophet then complains to God, asking how long this wicked nation will oppress Judah (1:2–4, 12–17). God's response is in Hab 2.[36]

Compare Cleaver-Bartholomew's argument with that of Walter Dietrich, who sees a more complex redactional development. He thinks that the original composition of Habakkuk included Hab 1:2–4, dated to the time of waning Assyrian power in the seventh century BCE. The next addition was Hab 1:5–8, which was an affirmation that God would judge the wicked Judahites at the hand of the Babylonians (again in the closing days of Assyrian power). This judgment did not occur in a timely fashion, however, leading to the response of Hab 1:12. God eventually raised up the Babylonians to judge Judah, effectively ushering in the exilic period for Judahites (ca. 586–515 BCE). During this time, the composition of Habakkuk undergoes another redaction, wherein the pro-Babylonian perspective of Hab 1:5–8 is changed to an anti-Babylonian tone in Hab 1:9–11, 2:5–19. And then finally, during the middle- to late-Persian period, Habakkuk undergoes its final editorial process in which the psalm of Hab 3 was added (along with the hymn of Nah 1:2–8). So, by the fourth century (ca. 550–330 BCE) Habakkuk has reached its final form.[37] Other scholars offer different redactional reconstructions for the development of Habakkuk as well.

33. James D. Nogalski, *The Book of the Twelve: Micah–Malachi*, SHBC (Macon, GA: Smyth & Helwys, 2011), 645–56.

34. Klaus Seybold, *Nahum Habakuk Zephanja*, ZBK 24/2 (Zurich: TVZ, 1991), 44–45.

35. Theodore Lescow, "Die Komposition der Bucher Nahum und Habakkuk," *BN* 77 (1995): 74–85.

36. David Cleaver-Bartholomew, "An Alternative Approach to Hab 1,2–2,20," *SJOT* 17 (2003): 206–25.

37. Walter Dietrich, "Three Minor Prophets and the Major Empires: Synchronic and Diachronic Perspectives on Nahum, Habakkuk, and Zephaniah," in *Perspectives on the Formation of the Book of the Twelve: Methodological Foundations—Redactional Processes—Historical Insights*, ed. Ranier Albertz, James D. Nogalski, and Jakob Wohrle, BZAW 433 (Berlin: de Gruyter, 2012), 147–57, esp. 150–55.

The radical divergence on the meaning, growth, and development of the book is enough to note the degree of difficulty that comes with such reconstructions! While recognizing the potential of historical analysis on the book, this commentary flags the limits to its achievement. It is appropriate to say the book did not stem from one historical moment but rather developed into its final form, but it is excessive for this commentary to become atomistic about the nature of this development. For example, Hab 3 may be an earlier composition that has been arranged to fit into the book that bears the prophet's name. Although disparate historical and literary material exists in the book, nonetheless with Roberts, it is reasonable to posit a unified composed corpus with a coherent message.[38] I shall emphasize how dialogic progression between the prophet and God, repetition of language, and thematic correspondence draw the book together to present God's address.

### The Structure of the Book of Habakkuk

In its final form, the book is a corporate unity composed of two major literary parts. The first is the "oracle" introduced in Hab 1:1 and the second is the "prayer" of Habakkuk in Hab 3:1. These two components are identifiable by the superscriptions. If the superscriptions are a means of accessing the macrostructure of the book, then the rest of the material comes more clearly into view.[39] On closer inspection, the book divides as follows:

> Oracle (Hab 1:1)
>> First Complaint (Hab 1:2–4)
>> First Divine Response (Hab 1:5–11)
>> Second Complaint (Hab 1:12–17; 2:1)
>> Second Divine Response (Hab 2:2–20)
> Prayer (Hab 3:1)
>> Programmatic Introduction (Hab 3:2)
>> The Divine March to Egypt (Hab 3:3–15)
>> The Prophet's Response (Hab 3:16–19)

38. Roberts, *Nahum, Habakkuk, and Zephaniah*, 82–85.

39. Michael H. Floyd divides the book into three rather than two parts, largely on the view that Hab 2:1–20 comprises a report of an oracular enquiry. This section, then, is form-critically distinctive from the other bits of the book and so comprises the second section; *Minor Prophets: Part 2*, FOTL 22 (Grand Rapids: Eerdmans, 2000), 81–86. The linguistic interaction as well as lack of superscription, however, lead to the conclusion that whatever its form-critical distinctiveness, 2:1–20 has nonetheless been incorporated within an "oracle" that begins with 1:1. This is then merged with the poem of Hab 3, eventuating into a bipartite structure for the book.

A couple of points arise from this structure. First, the complaint/response interaction between God and the prophet becomes evident. It is too much to argue that God answers the prophet's questions sufficiently one-by-one. But there is clear interaction at the level of theme, subject matter, and repetition of language. This reinforces the notion that the speeches of God and the prophet are related in a sequential manner. Second, I hold that Hab 2:1 belongs with the second complaint to which God responds in vv. 2–20. This somewhat unique view will be defended in the commentary, below.[40] Further, Hab 2:2–20 should not be subdivided into God's response (vv. 2–5) and prophetic woes (vv. 6–20), as some have argued.[41] Although the prophetic woe-form predominates these latter verses, these statements of judgment do not derive from another speaker or present a clear change in perspective. Therefore, the woe oracles are best understood as part of God's second response to Habakkuk's complaint.[42] The verses fit within the general oracle identified in Hab 1:1.

From the structure, it also becomes apparent that the prayer of Hab 3 functions well within the book of Habakkuk and secondarily within the larger testimony of the Minor Prophets. It is common today for redaction critics to identify Hab 3 and Nah 1 as a layer, added by scribes at some point (possibly the Persian period in Judah), that draws together Nahum and Habakkuk's teaching of God's justice against enemy nations (Assyria and Babylonia, respectively) to comfort those experiencing oppression under foreign power.[43]

A danger of such macrolevel redactional reconstructions lies in their inability to understand or communicate the function of Hab 3 within the book of Habakkuk. I take a book-internal approach and focus in the commentary, and argue that Hab 3 is a skillful addition that theologically reinforces the teaching of the previous oracle in Hab 1–2 and advances the lines of thought from them. Secondarily, the kerygma of Hab 3 functions within the testimony of Nahum-Habakkuk in the Minor Prophets.

---

40. This approach to Hab 2:1 is also similar to that of Cleaver-Bartholomew, "Alternative Approach," 206–25.

41. For a view that adopts the older scholarly consensus, see Brevard S. Childs, *Introduction to the Old Testament as Scripture* (Philadelphia: Fortress, 1979), 448.

42. Sweeney argues for Yahweh as the speaker in these verses as well: "Structure," 66–67.

43. See, e.g., Rainer Kessler, "Nahum-Habakuk als Zweiprophetenschrift: Eine Skizze," in *Gotteserdung: Beitrage zur Hermeneutik und Exegese der Hebraischen Bibel*, ed. Rainer Kessler, BWANT 170 (Stuttgart: Kohlhammer, 2006), 137–45; Dietrich, "Three Minor Prophets," 147–56.

### Habakkuk within the Minor Prophets

The above discussion of redactional processes within Nahum-Habakkuk draws us to recent research on Habakkuk within the Minor Prophets. Considering studies on the shaping of the Old Testament into distinctive corpora (whether the Pentateuch, Joshua–Kings, or prophetic books)—often identified as "canonical" concerns—it is appropriate to ask whether a modern commentary is remiss to avoid the broader canonical question of how Habakkuk exists as a book within a book of the Minor Prophets, often called the Book of the Twelve. From a variety of critical fronts, whether through historical and redactional, literary and thematic, or canonical approaches, scholars argue that the Twelve Minor Prophets have been intentionally arranged as a composite book and that Habakkuk plays a part in the larger framework of this book called the Book of the Twelve.[44]

An impressive amount of scholarly research advances the view that the Twelve may be coherently read together with Habakkuk fitting into its corporate testimony. Nogalski marshals three pieces of data: (1) chronological arrangement of the Minor Prophets, (2) Priority of Masoretic (Hebrew) sequencing over and above the Old Greek sequencing of the Twelve, and (3) the transmission of two preexisting corpora in the Twelve: the "book of the four" (Hosea-Amos-Micah-Zephaniah) and the corpus from Haggai to Zechariah 1–8.[45] The unified corpus of the Twelve presents (1) God's continuing work with his people

---

44. For the historical and redactional approach, see, e.g., James D. Nogalski, *Literary Precursors to the Book of the Twelve*, BZAW 217 (Berlin: de Gruyter, 1993); Nogalski, *Redactional Processes in the Book of the Twelve*, BZAW 218 (Berlin: de Gruyter, 1993); Aaron Schart, *Die Entstehung des Zwölfprophetenbuchs: Neubearbeitungen von Amos im Rahmen schriftenübergreifender Redaktionsprozesse*, BZAW 260 (Berlin: de Gruyter, 1998); Martin Beck, *Der "Tag YHWHs" im Dodekapropheton: Studien im Spannungsfeld von Traditions- und Redaktionsgeschichte*, BZAW 356 (Berlin: de Gruyter, 2005); Albertz, Nogalski, and Wohrle, *Perspectives on the Formation of the Book of the Twelve*. For the literary and thematic approach, see, e.g., Paul House, *The Unity of the Twelve*, JSOTSup 97 (Sheffield: Almond Press, 1990); Rolf Rendtorff, "Alas for the Day! The 'Day of the LORD' in the Book of the Twelve," in *God in the Fray: A Tribute to Walter Brueggemann*, ed. Tod Linafelt and Timothy K. Beal (Minneapolis: Fortress, 1998), 186–97. For the canonical approach, see, e.g., Christopher R. Seitz, *Prophecy and Hermeneutics: Toward a New Introduction to the Prophets*, STI (Grand Rapids: Baker Academic, 2007); Michael B. Shepherd, "Compositional Analysis of the Twelve," *ZAW* 120 (2008): 184–93; Donald C. Collett, "Prophetic Intentionality and the Book of the Twelve: A Study in the Hermeneutics of Prophecy" (PhD diss., University of St. Andrews, 2007). Note the variety of approaches on display in Paul L. Redditt and Aaron Schart, eds., *Thematic Threads in the Book of the Twelve*, BZAW 325 (Berlin: de Gruyter, 2003).

45. Ehud Ben Zvi and James D. Nogalski, *Two Sides of a Coin: Juxtaposing Views on Interpreting the Book of the Twelve/the Twelve Prophetic Books*, introduction by Thomas Römer, Analecta Gorgiana 201 (Piscataway, NJ: Gorgias, 2009), 12–16.

through preexilic Judah and Israel to postexilic Yehud as well as (2) provides a framework for which to understand the responsibilities and opportunities of God's people as they live in troubled times.

I have argued elsewhere that some Second Temple Jewish writers perceived the twelve prophetic books to cohere in some way.[46] Although texts of the Minor Prophets from Qumran are debated, other evidence points to Jews in the Second Temple period viewing the book as a whole. For instance, Sir 49:10 (ca. 200 BCE) describes the "bones" of the Twelve Prophets that comforted Jacob. This description necessitates that the Twelve is, at least in some manner, a coherent book (the bones serve as a framework for a body). Moreover, this body of text provides comfort and hope to those who read it.[47] And in the New Testament, Paul describes "the book of the prophets" (Acts 7:42) as he quotes some of Amos's prophecy. In his description, Paul speaks of "the prophets" (τῶν προφητῶν/*tōn prophētōn*) within a "book" (βίβλῳ/*biblō*). In his description, Paul plays upon a corporate understanding of the whole ("the prophets") while affirming its unity ("book"). Finally, I make mention of apocryphal and pseudepigraphal sources (4 Ezra 1:39–40, Martyrdom and Ascension of Isaiah 4:22, and the Lives of the Prophets). These texts also display a corporate or composite view of the Minor Prophets. The Second Temple sources indicate that from 200 BCE onward the Twelve often has been understood as a unified book.

These points have not been embraced by all because the data that demonstrates "the Twelve" are still too tenuous and methodologies (especially redactional models) drive conclusions. Philippe Guillaume rightly gives one pause before claiming the factuality of *a* book of the Twelve as a unified corpus. Guillaume addresses the tendency for scholars to overestimate the evidence that affirms *a* unitary scroll of the Twelve in the manuscript evidence, particularly in the Dead Sea Scrolls.[48] His analysis disrupts the scholarly view that there indeed was one book of the Twelve copied upon a single scroll, with the Dead Sea material being a hallmark (and early) example.[49] Important for our discussion

---

46. Thomas, "Hearing the Minor Prophets," 360.

47. For translation and discussion, see Patrick W. Skehan and Alexander A. di Lella, *The Wisdom of Ben Sira*, AB 39 (New York: Doubleday, 1987), 540–45.

48. Philippe Guillaume, "A Reconsideration of Manuscripts Classified as Scrolls of the Twelve Minor Prophets (XII)," *JHS* 7 (2007): 2–12; http://www.jhsonline.org/Articles/article_77 .pdf.

49. So Nogalski expounds the approach Guillaume rebuts: "Ancient traditions irrefutably establish that the writings of the twelve prophets were copied onto a single scroll and counted as a single book from at least 200 BCE": James D. Nogalski, "Intertextuality and the Twelve," in *Forming Prophetic Literature: Essays on Isaiah and the Twelve in Honor of John D. W. Watts*, ed. James W. Watts and Paul R. House, JSOTSup 235 (Sheffield: JSOT Press, 1996), 102.

is an outcome of his analysis: that at a very early time in the manuscript evidence, the Twelve likely may have been neither organized nor read as a unified corpus but rather as individual works, even if some manuscript evidence reveals that they appear on one scroll. Considering Guillaume's research, one must be cautious about trends that overplay the unity of the Twelve as a coherent book with a unitary message.

However, even if one affirms that there is a "book" of the Twelve, it does not follow necessarily that it should be read as *one* book akin to Isaiah, Jeremiah, or Ezekiel. Is the Twelve a unified book with a unified message? Is it a unified book with a series of messages? Or is it simply an anthology or compilation of prophetic books that each say their own thing, with no relation to one another? Ehud Ben Zvi argues against the redactional models put forth at present and instead thinks that the Twelve ought to be read as a compilation, or anthology, of twelve individual prophetic books. Even if books in the Twelve occur on a single scroll (*a* book of the Twelve), as evidenced by some Dead Sea Scrolls, it does not necessarily follow that a unitary scroll carries with it an internal reading-logic.[50] An anthology is a good analogy from modern literature of the kind of thing Ben Zvi (and Peterson) suggests. The Twelve is a collection of *individual* prophetic books with distinctive contributions.

Similarly, while recognizing that the Twelve can be read as a book, Peterson remains unconvinced that the diversity of models has provided a coherent picture of the redactional development of the Twelve along a unified theme. Instead, he argues that the Twelve is an anthology devoted to the theme of the Day of Yahweh without committing to the Twelve Hypothesis.[51]

Ronald Troxel, too, thinks that redactional models' use of "catchwords" as a key to trace the development of parts or all of the Twelve is unlikely. To be sure, he grants that connections between the books indicate some sort of editing processes in history, but then he says that "most of these processes are too inscrutable to permit a comprehensive account of how the Twelve came to be ordered as we know them."[52]

Although the data from redaction criticism is impressive, it is not the foundation for this commentary. Ben Zvi, Peterson, Troxel, and others raise

---

50. Ehud Ben Zvi, "Twelve Prophetic Books or 'The Twelve': A Few Preliminary Considerations," in Watts and House, *Forming Prophetic Literature*, 125–57, esp. 131. See also his contribution in *Two Sides of a Coin*, 47–86.

51. David L. Peterson, "Book of the Twelve?" in *Reading and Hearing the Book of the Twelve*, ed. James D. Nogalski and Marvin A. Sweeney, SymS 15 (Atlanta: Society of Biblical Literature, 2000), 1–10; Ronald L. Troxel, *Prophetic Literature: From Oracles to Books* (Chichester,: Wiley-Blackwell, 2012), 82–83.

52. Troxel, *Prophetic Literature*, 87.

questions that ought to generate more study on redactional models and their refinement. More research is needed to answer the following questions:

1. What exactly are the earlier forms of the texts under investigation? As Nogalski stresses in practice, it is not sufficient to stress later redactions without giving due account of previous editions and forms of texts prior to redactional development. But this needs to happen at the level of the individual book *and* its placement and function in the developing Twelve Prophets.

2. Despite the fact that redactors erased their tracks so we have limited access to earlier forms of the texts under investigation, one still must query whether or to what degree earlier texts were sensible and meaningful for specific communities *without* the redactional additions. This point goes to Ben Zvi's hesitations about the readerly communities that would have received this material.

3. Why was it necessary for scribes or schools to adapt previous texts and traditions for later communities? This says something about the assumed deficiency of earlier text traditions, to which we have limited access, that *necessitates* a later redaction. The historical situations from which redactional models are proffered remain suppositional.

4. Once we agree in principle that seams in the material exist, a follow-up question (that is not foregrounded as explicitly as it should) has to do with the hermeneutics of these seams: Would later communities read, hear, or interpret the Minor Prophets from the perspective of the redactional seams, or would the seams be a kind of second-order perception after perceiving the kerygmata of individual books within the collection of the Minor Prophets, akin to a kind of biblical theology?[53] The hermeneutics of the seams (whatever they may be or may have been) have been assumed by interpreters rather than argued rigorously.

Again, while not discounting the value of redactional models, the questions mentioned above invite further work in this field. Moreover, these questions lead us away from advancing a redactional approach to this commentary.

This commentary will read the book of Habakkuk as presenting a set of messages that can then be understood in the larger literary presentation of the Twelve. This commentary attends to Habakkuk's messages and then listens to them in concert with the larger testimony of the Twelve. Connections between

---

53. I use "seams" here as a term that indicates the redactional additions that give meaning and shape to specific text blocks.

Habakkuk and other books in the Twelve that appear here may overlap with some of insights of redaction criticism without reverting to redaction-critical explanations to give their sense.

The approach presented here is literary and theological. I read Habakkuk within its own horizons and then correlate it to how it might be heard in the Minor Prophets to investigate how Habakkuk discloses God and orients its readers to him. Such a listening does not necessarily devolve into an antihistorical synchronic reading that drives a wedge between the literary and the historical.[54] Nonetheless, this commentary will not engage in a redaction-critical reconstruction of Habakkuk within the Twelve to gain access to the messages of either Habakkuk or the Twelve. Nor do I want to delve into a full-scale historical reconstruction of the growth and development of Habakkuk in the light of socio-historical realities in ancient Judah or Persian Yehud (or beyond). Rather the focus here is a literary reading of Habakkuk within its own context, the larger context of the Twelve, and then within the horizons of a Christian biblical theology with the Old and New Testaments firmly in view.[55]

It follows from this point that Habakkuk's voice serves as part of the full testimony of the Twelve. The word of Habakkuk the prophet and the book that bears his name are set within a larger tapestry of God's word in the Minor Prophets that spans roughly four centuries. As such, in terms of a distinctive corpus, the Twelve may have been fixed in the postexilic period (fifth–second centuries BCE, with Sir 49:10 marking an extreme *terminus ad quem* at ca. 200 BCE). It was composed to formulate a theological basis for the future, for God's dealings with Israel, and for engendering hope in the face of present realities. The individual books connect with one another thematically and lexically (and perhaps historically) to complement the messages of both.

To come back to a previous example, similarities of language and form between Nahum and Habakkuk reveal that these two texts may have been conjoined prior to their incorporation in the Book of the Twelve. One notes the

54. John Barton's critique of antihistorical tendencies for some forms of literary approaches that may be deemed as canonical is apt, and may be applied, for instance, to John H. Sailhamer, *Introduction to Old Testament Theology: A Canonical Approach* (Grand Rapids: Zondervan, 1995). See John Barton, *Reading the Old Testament: Method in Biblical Study* (London: Darton, Longman, & Todd, 1984), 77–157. But Barton wrongly links the canonical approach of Brevard Childs to an antihistorical view that divorces the text from authors or readers (153–56).

55. I would argue that the canonical context of Habakkuk within the Old and New Testaments does not *obscure* the meaning of Habakkuk as much as *illumine* it even if in new ways. The canonical context obscuring the originating meaning of any biblical text is the language of Barton (*Reading the Old Testament*, 156; and Barton, *The Nature of Biblical Criticism* [Louisville: Westminster John Knox, 2007] 142–82). For another view that sees the canon *opening* the meaning of the text, see Seitz, *Prophecy and Hermeneutics*.

similarities of hymnic material opening Nahum and closing Habakkuk, taunt songs in Nah 2–3 and Hab 2, and then the problem of theodicy highlighted in Hab 1. On this reading, the message(s) of Habakkuk and Nahum work corporately to emphasize both theodicy and God's ultimate victory over foreign pagan nations. The message of Habakkuk to the Babylonians extends outward in a broader historical sweep, incorporating both Assyria and Babylonia, and presumably any other nation that taunts God and his people.[56]

### *Social and Historical Context of Habakkuk*

If God has spoken in the past to the prophet, then what is the best contextual and historical backdrop in which to set the book of Habakkuk? Many options are possible, but it is best to read Habakkuk against the backdrop of the last days of the Judahite state at the close of the seventh century BCE.

In the light of the mention of the Chaldeans in 1:6, the book presents a reading context that fits within the waxing of the Neo-Babylonian Empire and the waning of the Judahite state. Habakkuk, then, would minister within roughly 620–587 BCE. Several internal features within Habakkuk point in this direction. Of course, one is found with the reference to the Chaldeans in Hab 1:6. Also notable is the larger biblical context (like in Jeremiah) in which the Babylonians are raised up by God to punish Judah. This comports with the literary presentation in Habakkuk concerning a foreign nation that God empowers to do his bidding. Another internal feature that points to the context of the rise of the Neo-Babylonian state is reference to the violence done against Lebanon in Hab 2:17. David Vanderhooft recognizes that the acquisition of the prized cedars of Lebanon is a recurrent feature of Neo-Babylonian texts. As such, the biblical text may here be reflecting upon a Neo-Babylonian practice of exploiting the cedars of Lebanon in its rise to power. The violence then described in 2:17 accords with a prophetic denouncement of the Babylonian imperial war machine.[57]

Some argue for greater specificity within such a broad historical canvas. Keil situates Habakkuk's prophecy possibly within the reign of Manasseh (697–642 BCE) and points to internal idolatry as the rationale for God's raising up the Babylonians.[58] This view is difficult to maintain as the Babylonians did not rise

---

56. See the discussion of Paul Redditt, *Introduction to the Prophets* (Grand Rapids: Eerdmans, 2008), 198–99.

57. David S. Vanderhooft, *The Neo-Babylonian Empire and Babylon in the Latter Prophets*, HSM 59 (Atlanta: Scholars Press, 1999), 153–54.

58. Carl F. Keil, *The Twelve Minor Prophets*, vol. 2, trans. James Martin (Edinburgh: T&T Clark, 1878), 52.

to power until later in the century and thus would sit somewhat awkwardly in Habakkuk's presentation.[59] Theodore Laetsch prefers to read Habakkuk within the time of Josiah (639–609 BCE) and against the context of the prophet's future prediction of the coming of Babylonian power.[60] This view suffers in that it flies in the face of the Deuteronomic presentation of Josiah's faithfulness to Yahweh through his reform efforts (2 Kgs 22–23).

Recent work situates Habakkuk within the reign of Jehoiakim (608–598 BCE). Sweeney believes the prophecy of Habakkuk fits with this historical moment, particularly after the battle of Carchemish in 605 BCE. It is in the face of Babylonian threat and the impending defeat of Judah at the hands of this foreign nation that Habakkuk utters his prophecy. He believed Babylon to be a rebellious and idolatrous nation but was surprised to discover that God was using this nation as a punitive agent for his people. After this, he finally came on board with God's plan (e.g., Hab 3).[61]

With Sweeney, Robert Haak believes some of the book derives from the period of Jehoiakim, but thinks that Habakkuk the prophet was an opponent of royal policy. The "wicked" in Hab 1:1–4 refers both to royal Judahite policy and those who follow it, while 1:12–17 laments Babylon's might, and so is later and likely exilic. On Haak's view, for the final form of the book, what was a lament directed first against the royal Judahite court was incorporated into a larger lament about Babylon.[62] This view finds some support in the Deuteronomist and Jeremiah. The final forms of both texts are likely exilic as well and recognize Babylonian ascendancy as a mark of divine providence. So they reflect, as would Haak's reconstruction of Habakkuk, Jehoiakim's rebellion against Babylonian power coupled with his alliance with Egypt as a mark of rebellion against the will of the Lord (cf. 2 Kgs 23:37–24:6; Jer 22:13–19; 36:30). This view has problems as well.[63] More attention will be given to this in the comments on these verses, but it is sufficient at this point merely to note that Haak and Sweeney contextualize Habakkuk—in whole or in part—within the reign of Jehoiakim.

Some prefer to read otherwise. It has been common in historical-critical study to situate biblical books within wide-ranging historical milieus. So Haupt dates Habakkuk to the Maccabean period just after Judas Maccabeus's defeat of

---

59. See the discussion of J. Maxwell Miller and John H. Hayes, *A History of Ancient Israel and Judah* (London: SCM, 1986), 385–412.

60. Theodore Laetsch, *The Minor Prophets* (St. Louis: Concordia, 1956).

61. Sweeney, "Structure," 63–83; Sweeney, *Twelve Prophets*, 2:455–56.

62. Robert D. Haak, *Habakkuk*, VTSup 44 (Leiden: Brill, 1992), 107–49. This view nicely provides an explanation for the difficult crux of the audience of Hab 1:1–4.

63. Watson, *Paul and the Hermeneutics of Faith*, 138–42.

Nicanor in 161 BCE.[64] Bernhard Duhm and Charles C. Torrey date the historical milieu to the rise of Alexander the Great in the fourth century BCE.[65] Other options have been offered beyond these.

Key to the originating context debate is the identity of the wicked in Hab 1:4, 13. Other commentaries engage the historical questions in greater detail.[66] But some attempt must be made here to explain our view as well because the historical questions, to my mind, naturally impinge upon the theological. In the first place, about whom, in its originating context, is the complaint directed? Who are the wicked that surround the righteous? The first option understands the wicked as *internal* to Judah and the second option understands the wicked as *external* to Judah. The challenge of interpretation arises because of the nature of the relationship between the identity of the "wicked" in v. 4 and the identity of the "wicked" in v. 13. Are the wicked described in these verses from the same group or from different groups? If they are the same, then it is likely that the wicked are an external threat, likely the Babylonians. If they are different, then it could be that the wicked of v. 4 are rebellious Judahites, while the wicked of v. 13 are the Babylonians.[67]

The wicked of v. 4 could refer to rebellious Judahites. It is possible to situate Habakkuk's lament within the reign of Jehoiakim so that his complaint is resonant with the complaint of Jeremiah (and God) concerning Judah's leadership. The divine response that follows in 1:5–11 is one of divine judgment against rebellious Judah through the hand of the Neo-Babylonian Empire. Some Judahites spurn God and his torah in the last years of the Judahite monarchy, perhaps under the auspices of King Jehoiakim and those in league with him (cf. Jer 22:1–23:2). Wicked Judah's general disregard for God and his law reveal that the torah is paralyzed from its effectiveness in leading people in God's paths. As a result, justice never goes forth. Crooked justice is the order of the day.[68] This leaves the righteous prophet and those like him questioning God about this state of affairs.

---

64. Paul Haupt, "The Poems of Habakkuk," *Johns Hopkins University Circular* 39/325 (1920): 680–84.

65. Bernhard Duhm, *Das Buch Habakuk* (Tübingen: Mohr, 1906); Charles C. Torrey, "The Prophecy of Habakkuk," in *Jewish Studies in Memory of George A. Kohut*, ed. Salo W. Baron and Alexander Marx (New York: Alexander Kohut Memorial Foundation, 1935), 565–82. See the discussion of Marshall D. Johnson, "The Paralysis of Torah in Habakkuk 1:4," *VT* 35 (1985): 257–59.

66. For discussion, see Andersen, *Habakkuk*, 24–29, 123–34.

67. Budde thought the wicked of v. 4 were the Assyrians, while v. 13 referred to the Babylonians; Budde's view has been abandoned. Cf. K. Budde, "Die Bucher Habakuk und Zephanja," *TSK* 66 (1893): 383–93.

68. This interpretation is sensible as well because the king was responsible for administering sound judgments for his people rather than perverse ones (cf. Ps 72).

Theologically, this reading pits the faithful prophet against his own people and culture, and this fits well with the general thrust of Jeremiah's life and preaching. It also comports with the picture of God's prophet as being fundamentally countercultural rather than overly accommodating to it. As a result, in vv. 5–11 God informs the prophet that he will raise the Babylonians for judgment, even if the Babylonians are not the greatest of nations. In fact, they are rebellious against God and his divine order—wicked in v. 13. That God would use a wicked nation to do his bidding leads to the prophet's second complaint in vv. 12–17. This represents a two-party understanding of the wicked in Hab 1: Judahite (v. 4) and Babylonian (v. 13).

A nuance to the two-party view advocated above places the book *earlier* than the reign of Jehoiakim. On this view, the Assyrian Empire in the mid-sixth century BCE ruled supreme in the Levant, with King Manasseh in charge of a rebellious Judah.[69] Rebellious Judahites compose the wicked in v. 4. Because of Manasseh's rule (cf. 2 Kgs. 21:1–16), the prophet decries Judah's rebellion against God and his law and awaits divine judgment on Manasseh's iniquitous rule. Like the former view elaborated above, the prophet critiques his own sinful people and awaits divine judgment.[70] Judgment comes at the hands of the Babylonians, who again are identified as the wicked in v. 13. So the same two-party view of the wicked is held as the one above—Judahite (v. 4) and Babylonian (v. 13)—but with the time frame being earlier than the reign of Jehoiakim.

Alternatively, Hab 1:4 generally could describe a failure of God's torah in the face of an external threat, likely the Neo-Babylonian Empire. On this account, God's Deuteronomic torah promises to bless God's people if they remain faithful to him (cf. Deut 28:1–14; 30:11–20), but they are "paralyzed" because of the reality of foreign ascendancy. God's people are not blessed but dominated. The wicked foreigners oppress the righteous Judahites, preventing the justice of God's people from ever going forth.[71] This external view of the wicked in v. 4 places the prophet as a spokesman for his people, who suffer because of a perceived failure of God's word. Historically, this position is cogent if, following Johnson, the torah promises are closely connected to the Josianic reform movement. Reform theology has failed in the face of historical reality.[72] As a result, the wicked in vv. 4 and 13 are the Babylonians. This would make good

---

69. Richard D. Patterson, *Nahum Habakkuk Zephaniah: An Exegetical Commentary* (Richardson, TX: Biblical Studies Press, 2003), 109–10; Patterson, "Habakkuk," in *Minor Prophets: Hosea–Malachi*, ed. Philip Comfort, Cornerstone Biblical Commentary 10 (Carol Stream, IL: Tyndale House, 2008), 395–444.

70. For some, then, Hab 1:5–11 represents a celebration of God's instrument of judgment, Babylon. This view fails, however, in that the Babylonians are not set in positive terms (cf. vv. 6, 7, and 9).

71. See the discussion of Johnson, "Paralysis," 257–66.

72. Johnson, "Paralysis," 262–63.

sense in a period after 609 BCE (death of Josiah at Megiddo) and particularly after the battle of Carchemish in 605 BCE. The death of Josiah and the loss of momentum of Josianic reforms coupled with the imperialistic policies of Babylon led to a critique of this foreign invader. But in fact, this view suffers from a myopic understanding of torah: there is no reason to suppose that torah necessarily references the Josianic reform movement. And further, glossing the Josianic reform movement with the simple term "torah" simply occurs nowhere else in the Old Testament. It is better to read torah as either wisdom instruction or Mosaic torah rather than Josianic reform.

Apart from these distinctive views, another option is possible as well. It is possible to see vv. 5–11 as an elaboration of the general description of trouble identified in vv. 2–4. Sweeney and Watson argue that the problem of injustice and violence identified by Habakkuk finds its source in Babylonia, both in vv. 2–4 and 5–11.[73] The wicked identified by Habakkuk throughout are the Babylonians and their ascendancy in the waning years of the sixth century BCE. In the wake of Neo-Babylonian ascendancy in the latter days of Judean monarchy, Habakkuk addressed the general breakdown of the moral order in his society—especially in the reign of Jehoiakim. The complaint of vv. 2–4, then, introduces a theological and practical problem in a general way, upon which the rest of the book elaborates. On this reading, there is not a sequential call and response between vv. 2–4, 5–11, and 12–17. Rather, vv. 2–4 introduce a general problem of the wicked surrounding the righteous. This problem inverts some biblical wisdom instruction but coheres with the generic description of distress in some psalms (Prov 10–15; Ps 7:9; Ps 37; cf. Jer 12:1; Gen 18:23–25).

It is best to read Habakkuk and his prayers against the context of the reign of Jehoiakim prior to the fall of Jerusalem in 587 BCE.[74] The reasons for this are as follows:

1. The presentation of the righteous and the wicked in Hab 1:2–4 presents the wicked as those who are presently Judahite and oppressing the righteous in Judah. This context fits the reign of Jehoiakim in the waning days of Judah.

2. The mention of the Chaldeans in Hab 1 gives further support to the notion of the rising Neo-Babylonian threat, which fits with the reign of Jehoiakim.

3. The imminence of the Judean exile in Hab 1 provides an ominous foregrounding for destruction rather than mourning over past destruction,

---

73. Watson, *Paul and the Hermeneutics of Faith*, 139–41; Sweeney, "Structure," 66–67.
74. So too Grace Ko, *Theodicy in Habakkuk*, PBM (Milton Keynes: Paternoster, 2014), 9–10.

as one sees in Lamentations, which is a Judahite text that belongs to the period of the exile (587/6–515 BCE).[75] Such anticipatory threat fits well within the waning days of Judah. Through Habakkuk's eyes we see the sin of Judah as well as the greed of Babylon as they gobble up people and resources down the Levant with the efficiency of a wood-chipper, spitting out the refuse in a garbled mess. Babylon, however, cannot come to grips with their tyranny's collateral damage—the sustenance of strife in an unceasing procession of suffering.

### Yahweh and the Logic of Empire

Books like Habakkuk emerge from the crucible of warring empires burning to secure international power. In Habakkuk's day, Babylon and Egypt battled over the contested supremacy of the Levant in general but specifically grappled over the little region of Judah. Yahweh's description of Babylon as a "bitter and hasty nation" that seizes land that does not belong to them (Hab 1:6) presents Babylon as a bloodthirsty and greedy nation bent on evil. As an imperial power, Babylon's justice is self-serving: it "proceeds from itself" (Hab 1:7). The image here is of an imperial power whose logic of empire is rooted in self: it serves neither God nor good, but is interested only in the development and expansion of its own interests.

From the perspective of Babylon, imperial expansion was a savvy move. Oded Lipschits shows that Babylonian policy in the Levant in the late seventh to sixth century BCE was in part motivated by economic factors. The raw goods of the Levant (particularly wine, oil, and grain) as well as potential tribute and tax revenue would resource the rebuilding of the depleted Babylonian state from decades of struggle with the waning Assyrian Empire. In terms of security, by moving into the Levant, Babylon would safeguard its power by providing an extensive buffer zone against its main rival in the southwest, Egypt. And finally, through an active imperial policy Babylon would expand its borders.[76] All this

---

75. For Lamentations' outlook, date, and provenance see Heath A. Thomas, *Poetry and Theology in the Book of Lamentations: The Aesthetics of an Open Text*, HBM 47 (Sheffield: Sheffield Phoenix, 2013), 8–14; Thomas, "'I Will Hope in Him': Theology and Hope in Lamentations," in *A God of Faithfulness: Essays in Honour of J. Gordon McConville on His 60th Birthday*, ed. Jamie A. Grant, Alison Lo, and Gordon J. Wenham, LHBOTS 538 (London: T&T Clark, 2011), 203–5.

76. Oded Lipschits, *The Fall and Rise of Jerusalem: Judah under Babylonian Rule* (Winona Lake, IN: Eisenbrauns, 2005), 29–35, 104. David Vanderhooft emphasizes that Babylon's motivation for its policy in the Levant was to secure a buffer zone from Egypt in "Babylonian Strategies of Imperial Control in the West: Royal Practice and Rhetoric," in *Judah and the Judeans in the Neo-*

activity, in theory, would serve to reinforce imperial power back home. Babylon's policy of invasion into the Levant makes good political sense. But good politics does not always good policy make.

The biblical account presents little of Babylon's reasoning. This is understandable because the focus of the text is decidedly different. Rather than an independent and fully self-governing empire in the book of Habakkuk, the Babylonian state remains an agent of Yahweh's purposes for Israel in the biblical account. The *theological* characterization of Babylon as a power is important for several reasons, but not least is the fact that as an empire, Babylon is subservient to Yahweh's universal rule.

Babylonian invasion on Habakkuk's account is not haphazard, nor is it due to political, social, or economic factors. Rather, the Babylonian rise to power and its campaign westward into the Levant is both providential and punitive. The God of Israel has orchestrated world events, and he is supremely in charge of the movements of history. God sets history into motion and bends it for his purposes, namely, the outworking of his covenant within the created order. God's judgment and salvation of Habakkuk and the people of God are part and parcel of *God's rule, God's kingdom,* working itself in the world. God raises up the Babylonians for his own purposes (Hab 1:5). But Babylon's wicked empire will not survive; it is not fitting within the kingdom of God and the purposes of God in universal history. Rather, the Lord of the universe will call all nations to account, as Hab 2:6–20 testifies.

This logic of Yahweh's universal rule is important for a people who see cities of blood as commonplace. Although it appears these bloody empires will have the final say in the world, Habakkuk presents Yahweh's rule as one of justice that, in a sense, swallows up evil empires in a great eschatological reversal. Empires built on blood are doomed because injustice and unrighteousness are not fitting for the kingdom of God. Yahweh will establish his own kingdom, saving the righteous and punishing the wicked.

In Habakkuk's vision, Yahweh's rule declares that the logic and imperial policies of a wicked nation will not stand. Yahweh's reign and his verdict from the temple (Hab 2:20) declare that wicked nations will be swallowed in their wickedness and Yahweh will put them to rights. This is true, we should say, whether that nation is Judah, Babylon, or the United States. Habakkuk presents a view of empire that looks beyond the current national and political goings-on to see the complete authority of the Lord over all kingdoms. His salvation and vindication of the suffering righteous are sure because his justice is assured.

---

*Babylonian Period*, ed. Oded Lipschits and Joseph Blenkinsopp (Winona Lake, IN: Eisenbrauns, 2003), 242–43.

## Biblical and Systematic Theology

This commentary correlates two fields of enquiry sharply differentiated in the past three hundred or so years: systematic and biblical theology. Since the famous lecture of Johann Philipp Gabler, biblical theology often has been understood as the historical investigation of the evolving religious beliefs of God's people in various eras. The aim of biblical theology on this model was to identify the essential religious beliefs of Israel at various points in their history. From this goal, the findings of biblical theologians were then handed over to systematic theologians to systematize and organize in a rational, coherent, and timeless manner (dogmatic theology). The two disciplines were related, but at different planes in theological discourse. These hardened distinctions are softening within some circles in the present, and the state of biblical theology as a discipline is somewhat in flux.[77] If this is a commentary that aims to relate biblical and dogmatic theology, one must press the crucial question of why and how one ought to *achieve* such a dialectic. While an adequate response would take us too far beyond the confines of the introduction, I offer some initial considerations.

I have used the term "dialectic" between the disciplines, and dialectic is aimed for because, hermeneutically, theological commitments serve to open Habakkuk constructively for interpretation rather than being an impediment to understanding. After all, philosophical hermeneutics in the past sixty years or so have highlighted the impossibility of completely bracketing out from one's interpretation of any text one's own preunderstandings or faith commitments, theological or otherwise. Preunderstandings are vital in the process of understanding.[78] Presuppositions infuse the study of anything, including both dogmatic and critical studies of the Bible.

The typical division in the modern era between biblical theology and dogmatics remains difficult to maintain hermeneutically. Walther Eichrodt saw many years ago the reality and necessity of preconceived commitments in the

---

77. Craig G. Bartholomew, *Introducing Biblical Hermeneutics: A Comprehensive Framework for Hearing God in Scripture* (Grand Rapids: Baker Academic, 2015), 51–112, 431–62; Watson, *Text and Truth*; Michael Williams, "Systematic Theology as a Biblical Discipline," in *All for Jesus: A Celebration of the 50th Anniversary of Covenant Theological Seminary*, ed. Robert A. Peterson and Sean Michael Lucas (Fearn: Mentor, 2006), 167–96; Christopher R. Seitz, *The Character of Christian Scripture: The Significance of a Two-Testament Bible*, STI (Grand Rapids: Baker Academic, 2011); Edward W. Klink III and Darian R. Lockett, *Understanding Biblical Theology: A Comparison of Theory and Practice* (Grand Rapids: Zondervan, 2012).

78. Hans-Georg Gadamer, *Truth and Method*, trans. Joel Weinsheimer and Donald G. Marshall, 2nd ed. (New York: Continuum, 2003), 277–85.

discipline of biblical theology, then perceived to be a science, and it is sensible to extend these presuppositions to faith commitments as well.[79] The idea of putting into brackets religious convictions in biblical interpretation (James Barr's terminology) becomes much more challenging than one might assume at first blush.[80]

There is sufficient reason to suppose that theological commitments can helpfully open readers to biblical meaning rather than close them off from it. This is so because the very *substance* of Scripture is God. God, who reveals himself in and through Scripture, is not so much a theme or an idea conveyed in the Bible as the reality to which the Scripture testifies and the one with whom its readers must deal. For this reason, a presupposition that the Scriptures testify to this real God who addresses the reader is helpful to understanding the meaning of the text.

Now this will not be a presumption that some interpreters hold. Yet assuming a faith-neutral reading of the biblical text will yield a truer understanding of the biblical text is simply that—an assumption. And this assumption is not adopted here, though I recognize and affirm the many works in scholarship that build out from a premise of a "neutral" reading, whatever that may be.

But it is also important to recognize that allowing faith commitments to inform the reading here does not necessarily eventuate theology running roughshod over the historical meanings of the biblical text. The present commentary does not aim to neutralize the benefits and gains of criticism, as I hope the exegesis of the text bears out. The interpreter engages the biblical text not merely for insight into systematic theology or as an apologetic for particular systematic positions, but to hear the voice of God who addresses his people. Attentiveness to the philology and historical situation of the book helps to inform that address. Theological interpretation reads to be captured by his word, to be captured by God who has spoken in and through his prophets and Scripture in historically and contextually defined and circumscribed situations that are different from our own. This basic insight helps us to hear the biblical text with its own voice, rather than simply hearing ourselves.

Barr's insight on the proper distinction between dogmatics and biblical theology carries with it some positive force. It is right to respect the givenness of the biblical text as speaking a word that ought to be heard. Moreover, biblical theology, insofar as I understand it to be a discipline that attends to the storied

---

79. Walther Eichrodt, "Hat die alttestamentliche Theologie noch selbständige Bedeutung innerhalb der alttestamentlichen Wissenschaft?" *ZAW* 47 (1929): 83–91.

80. James Barr, *The Concept of Biblical Theology: An Old Testament Perspective* (London: SCM, 1999), 208.

shape of Scripture in all its diversity and particularity, presents a redemptive account of Yahweh, the Creator of the world, who reconciles a broken world back to himself in and through his Son, Jesus. Systematic theology is a kind of analysis of Scripture that attempts to set out systematically, logically, and in an orderly way a topic or teaching, be it a doctrine of God, sin, humanity, or the like, especially engaged with contemporary currents of thought, whether theological, philosophical, or the like. Because of its aims and approach, systematic theology necessarily abstracts from the biblical contexts for a logical and systematic accounting. This is a helpful and necessary endeavor for the church, but Craig Bartholomew is correct to say that a good test for dogmatic formulation is whether it deepens the reading of Scripture and thereby the love of and fidelity to God.[81]

It is true that systematic theological categories *may* occlude the testimony of the text in its own voice, to be sure. For example, a strong antinomian position on the role of law in the Bible may in fact prevent the beauty and benefit of God's law from having its effects both in the Scriptures and for the Christian life. In this way, dogmatics *can* impede one from hearing the text. As the Catholic theologian Karl Rahner suggests, the Bible ought to be the norm that norms theological construction.[82]

However, the opposite is just as true as well. Systematic categories may usher us more deeply into the testimony of Scripture and thereby enable us to hear the voice of God better! For example, the early church formulation on the doctrine of the Trinity was deeply rooted in Scripture and drove the church more deeply to know and love God and read Scripture in the light of the Triune God.[83] Thus, dogmatic categories and the theological traditions that proffer them will offer guidance and productive engagement with the text insofar as they deepen the reading of Scripture to hear God's address through Habakkuk.

While there are many ways to enter the biblical testimony, a productive question is, "Which entry points are most helpful for understanding the material?" I judge it better to admit that this work is a theological commentary written by a Christian from a Christian stance, and this is the entry point for reading Habakkuk. Christian tradition that stems from apostolic witness forward to the present day becomes a resource to be embraced rather than avoided.

---

81. Bartholomew, *Introducing Biblical Hermeneutics*, 436. I am indebted to Bartholomew for his very good work on the relationship between biblical theology and dogmatic theology.

82. Karl Rahner, "Scripture and Theology," in *Theological Investigations: Volume 6* (Baltimore: Helicon, 1969), 89–97. Cf. Joseph A. Fitzmyer, *The Biblical Commission's Document "The Interpretation of the Bible in the Church": Text and Commentary*, SubBi 18 (Rome: Pontifical Biblical Institute, 1995), 145.

83. Matthew W. Bates, *The Birth of the Trinity: Jesus, God, and Spirit in New Testament and Early Christian Interpretations of Old Testament* (Oxford: Oxford University Press, 2015).

The hope is that the Christian faith provides the hospitable space from which to read the book and allow the biblical text to inform my presuppositions and potentially transform them in the process of reading and interpreting Habakkuk. This perspective, however, is not meant as an intentional slight to other reading practices or reading traditions. Rather, the view held here is that after an interpretative stance is clearly articulated (root and branch), disagreements over foundational precommitments emerge and meaningful dialogue ensues.

This commentary aims at a productive dialectic between biblical theology and systematic theology. This construction theoretically serves to guard against collapsing systematic categories onto the biblical text in a way that obscures rather than clarifies its meaning. It is true that a powerful insight of modern biblical study lies in its aims to hear the text in its own historical and cultural particularity, an insight that should not be discarded as too modernistic on the one hand or untheological on the other.[84] The historical, philological, and grammatical meaning of the text is an essential component to textual meaning that serves to inform broader theological concerns.

What is attempted here is a kind of theological reading that achieves a hard-won "thick" analysis of the biblical text that takes account of faith commitments in reading the Bible. Through the dialectic between biblical text and theology, it is hoped that the reader will come away with an enlarged and truer account of the meaning of Habakkuk and a deeper love of God. N. T. Wright has suggested such an approach, with some success in my estimation, in his work on the world of Judaism in the first century CE and the New Testament. Craig Bartholomew and Ryan O'Dowd's similar approach has produced extraordinary theological research on Old Testament wisdom literature.[85] Bartholomew has also advocated for such a thick analysis constructively in his insightful biblical hermeneutics.[86] A stimulating example of the dialectic between theology and exegesis in Old Testament study is Gary Anderson's excellent monograph illustrating such an approach.[87]

---

84. Any dichotomization here leads to an unhelpful characterization of the challenges of interpretation. For different ways of engaging the issue, see Stephen Fowl, *Engaging Scripture: A Model for Theological Interpretation*, CCTh (Oxford: Blackwell, 1998); Watson, *Text and Truth*; Barr, *Concept of Biblical Theology*; J. Todd Billings, *The Word of God for the People of God: An Entryway to the Theological Interpretation of Scripture* (Grand Rapids: Eerdmans, 2010).

85. N. T. Wright, *The New Testament and the People of God*, COQG 1 (Minneapolis: Fortress, 1992), 3–46; Craig G. Bartholomew and Ryan P. O'Dowd, *Old Testament Wisdom Literature: A Theological Introduction* (Downers Grove, IL: InterVarsity Press, 2011).

86. Bartholomew, *Introducing Biblical Hermeneutics*, esp. 3–112, 431–62.

87. Gary A. Anderson, *Christian Doctrine and the Old Testament: Theology in the Service of Biblical Exegesis* (Grand Rapids: Baker Academic, 2017).

## The Poetry of Habakkuk

Attending to the particularities of the text of Scripture is crucial for interpreting Habakkuk. One of the particularities for Habakkuk is its poetry. Samuel Meier recognizes a connection between prophecy, poetry, and psalmody. Prophets in Israel regularly spoke their words in poetry, and music accompanied their speeches.[88] At the very least, their words were set to music later on. This is true for the musical notation in Hab 3:1, 19. The remainder of the book does not have the same notation, but it is interesting to think that the poetry of Habakkuk may have been accompanied by music. At any rate, it is true that the poetic form remains important to consider in interpreting the meaning of the book. Several features in the poetry—form, repetition, use and adaptation of traditional material, and imagery—inform the meaning of Habakkuk. Unlike Haggai and Zechariah 9–14, our book is entirely composed in poetic verse. Meier rightly says that poetry in prophetic texts is significant for several reasons, not the least being that poetic form is informative for comprehension of the prophetic message.[89] Attending to the poetry of Habakkuk remains vital for comprehension of its theology.

*Sound and Sense.* The very sound of words in the poetry, and their interplay, expresses meaning in Habakkuk. In Hab 1:6, Babylon is identified as the "bitter and hasty" nation, which in Hebrew is *hammar wĕhannimhār*. The phonetic congruence between the words gives a distinctive way to identify the nation, and mark their terror. The use of the same Hebrew root in fixed grammatical construction (substantive participle + noun) marks another way the poetry exploits form. In Hab 1:5, God says that he is "working a wondrous work" which in Hebrew is *kî-pōʿal pōʿēl*/כִּי־פֹעַל פֹּעֵל. The idea could have been expressed with the verb "to do" (*ʿśh*/עשה), but the repetition of the same root and the sound of God's work become a way for the hearers to understand it. A similar phenomenon occurs in Hab 2:9, where a woe oracle is given over the one who "makes an evil profit for his house." But the phrase that describes this in Hebrew is *bōṣēaʿ beṣaʿ*/בֹצֵעַ בֶּצַע, again a participle followed by a noun. Here as well, the injustice that is described is meant to be heard and remembered clearly. Sound and sense go hand in hand.

*Dialogical Style.* Most scholars recognize the question-and-response form of the first two chapters of Habakkuk. The dialogical style of question and response occurs throughout the book, which creates a forward movement for

---

88. Samuel A. Meier, *Themes and Transformations in Old Testament Prophecy* (Downers Grove, IL: InterVarsity Press, 2009), 82–86.

89. Meier, *Themes and Transformations*, 86.

the reader. A question is raised by Habakkuk (Hab 1:1–4), only then to be answered by God (1:5–11). Following upon this, Habakkuk raises another question (Hab 1:12–2:1), to which God responds a second time (Hab 2:2–8). In the construction of the book as a whole, the third chapter may be understood as a final response to God's disclosure in chapter 2, providing a kind of bookend of divine questioning (Hab 1) and human response in light of God's answer (Hab 3). The dialogical nature of call and response opens a relational facet to the poetry and leaves the reader expecting divine response to the questions in a way somewhat unique in biblical prophecy. Of course, Jeremiah and Ezekiel demonstrate a call-and-response format in their works, but nowhere in those prophets does this form predominate as in Habakkuk.

*Intertextual Connections.* Habakkuk's language echoes language from other texts in the Minor Prophets and the remainder of the Old Testament. The language of "woe" that occurs in Hab 2:6–19 clearly echoes the woe oracles of judgment across the prophetic corpus. The use of the oracles in Habakkuk, however, takes a sapiential focus, as the woes in Hab 2:6–20 compose the great reversal that accompanies a life of folly rather than faith. These indicate that Babylon's veritable pride comes before their fall, and guarantees it. It is also apparent that there are linguistic ties that bind Habakkuk to the broader Old Testament, drawing our prophetic book into rich dialogue with the canon:

"Look and see" (Hab 1:3; Lam 2:20; 5:1)
"Evening wolves" (Hab 1:8; Zeph 3:3)
"The earth will be filled to know the glory of Yahweh" (Hab 2:14; Isa 11:9)
"The Lord is in his holy temple" (Hab 2:20; Mic 1:2; Jonah 2:4, 7; Ps 11:4)
"Be silent all the earth" (Hab 2:20; Zeph 1:7; Zech 2:12)
"Building a city of bloodshed/violence" (Hab 2:12; Mic 3:10)
"He makes my feet like the deer's feet" (Hab 3:19; Ps 18:33)

*Poetic Use of Repetition.* This commentary will explore the deep and rich structures of repetition that occur in different levels in the book. There are several repeated phrases in the book. Rather than treating them as dittography or accidental insertions, we take the repetition to be significant exegetically. So, the repeated phrase in Hab 2:8, 17 heightens the emphasis on Babylon's reversal ("from the blood of humanity, and the violence of the ground of the city, and all the inhabitants in her"). Repetition occurs at the level of the poetic line, following normal patterns of Hebrew poetry.[90] But it should also be recognized that repetition drives the reader reflexively backward, creating a new perspec-

90. Cf. Bliese, "Poetics."

tive on repeated elements. This repetition can occur at the level of the poetic line as scholars since Robert Lowth (and before) have recognized, but reflexive movement due to repetition can occur within and across poems as well. In this way, Habakkuk is tied together lexically through repetition of roots, terms, and clauses. These have the effect of drawing the reader to reflect upon the correlation between repeated elements. Repetition creates interpretative depth. Such repetition of elements throughout the book exceeds the bounds of what is often understood as discrete traditional material: such as hymnic tradition, wisdom tradition, cultic and prophetic tradition, and perhaps Canaanite mythological tradition. Even if Habakkuk is a composite text, repetition of elements within its poetry binds the book together. Poetic deployment of repetition creates a new interpretative environment for what was once disparate material, deepening and enriching the meaning of the poetry.

*Metaphor and Imagery.* Finally, imagery plays a significant role in developing the meaning of the book. The imagery taps a rich vein of theological metaphors for God and enemies, idolatry and faithfulness. As such, the imagery in the book drives the interpreter outward into the canon of Scripture. In Habakkuk God is typified as a warrior for his people (Hab 3), as he is in Exod 15. Further, the implicit imagery of God as a judge who hears the laments of Habakkuk is founded upon Israel's lament tradition, where God is depicted as a just judge who is powerful to hear and save. It is Yahweh's divine verdict that comes from Zion, where the wicked are judged and the righteous vindicated. Israel's enemies are not left out of the imagery in the book. They are pictured with metaphors of predation: "evening wolves" and ravenous birds hastening to eat. Interestingly, they are also designated as fishermen who trawl up the bounty of nations and sacrifice their catch to their idols. In Hab 2, personification is used to describe the great reversal of the Babylonian threat. The houses that they gobble up in destruction cry a woe oracle over them. That a house can speak is an effective use of personification that highlights Babylon's demise.

## The Theology of Habakkuk

Habakkuk has a voice in Scripture, and we should take care to listen to it without occluding its contribution. As readers, we tend to interpret unfamiliar texts in the Scriptures by and through texts that are more familiar. For many readers, Habakkuk is only familiar because the New Testament quotes it at several points. So functionally, the "theology of Habakkuk" becomes what is said in Rom 1:17 or equivalent New Testament cotexts in Galatians or Hebrews.

A more nuanced approach to the book treats the theology of the book within its own horizons and then observes how it is received in the New Testament, which is the approach favored here. Then, the two parts of the canon are related in a robust canonical biblical theology in the light of the full revelation of Scripture: reading from Habakkuk through to the New Testament books, and then from the New Testament books back to Habakkuk. Watson's reading of Habakkuk is such an attempt, though it is difficult to reduce the meaning of this book (or the Twelve) to one theological message as he has proposed.[91] Rather, many realities about God emerge in the book.[92]

### The Revelation of Yahweh, the Creator God and Covenant Lord

The first theological reality that Scripture proclaims is central to its testimony: Who is God? The book of Habakkuk testifies about God in two complementary ways: he is the God of creation, who created and governs the world and its inhabitants, and he is the God of the covenant, who relates with his particular people in a particular way for a particular purpose. Both facets of God in Habakkuk ground the prophet's complaints concerning (in)justice, violence, and the world gone upside down. Interestingly, this presentation of God in the book is achieved largely through the prophet's complaints. God's nature as a life-giving and death-defeating Lord is assumed, not explained, and becomes the ground of Habakkuk's hope. Because of this, Habakkuk presents knowledge of God as creator and covenant Lord through the interchange between the prophet and God.

### Prayer, Divine Justice, and the Future Hope

If God is the reality proclaimed in Habakkuk, the book invites human response to this covenantal and creator Lord. Yehezkel Kaufmann has described Habakkuk as "the prophetic Job" because of his suffering and response.[93] Like Job, the prophet's response to his suffering was prayer. Job was the only person in the story to address his pain to God in prayer, and so too Habakkuk prays in a way unique in the prophets. The dialogic call-and-response format of Habakkuk

---

91. Watson, *Paul and the Hermeneutics of Faith*, 125–57.

92. See the chapter on Habakkuk's presentation of God in Heath A. Thomas, *Faith amid the Ruins: The Book of Habakkuk* (Bellingham, WA: Lexham, 2016), 35–46.

93. Yehezkel Kaufmann, *The Religion of Israel: From Its Beginnings to the Babylonian Exile*, trans. Moshe Greenberg (Chicago: University of Chicago Press, 1960), 399.

underscores a theology of prayer at work in the book. Prayer is the first and best reflex for negotiating pain in the life of faith.

However, the kind of prayer that we find in the book is problematic, because it teeters on the edge of impertinence. Jewish and Christian interpreters through the centuries struggled mightily with Habakkuk's prayers. According to Dov Weiss, "Habakkuk sees a gap between God's essential nature and the reality of human suffering. For Habakkuk, while God cannot theoretically countenance wrongdoing [see Hab 1:13] we live in a world in which God does 'countenance treachery' [see Hab 1:3]."[94] Although God never reprimands Habakkuk for his complaints in the book, in the midrashic tradition the rabbis saw the prophet speaking impiously to God. In the midrash on Ps 90, the rabbis argue that Habakkuk spoke to God in error because he did not affirm the clear teaching of Deut 32:4, where God's ways are proclaimed perfectly just and God is affirmed as faithful and never false.[95] In other words, Habakkuk should never have questioned God's justice through his prayers. Some Christian readers recognized the same challenge that Jewish readers saw in regard to Habakkuk's prayers, especially Jerome.

Jerome's commentary influenced Christian interpretation of the book for centuries. In his comments on Hab 1:2, Jerome addresses the prophet's complaint. Jerome thinks Habakkuk's prayer is understandable but not necessarily admirable. The prophet prays because he has forgotten "the unsearchable judgments of God and the depth of the riches of his wisdom and knowledge, because God does not see as man sees."[96] Like the midrash Tehillim, Jerome reminds the reader that God is just and that Habakkuk has spoken with a "rash voice" and teeters on "blaspheming, in a way calling out his Creator into judgment."[97] He reminds the reader that God sees past, present, and future. Suffering and tribulation are part and parcel of the Christian life, and the ones who persevere through suffering by faith are those most commended. He uses 1 Cor 7:25, Eph 3:13, and Matt 10:22 as examples to bolster his case. In conclusion to his comment on Hab 1:2, Jerome admonishes: "Thus just as one man calls upon God, so the holy man and undefeated warrior desires to come into tribulation and misery in order to train himself and be put to the test."[98] Jerome's comments emphasize the way that suffering produces patience and endurance

94. Dov Weiss, *Pious Irreverence: Confronting God in Rabbinic Judaism*, Divinations (Philadelphia: University of Pennsylvania Press, 2017), 47.

95. August Wünsche, ed., *Midrasch Tehillim: Oder haggadische Erlkärung der Psalmen* (Trier: Mayer, 1892), 1:61.

96. Jerome, *Commentaries on the Twelve Prophets*, 187.

97. Jerome, *Commentaries on the Twelve Prophets*, 186.

98. Jerome, *Commentaries on the Twelve Prophets*, 187.

in the trial. Trials make one holy and refine the sufferer. The "holy man" is contrasted against the "one man" who "calls upon God" in complaint. In Jerome's understanding, prayers of complaint that raise the issue of divine justice are understandable for mere mortals, but they are not fitting for the true life of faith. But is his configuration of the problem appropriate for the life of faith?

James Garrett rightly says that prayer is a human mode of reaching out to God, to hear from him and obey him. "In prayer, there is both the reaching out in thought, aspiration, and spoken word after God and the waiting upon and listening to God in an attentive, receptive, and obedient attitude."[99] The kind of prayer found in the book of Habakkuk, particularly in chapter 1, is engaging prayer that believes God and knows of his saving power. Moreover, it is a kind of prayer that looks for God's just rule to be real in the real world. But this kind of prayer is not constitutive of *all* prayer, because many different forms of prayer occur in the Bible and the Christian tradition: praise and thanksgiving, meditative or mystical prayer, confession, petition, or intercession.[100] Henry Trevor Hughes says that prayer in the Christian tradition navigates between "mystical and prophetic elements in prayer."[101] Garrett explains the difference between mystical and prophetic in the thought of Hughes: "The former, which aims for absorptive union with God, enjoins passivity and withdrawal from the world, especially through the monastic life, whereas the latter, which seeks communion with God, involves redemption that issues in active work in a social context."[102] Habakkuk's complaints in chapter 1 constitute the prophetic pole of prayer: that God's justice and redemption might be actualized in his social context.

The prophet can identify what has gone wrong in the world precisely because he knows of God, his order, and his justice instilled in the creation itself. For instance, Habakkuk clearly invokes God's creation order (see the discussion on Hab 1:14) to frame his second complaint. Without the prophet's understanding of a God who founds the world with a sense of justice or rightness to its working, it becomes difficult to understand why the prophet calls upon God to do something in accord with how he has established his creation. The goodness of the Creator God becomes the ground by which the prophet can raise his voice in prayer.

99. James Leo Garrett Jr., *Systematic Theology: Biblical, Historical, and Evangelical* (Grand Rapids: Eerdmans, 1995), 2:394–95.

100. Garrett, *Systematic Theology*, 2:402–5. See also Heath A. Thomas, "Relating Prayer and Pain: Psychological Analysis and Lamentations Research," *TynBul* 61 (2010): 183–208.

101. Henry Trevor Hughes, *Prophetic Prayer: A History of the Christian Doctrine of Prayer to the Reformation* (London: Epworth, 1947), 2, cited in Garrett, *Systematic Theology*, 2:401.

102. Garrett, *Systematic Theology*, 2:401.

In his prayers in chapter 1, the covenant between God and Israel emerges as central to Habakkuk's vision of divine justice. In the covenant with his people, Israel, God can discipline them for sin because of his justice in their covenant relationship. Equally, out of that relationship, God can and does deliver his people from sin and suffering; this too is a manifestation of his justice. The affirmation of Hab 2:20 makes clear that justice is a characteristic of God and his judgments go forth from the temple where God has heard the cries of his people and responds with justice. He will be known as the covenant Lord of Israel precisely because of the righteousness that he dispenses for them. His verdict from his holy temple verifies his just word and his just world.

But exactly when is God's justice manifested? The *timing* of God's manifest justice is another major theological theme. Habakkuk's prayer reveals that God's justice appears in the raising up of the Babylonians to punish the wickedness of his own people. Habakkuk 1:5 clearly demarcates the advent of the Babylonians as the demonstration of divine justice. This can be put on a timeline: from 597 to 582 BCE, when the Neo-Babylonians invaded, besieged, and ultimately destroyed the Judean capital and many of its people. The prophet affirms Babylonian ascendancy as the exercise of God's justice when he recognizes that God raises up the Babylonians to reprove his people in Hab 1:12.

However, Habakkuk also presents a time of God's justice that cannot be firmly set on a timeline. God's justice is carried forward to a future time in which the righteous will be vindicated and the wicked punished in Hab 2:2–3. This period of time is an *eschatological* era. This eschatological time described in Hab 2:2–3 is pronounced from God's holy abode, the temple (Hab 2:20). God's vindication of the righteous and punishment of the wicked occur, according to Hab 2:2–3, at an "appointed time" which is also called the "end." This is a future time that cannot be relegated to one period in Israel's history. This end is closely attuned to the "day of Yahweh," a day of judgment and/or salvation for Israel and/or the nations that accords with both the justice and mercy of God. The end is the day when God will make his vision for future vindication come to pass. The Minor Prophets depict the righteous who remain on the day of judgment as the remnant of Israel, and indeed, it is this people that should be understood as those who will live faithfully as they come to trust in God's faithfulness to them, as Hab 2:4 describes.

God's justice will be made manifest at the end from his holy hill, but its effects will be cosmic in scope. Habakkuk 3:3–15 shows how God's judgment against wicked nations on behalf of his suffering people carries with it cosmic effects. Habakkuk 2:14 reinforces that God's enactment of justice will eventuate to this reality: "the earth will be filled to know the glory of Yahweh, as waters cover the sea." The glory of God is pervasive, and reveals that God's good work swallows up oppression and sin. The eschatological picture of divine justice, which is anticipated and revealed in prayer, is important for the theology of the book.

The prayers of Habakkuk expose his deep desire: a time in which God's goodness, justice, and glory cover the world. So, we begin to see that the kind of justice aimed at in Habakkuk is a profound *defeat* of evil. What is the defeat of evil? Jeremy Evans describes it: "The defeat of evil, in addressing evil *as evil*, seeks to restore the goodness of being that evil snatched away."[103] This is the picture of justice that we see in Habakkuk. Divine justice *undoes* the horrible sins of God's own people as well as the horrors of Babylon so that God's glory becomes manifest everywhere. The sin of God's people, as well as the sin of the Babylonians, is reckoned through the justice of God. He punishes the wicked but vindicates the righteous. The comprehensive vision of God's restorative act in Hab 2:14 suggests that what God does at the end (promised in Hab 2:2–3) will not be localized to Israel, but will be effective for the world. What is manifest in the "glory of Yahweh" covering the earth as "waters cover the sea" is a defeat of wickedness, injustice, and evil. The world will no longer embody these negative characteristics in the future. By his divine verdict, God's glory will be made manifest everywhere. At his divine verdict from Zion, all the earth is commanded to silence (Hab 2:20).

The view of justice and future hope espoused in Habakkuk is not perceived without the prayers of the book. Prayer gives the prophet, and us, the frame by which to affirm the goodness and justice of God, cry out for his justice to be manifest in the real world, and look for his justice to be exercised ultimately, in the future. Prayer provides the vocabulary to voice pain. Prayer provides the frame to affirm God's righteousness while simultaneously pleading for that justice to be actualized amid suffering. But prayer also gives the frame by which to look forward to a deeper future hope, a hope when God's justice will be revealed at the end and all shall be well.

### Faith and Faithfulness

In addition to prayer, the book of Habakkuk helps to elucidate the nature of faith. Faith is a crucial teaching of Habakkuk and crystallizes in Hab 2:4b: "The righteous will live by his faith" (ESV). But the concept of faith, it turns out, is not so

---

103. Jeremy Evans, *The Problem of Evil: The Challenge to Essential Christian Beliefs*, BHSCA (Nashville: B&H Academic, 2013), 46.

easily pinned down.[104] It is tempting to identify Hab 2:4b as a cognitive assent to God and his ways. It is a subjective apprehension of God's objective revelation. One "believes" what God has revealed and therefore "faith" is what the subject (humanity) apprehends of the object (God) in the rational mind. Of course, cognitive belief in God is important, but that is not the full measure of what is conveyed by faith in Habakkuk. Theodoret of Cyrus's apprehension of Hab 2:4 pushed a direction that both assented to God's faithfulness and lived a faithful life to him as a way to understand faith. James's teaching is instructive as well: "You believe that God is one; you do well. Even the demons believe—and shudder!" (Jas 2:19). The verb for "believe" there is the same root as one finds in the Greek translation of Hab 2:4: πίστις/*pistis*//πιστεύω/*pisteuo*.

The faith on display in Habakkuk is a commitment to God that yields acceptance, even embrace, of God and his ways. It is a commitment to God that engenders human fidelity to God in the face of hardship and pain. It is the embrace of God and his ways in the contested arena of God's world. *Faith in Habakkuk is the faithfulness of God's people to him, which is their fitting response to God's faithfulness to his people.*

The faith on display in Habakkuk is rooted first and foremost in an unwavering trust in the fidelity of God to his word, which leads to an absolute abandonment to the providential care of God himself. Faith, then, in Habakkuk is better understood as *faithfulness.* Adherence and fidelity to God in lieu of what he has revealed, despite all obstacles or in the face of impending death, are the substance of faithfulness for Habakkuk. This is not to disparage cognitive assent but to take it further. To gloss James's teaching as the way to describe faith and faithfulness in Habakkuk: faith (cognitive assent) without works (faithfulness to God in the whole of life despite obstacles) is dead. Faith means entrusting oneself wholly to the faithfulness of God. The comments on Hab 2:2–5 advance this line of thought further.

## Habakkuk in the Church

Habakkuk is a vital source of hope and inspiration for the life of the Christian church. The theme of faith and of faithfulness indicated above appears in the church's reading of Habakkuk, particularly from the Reformation forward, but also in earlier reception of Habakkuk: Irenaeus, Theodore of Mopsuestia, Augustine, and the Venerable Bede. Beyond this, Habakkuk was read

---

104. See, for instance, Matthew Bates, *Salvation by Allegiance Alone: Rethinking Faith, Works, and the Gospel of Jesus the King* (Grand Rapids: Baker Academic, 2017).

christologically, as a prophetic work that revealed (in many ways) Jesus as the messiah.

What proceeds is a rather impressionistic survey of Habakkuk in the reading of the church, focusing upon major thinkers and significant works. This is in no way exhaustive. I omit, for instance, the significant work of Rupert of Deutz, whose commentary on the Twelve influenced the church in the Middle Ages. Others, no doubt, will be excluded as well. There is much work to be done in the reception of the book of Habakkuk in the church, both in the expository/commentary tradition and in the ways the church employs Habakkuk in theological reasoning. In this light, the present survey is meant to spur more research and reflection on the reading of Habakkuk in the Christian tradition. I highlight the commentary tradition here, but Fowl certainly is correct to note the rich homiletical tradition that reveals the reception and interpretation of the Bible in the church.[105] Other overviews of the reception of Habakkuk, both ecclesial and academic, are found in Jöcken, Childs, Dangl, Kealy, and Coggins and Han.[106]

### *Apostolic Period*

The LXX of Habakkuk is used in the books of Romans, Galatians, and Hebrews to relate two realities: the faithfulness of God and the call for faith in God's vindication that comes through his messiah, Jesus. In this way, faith in God's faithfulness is contrasted, especially in Galatians, against salvation that comes by obeying God's law. Obedience in this latter way, as Israel's history shows, is a futile pursuit. If nothing else, Israel's cultic law reveals that God knew Israel could not achieve salvation by obeying the law—regular sacrifice supposed Israel's persistent problem with sin! The apostle Paul contrasts those who think that there is such a salvation (Judaizers) against those who recognize that salvation that comes by faith alone (Gal 3:11). Habakkuk in the New Testament will be addressed more fully in my chapter on biblical theology in part two of this commentary, below. Because of this, it is appropriate to turn to the second century CE to see how the church received Habakkuk.

---

105. Stephen E. Fowl, *Theological Interpretation of Scripture*, Cascade Companions (Eugene, OR: Cascade, 2009), 73.

106. Jöcken, *Buch Habakuk*; Childs, *Introduction to the Old Testament*, 447–56; Oskar Dangl, "Habakkuk in Recent Research," *CurBS* 9 (2001): 131–68; Sean P. Kealy, *An Interpretation of the Twelve Minor Prophets of the Hebrew Bible: The Emergence of Eschatology as a Major Theme* (Lewiston, NY: Mellen, 2009), 136–61; Richard Coggins and Jin H. Han, *Six Minor Prophets through the Centuries: Nahum, Habakkuk, Zephaniah, Haggai, Zechariah, and Malachi*, BBC (Chichester: Wiley-Blackwell, 2011), 36–91.

### Patristic Period

The church fathers saw in Habakkuk prophecies about the coming of Jesus. In his treatise against the Marcionite heresy, Irenaeus (ca. 125–202 CE) argues that it is impossible that the New Testament testifies to a different deity than does the Old Testament. His proof of this is the prophetic witness of Jesus Christ, which foretold all of Christ's works and even pronounced the end of the law. It is here that Irenaeus draws in Hab 2:4, and says, "But this point, that the Just shall live by faith had been foretold by the prophets."[107] Irenaeus suggests that the "Just" is none other than Jesus Christ, so that this verse proclaims the gospel. Irenaeus here is reading the Greek version of Habakkuk and interprets the noun δίκαιος/*dikaios* "righteous one" or "just one" as a proper title for Jesus: "The Righteous One" or "Just One." He believes that the vision which is appointed for the end in Hab 2:2-3 is a prophecy about the coming of Jesus. This is not an early affirmation about the doctrine of justification by faith as one finds in the Reformed tradition, but rather typical of the early church recognizing an Old Testament prophetic text as predicting the coming of Jesus, the messiah. Irenaeus used Hab 2:4 as a key text to identify the kind of faith that Abraham displayed, and the kind of faith that justifies believers in Christ, apart from obedience to the law.[108]

In the first four centuries of the church, Habakkuk was used prominently among other leading lights.[109] The great Old Testament exegete Origen apparently wrote a full commentary on Habakkuk and the rest of the Twelve, and it was known to Eusebius, but it has been lost. Only a fragment on Hosea remains in Origen's *Philocalia*. Extant commentaries on Habakkuk appear from Jerome (340–420 CE) along with his work on the remainder of the Minor Prophets, Theodore of Mopsuestia (350–428 CE), Cyril of Alexandria (378–444 CE), and Theodoret of Cyrus (393–458 CE).[110] Jerome's commentary made a significant impact, influencing the Latin West of Christendom, and his interpretative ap-

---

107. Saint Irenaeus, *Five Books of Saint Irenaeus against Heresies*, trans. John Keble (Oxford: Parker, 1872), §4.34.2-3, pp. 414-15.

108. Saint Irenaeus, *The Demonstration of the Apostolic Preaching*, trans. J. Armitage Robinson (London: SPCK, 1920), §35, p. 102.

109. For a helpful overview, see Alberto Ferreiro, *The Twelve Prophets*, ACCS 14 (Downers Grove, IL: InterVarsity Press, 2003), xvii–xxv, 186–206.

110. For Jerome's commentary on Habakkuk, see *Commentaries on the Twelve Prophets*; Jerome, *Commentarii in Prophetas Minores*, CCSL 76, 76a (Turnholt: Brepols, 1969-1970). Theodore of Mopsuestia, *Commentary on the Twelve Prophets*, ed. Robert C. Hill, FC 108 (Washington, DC: Catholic University of America Press, 2004); Cyril of Alexandria, *Commentary on the Twelve Prophets*, trans. Robert C. Hill, FC 116 (Washington, DC: Catholic University of America Press, 2008); Theodoret of Cyrus, *Commentaries on the Twelve Prophets*.

proach is deeply indebted to Origen. Cyril of Alexandria's commentary can be read alongside his contemporary Theodore of Mopsuestia and the later Antiochene, Theodoret of Cyrus, as one notes differences between Alexandrian and Antiochene exegesis in the Christian tradition. The Antiochenes read Habakkuk as a great resource to teach faithfulness to the Lord, even in the face of hardship and pain. Theodore of Mopsuestia, typical of Antiochene interpretative practice, explores the literal sense of Habakkuk and finds that Hab 2:4 is a picture of, and encouragement toward, faith in God. He writes, "I define a righteous person as the one who trusts in the promises [of God, given in Hab 2:2–3] and gets benefit from them."[111] Cyril followed the Alexandrian tradition and resourced Habakkuk as teaching a twofold "level of meaning, both spiritual and factual," as he says in the preface to his commentary on Habakkuk.[112]

Although he did not write a commentary on the book, Augustine (354–430 CE) plumbed the riches of the book to inform his understanding of salvation of God in Christ, as well as the nature of faithfulness in the Christian life. Augustine thinks that Habakkuk saw the climax of God's story in the advent of Christ in Hab 2:2–4 in his *The City of God*.[113] He sees in Hab 3:2 a prophecy that Jesus is born in between the two living creatures, which means (allegorically) that Jesus is born between the testaments, placed between the two thieves on the cross, and sits between Moses and Elijah on the mount of transfiguration.[114] Augustine's interpretation of Hab 3 is an extended Christological reading using an allegorical approach.

Coggins and Han describe the various ways that Augustine uses Hab 2:4 in his theological treatises, exegetical tractates, and letters. They find that Augustine routinely sees Hab 2:4 as foundational for understanding the life of faith. It is by faith that Christians find life, Augustine argues. The Christian faces uncertainty as part of human existence, but he argues that faith in Christ leads us to the happy and eternal life to come. In *The City of God,* Augustine uses Hab 2:4 in a number of places. It is by faith that the church lives in the city of God while on earth; even though the church cannot see the good in the world today, it is by faith that the life to come is made evident. In one of his letters (Letter 190.2), he argues that faith is the mechanism for salvation in the eras before and after Christ. In this way, faith is essential for the people of God.[115]

---

111. Theodore of Mopsuestia, *Commentary on the Twelve Prophets*, 274.

112. Cyril of Alexandria, *Commentary on the Twelve Prophets*, 331.

113. Saint Augustine, *City of God*, §31 (*NPNF* 1/2:377–78).

114. Augustine understands the "two living creatures" here in Hab 2:3 based on the Latin translation of the Greek. It is not original to the Hebrew text. See *City of God*, §31.

115. For a fuller description of Augustine's use of Hab 2:4, see the very good work of Coggins and Han, *Six Minor Prophets*, 71–73.

### *Medieval Period*

For western Christianity, the transitional figure between the patristic period and the Carolingian interpreters is the Venerable Bede, who lived in England and was a significant exegete in his own right. On his own testimony, the Venerable Bede composed two major works on Habakkuk in his life (672–735 CE): one on Hab 3 as well as a full commentary on the book within a running exposition on the Twelve Minor Prophets.[116] His commentary on Hab 3 is available in Latin, but his full commentary on the Twelve (including Habakkuk) is lost, though mentioned by other medieval Christian commentators who apparently knew of the work.[117] We do not know precisely where in England Bede produced these works, whether in Wearmouth or Jarrow, though likely it was in Jarrow because the majority of his adult life was spent there at the Monastery of St. Paul. It is interesting to note that Bede finds in Hab 2:4 the link between the testaments: salvation and life that come through faith in Christ.[118] In his expositions on Habakkuk, it is apparent that Bede follows the patristic tradition (particularly Jerome) of making links to Christ through Habakkuk.[119]

In Eastern (Syriac) Christianity, Habakkuk received attention from Išoʻdad of Merv (ca. 850 CE). He was the bishop of Hadatha, in Assyria. He wrote one of the few full-length commentaries on the Minor Prophets in Eastern Christianity, and it is part of his larger commentary corpus.[120] His comments on Habakkuk comprise only 150 lines in Syriac, and are occasional rather than comprehensive. For instance, he only comments on a few verses from Hab 1 (1:1–2, 4, 7, 10, 11–12, 16), a few in Hab 2 (2:1, 6–7, 11, 15), and some from Hab 3 (3:1–7, 9, 11, 13–16). The analysis that he does give is brief, especially when comparing his work on Habakkuk against his other commentaries in the Minor Prophets. It is fascinating that he does not comment directly on Hab 2:4 in his work when one notes its importance in other leading lights from the earlier centuries.

116. Venerable Bede, *The Complete Works of Venerable Bede, In the Original Latin, Volume 9: Commentaries on the Scriptures*, trans. John A. Giles (London: Whittaker and Company, 1846), 405–26. For his life, and his listing of the writings, see George Forrest Browne, *The Venerable Bede: His Life and Works* (London: SPCK, 1919), 15.

117. Bede, *Complete Works, Volume 9*, x–xi.

118. Coggins and Han, *Six Minor Prophets*, 64.

119. Bede, *On Tobit and the Canticle of Habakkuk*, trans. Seán Connolly (Portland, OR: Four Courts Press, 1997); Sarah Foot, "Women, Prayer and Preaching in the Early English Church," in *Prayer and Thought in the Monastic Tradition: Essays in Honour of Benedicta Ward, SLG*, ed. Santha Bhattacharji (London: Bloomsbury, 2014), 59–76, esp. 59–62.

120. Ceslas van den Eynde, ed., *Commentaire d'Išoʻdad de Merv sur l'Ancien Testament, IV. Isaïe et les Douze*, CSCO.S 128 (Louvain: Secrétariat du CorpusSCO, 1969), 109–14.

Among the Carolingian interpreters, it is unfortunate that Hrabanus Maurus (780–856 CE) did not write a commentary on the Minor Prophets or Habakkuk, as he wrote on much of the Old Testament. Neither did the great theologian of Charlemagne's court, Alcuin (ca. 735–804 CE), though he wrote on other Old Testament texts.

However, those working in the monastery of St. Germain in Auxerre, France, produced a full commentary on the Minor Prophets, Habakkuk included, entitled *Enarratio in duodecim prophetas minores.*[121] It is unclear who exactly wrote the commentary, either Haimo of Halberstadt (died ca. 855 CE) or Remegius of Auxerre (841–908 CE). Jerome's influence is felt in this work.

Theophylact, the Archbishop of Ochrid (1088–1120 CE), wrote on Habakkuk in his commentary on four of the Minor Prophets (Hosea, Jonah, Nahum, and Habakkuk). As a light of Eastern Christianity, his works on these prophets were highly popular and influential for Byzantine Christians. The work is in Greek and the influence of John Chrysostom is felt in it.[122]

Of the exegetes who labored at the Abby of St. Victor in France, Andrew of St. Victor (1110–1175 CE) wrote a full-length commentary on Habakkuk that searched the literal sense of Scripture and used Jewish interpretation systematically as a guide in his work.[123] The mechanics of the commentary are fascinating, as the Victorines inserted explanatory notes (*glossa*) between the lines of Jerome's Latin Vulgate to explain or interpret the text. In addition, more extended interpretations of the biblical verses (*postilla*) were added to the glossed text.

A good example of Victorine combination of explanation and interpretation in Habakkuk, is what Andrew says of Hab 3:1, which reads (in the Latin), "A prayer of Habakkuk the prophet, for ignorances." Andrew supposes that the "ignorances" of which the verse testifies is the fact that Habakkuk had upbraided the Lord for his lack of compassion and action on behalf of Israel (in Hab 1). But the Lord responded in Hab 2, and now the prophet is embarrassed by his lack of trust, and so confesses his ignorance of God's ways. So this is the meaning of the "ignorances" in the text. Of course, the Hebrew word is obscure (see commentary, below), but Andrew's attempt is rooted in a literal reading of the text rather than something else.[124]

---

121. See Andrew T. Sulavik, *Guillelmi de Luxi Postilla super Baruch, Postilla super Ionam,* CCCM 219 (Turnhout: Brepols, 2006), xxx; PL 117.

122. Theophylact of Bulgaria, *Expositio in prophetam Habacuc* (PG 126:819–906).

123. Andrew of St. Victor, *Expositio super duodecim prophetas,* ed. Franciscus A. van Liere and Mark A. Zier, CCCM 53G (Turnhout: Brepols, 2007).

124. See Frans van Liere, "Andrew of Saint-Victor and His Franciscan Critics," in *The Multiple Meaning of Scripture: The Role of Exegesis in Early-Christian and Medieval Culture,* ed. Ineke van't Spijker, Commentaria 2 (Leiden: Brill, 2009), 291–310, esp. 301–3.

From the heritage of patristic exegetical tradition, the work of Carolingian interpreters and the influence of the school of Auxerre, the *Glossa ordinaria* emerged in the twelfth and thirteenth centuries in and for the church. Jerome's commentary on the Minor Prophets coupled with the mediating commentators of the school of Auxerre provided a foundation on which later scholars would incorporate a series of glosses on the biblical text of Habakkuk that informed Christian interpretation of the book for the next three hundred years. Through marginal notes that surrounded the biblical text, interpreters were given a window into the views of the fathers of the church on Habakkuk. By the middle of the thirteenth century CE, however, the gloss was supplemented by the *postilla,* a running commentary on Scripture that drew in insights of the fathers (like the gloss) but also the insights of twelfth- and early thirteenth-century theologians.

Nicholas of Lyra (1270–1349 CE) formalized the *gloss* and *postilla* tradition from Carolingian exegetes, interpreters at Auxerre, and Victorine scholars in two major works: the *Biblia sacra cum glossa ordinaria,* "The Holy Bible with ordinary gloss," and *Postilla litteralis in Vetus et Novum Testamentum,* "Literal postils on the Old and New Testament." His work lends him the reputation of being the greatest Christian commentator of the fourteenth century and "perhaps the greatest in the West since Jerome."[125] His work, as is well known now, is heavily influenced by the interpretation of medieval Jewish commentators.[126] But of interest to our discussion is the way that he disagreed with Andrew of St. Victor's comments on Hab 3:1 in his reading on the book. His comments on this verse emerge on his *postilla* on Habakkuk, which are embedded in the larger notes on the entirety of the Scriptures. For Nicholas the idea that the prophet Habakkuk (who was inspired by God) could be ignorant of God or his plans was unconvincing.[127] In an interesting hermeneutical move, he believes that Habakkuk took on the persona of a faithless person only to contravene that perspective. He says of Hab 1:1:

> It does not seem very likely that the prophet, enlightened and inspired by God, would not know that God's judgments are righteous, at least in a general sense, even though he did not know exactly in what sense they would be righteous. Hence it is not very likely that he was complaining against

125. The quotation comes from the introduction of the volume by Philip D. W. Krey and Lesley Smith, eds., *Nicholas of Lyra: The Senses of Scripture,* SCHT 90 (Leiden: Brill, 2000), 1.

126. Deanna Copeland Klepper, *The Insight of Unbelievers: Nicholas of Lyra and Christian Reading of Jewish Text in the Later Middle Ages,* JCC (Philadelphia: University of Pennsylvania Press, 2007).

127. Van Liere, "Andrew of Saint-Victor," 302–3.

God on behalf of himself, but rather, that he assumed the role of one of the feeble ones who did complain about God's judgments.[128]

Thomas Aquinas (1224–1274 CE) rounds out the discussion of the medieval period. Although he did not write a commentary on Habakkuk, Aquinas drew upon Hab 2:4 to help him elucidate the nature of justification and to relate it to, but distinguish it from, the forgiveness of sins in his *Questiones Disputatae de Veritate*.[129] Still, for Habakkuk his interpretation is not as significant as that of Bede, the school of Auxerre, Andrew of St. Victor, Nicholas of Lyra, or even Išoʿdad of Merv.

### Reformation Period

The present survey focuses upon Luther and Calvin. Others no doubt could be brought into the discussion as well, but constraints of space prevent it. Martin Luther (1483–1546 CE) is the wellspring of the Reformation, and Hab 2:4 especially influenced his thought and theology. Luther found that the way to salvation lay not in the works of the law but in salvation by grace alone by faith alone in Christ alone. By 1519, Luther was absolutely burdened and bludgeoned by his guilt over sin, and in his misery he discovered Hab 2:4 employed in Rom 1:17. From his understanding of Paul's use of Hab 2:4 and the "righteousness of God" from Rom 1:16, Luther began to see that the justice of God is a gift-righteousness conferred on him. "Then and there, I began to understand the justice of God as that by which the righteous man lives by the gift of God, namely, by faith, and this sentence 'The justice of God is revealed in the gospel' to be that passive justice with which the merciful God justifies us by faith, as it is written, 'The just will live by faith.'"[130] In this understanding, God granted to sinners a gift-righteousness that he conferred on those who embraced Christ by faith. For the believer, life is attained only by faith. So Luther says in summary of Hab 2:4:

> The godly people are waiting for Yahweh; therefore they live, therefore they are saved, therefore they receive what has been promised [namely, life

---

128. Nicholas of Lyra, *Postillae litteratum*, vol. 4, fol. 393v; quoted in van Liere, "Andrew of Saint-Victor," 302.

129. Thomas Aquinas, *Quaestiones Disputatae de Veritate*, trans. R. W. Schmidt (Chicago: Regnery, 1954), §28.I.5.

130. Martin Luther, *Lectures on Romans*, ed. Wilhelm Pauck, LCC (Louisville: Westminster John Knox, 2006), xxxvii.

through the good news of Jesus Christ]. They receive it by faith, because they give glory to the God of truth, because they hold the hand of Yahweh. And so the prophet is looking not only to this promise but to all the other promises about preaching the Gospel or revealing grace.[131]

Luther gains this interpretation of Hab 2:4 because he believes what is written on the tablets of the vision in Hab 2:2 is nothing short of the salvation that comes through Jesus Christ. Luther thinks the vision that God gives is "a prophecy about the Christ and the kingdom of the Christ, which had been prophesied earlier in all the prophets."[132] In this way, Luther reads Habakkuk as a prophecy concerning the prophet's own day, to be sure, but ultimately a prophecy concerning the coming of the messiah. Moreover, this prophecy enjoins the believer to embrace the Lord by faith and not works.

Luther's insight is picked up by John Calvin (1509–1564 CE), who agrees with Luther's interpretation of Rom 1:17 and Hab 2:4, yet takes it further. He argues that the verse, as it is used in Romans, speaks about justification by faith, which is God's gift.[133] For Hab 2:4, in his commentary on the book, Calvin says that the faith mentioned there is that which is "in opposition to all those defences by which men so blind themselves as to neglect God, and to seek no aid from him."[134] Humanity, then, trusts not in God for salvation and life but in other things. Habakkuk, however, gives a different word, according to Calvin, who is worth quoting at length to understand his thought:

> [In Hab 2:4] faith is not to be taken here for man's integrity, but for that faith which sets man before God emptied of all good things, so that he seeks what he needs from his gratuitous goodness: for all the unbelieving try to fortify themselves, thinking that anything in which they trust is sufficient for them. But what does the just do? He brings nothing before God except faith: then he brings nothing of his own, because faith borrows, as it were, through favor, what is not in man's possession. He, then, who lives by faith, has no life in himself; but because he wants it, he flies for it to God alone.[135]

---

131. Martin Luther, *Luther's Works, Volume 19: Lectures on the Minor Prophets II*, ed. Hilton C. Oswald (St. Louis: Concordia, 1974), 123.

132. Luther, *Luther's Works*, 121.

133. John Calvin, *The Institutes of the Christian Religion*, trans. Henry Beveridge (repr., Peabody, MA: Hendrickson, 2008), § 3.11.18, p. 488.

134. John Calvin, *Commentaries on the Twelve Minor Prophets*, trans. John Owen (repr., Grand Rapids: Baker, 2009), 4:73.

135. Calvin, *Commentaries on the Twelve Minor Prophets*, 4:75.

How does Calvin square Habakkuk's thought with Paul's in Rom 1:17? Although it seems Paul has misapplied the prophet's words, in fact Paul has applied the principle of Habakkuk: "that men are emptied of all works, when they produce their faith before God: for as long as man possesses anything of his own, he does not please God by faith alone, but also by his own worthiness."[136] So Paul teaches in principle what is clearly demonstrated by Habakkuk: "eternal salvation is to be attained by faith only; for we are destitute of all merits by works, and are constrained to stand naked and needy before God; and then Yahweh justifies us freely."[137] Those who are justified by faith are given a righteousness that satisfies God's wrath against the sinner. As Calvin says in his *Institutes,* "Christ ever remains a Mediator to reconcile the Father to us, and there is a perpetual efficacy in his death."[138]

This basic insight on the nature of faith and justification carries through in Reformed communities of Christian tradition today, whether in mainline denominations such as Lutheran, Presbyterian, Anglican, or in free-church traditions such as charismatic, Pentecostal, Bible-church, or Baptist. It should be noted that the Catholic Church's Counter-Reformation set the issue of faith as a central plank in their platform, and so Hab 2:4 was squarely set in the discussion. This disagreement was wide and only recently came to uneasy concord in 1999 with the "Joint Declaration on the Doctrine of Justification."[139]

### The Modern Period

After the Reformation, scholarship increasingly attuned its ears to hear the historical message of Habakkuk, but sometimes with the effect that that word was divorced from the life of the church. The circumstances that led to this situation are well known: the rise of academic biblical criticism, the historical turn in biblical studies, the division between dogmatics and biblical theology

---

136. Calvin, *Commentaries on the Twelve Minor Prophets,* 4:77.

137. Calvin, *Commentaries on the Twelve Minor Prophets,* 4:77.

138. Calvin, *Institutes,* § 3.14.11, p. 509.

139. See Wayne Stumme, ed., *The Gospel of Justification in Christ: Where Does the Church Stand Today?* (Grand Rapids: Eerdmans, 2006), 27–41, 69–84. See the declaration on: http://www.lutheranworld.org/LWF_Documents/EN/JDDJ_99-jd97e.pdf; http://www.vatican.va/roman_curia/pontifical_councils/chrstuni/documents/rc_pc_chrstuni_doc_31101999_cath-luth-joint-declaration_en.html. For analysis and critique, see Ted M. Dorman, "The Joint Declaration on the Doctrine of Justification: Retrospect and Prospects," *JETS* 44 (2001): 421–34; Stumme, *Gospel of Justification in Christ.* See also Eduardus van der Borght, ed., *The Unity of the Church: A Theological State of the Art and Beyond,* SRTh 18 (Leiden: Brill, 2010).

as an academic methodological necessity, the list goes on. Because of these factors, scholars interpreted Habakkuk to get a glimpse of an ancient prophet belonging to a distant past. Whatever he said to the church came to be a secondary matter. Still, Habakkuk as a resource that inspired the church never diminished.

Matthew Poole (1624–1679 CE) wrote a number of works, his most famous being a commentary on the Scriptures. In it, he interprets Habakkuk as a book that teaches the providence of God and the way for the faithful to trust in God. The righteous is the one who "adores the depth of Divine Providence, and is rewarded with the Truth of Divine Promises," which God fulfills at the appropriate time.[140]

This is seen in the commentary of Matthew Henry (1662–1714 CE), who says Hab 2:4 encourages faithfulness among God's people; that faithfulness looks to God and trusts in his promises concerning the vision (in vv. 2–3). Yet Henry also marks this verse as being the foundation of the Reformation doctrine of justification by faith alone in Christ alone.[141]

E. B. Pusey (1800–1882 CE) wrote a commentary on the Minor Prophets that still stands as a major resource for the church. In Pusey's understanding, Habakkuk teaches many things, but for all of them, it is a teaching that contrasts those who falter and do not believe in God's work (Hab 1:5) against those who are just and live by faith (Hab 2:4b).[142] Pusey also provides an extensive apologetic for the rationality of Habakkuk's predictive prophecy concerning the Babylonians. He commends Habakkuk finally because of his radical teaching on fidelity to God: "His faith triumphs most, when all, in human sight, is lost."[143]

The twentieth century saw an extraordinary rise in the number of works devoted to the interpretation of Habakkuk that hold relevance for the life of the church. Gerhard von Rad's *The Message of the Prophets* is exemplary in this regard. He saw in the prophets a book of expectation that leads the church to Christ, wherein Christ then fulfills the expectation of the prophets.[144] Habakkuk 2:4 is characteristic of this expectation in terms of its call for faith in light of God's announcement in Hab 2:2–3.[145]

---

140. Matthew Poole, *Annotations upon the Holy Bible*, 4th ed., vol. 2 (London: Poultrey, 1700).

141. Matthew Henry, *The Comprehensive Commentary on the Holy Bible: Vol. 3; Psalm LXIV–Malachi*, ed. William Jenks (Philadelphia: Lippincott, 1849), 111.

142. E. B. Pusey, *The Minor Prophets: With a Commentary Explanatory and Practical and Introductions to the Several Books* (Oxford: Parker, 1860), 397.

143. Pusey, *Minor Prophets*, 405.

144. Gerhard von Rad, *The Message of the Prophets* (London: SCM, 1969).

145. Von Rad, *Message of the Prophets*, 159.

Although not of the Christian church, two major Jewish names need to be mentioned, not only for their impact on Christian interpretation, but also for their exploration of the prophets: Martin Buber and Abraham Heschel.[146] Buber does not treat Habakkuk at all, though his exposition of prophetic suffering applies to the experience of Habakkuk: "God offers himself to the sufferer who, in the depth of his despair, keeps to God with his refractory complaint; He offers Himself to him as an answer."[147] Heschel's chapter devoted to Habakkuk presents the essence of prophetic faith: "Prophetic faith is to trust in Him, in Whose presence stillness is a form of understanding."[148] In both Buber and Heschel, prophetic faith is reliance and stillness before the God of Israel. The encounter with God is a sufficient response to the questions and troubles that the prophets face.

Finally, in his major exploration on the mercy and righteousness of God, Karl Barth draws upon Hab 2:4 to describe the extraordinary power of the righteousness of God. The one who leans upon God utterly and rests in the salvation that comes *only* through God and his righteousness, to this one the day of judgment (or the "Day of the Lord" in Barth's exposition) will not be a day of darkness or terror but rather a day of "light and joy." Why? Because, and only because, that person has placed his faith in the righteous God who saves. Hence Barth's climactic quotation: "On that day—in accordance with the saying in Hab 2:4 which is cited in Rom 1:17 and which assumed such importance for Luther—he will remain alive in virtue of his faith: *iustus ex fide vivet*."[149] Yet Barth goes further to suggest that faith in God is nothing other than faith in Jesus Christ, because it is in Christ "that God reveals and does what is worthy of himself. It is in Him that He reveals and exercises His own righteousness in favor of those whom He has called and chosen, even though their own righteousness is as filthy rags. . . . It is faith in Him which God reckons to the ungodly as righteousness, and in which he becomes and is truly righteous."[150]

## Habakkuk Today

The present day sees a veritable renaissance of interpretation from the heart of the church. This is often identified as "theological interpretation," which is a

146. Martin Buber, *The Prophetic Faith* (New York: Macmillan, 1949); Abraham J. Heschel, *The Prophets: An Introduction*, vol. 1 (New York: Harper, 1962).

147. Buber, *Prophetic Faith*, 195.

148. Heschel, *Prophets*, 143.

149. Karl Barth, *CD* II.1:390.

150. Barth, *CD* II.1:390.

term that applies to the present commentary. Other works are devoted to this theme, and this commentary highlights many of these.

Gowan's monograph and interpretation of the book still stands out for its theological depth.[151] His work is academic, but it is tooled to speak to the church and to address the theology of Habakkuk. He finds here a resource for the church as she deals with extraordinary pain, and while it is not a theodicy, he suggests that Habakkuk does provide a way to work through suffering and triumph in faith.

Childs's chapter on Habakkuk remains influential, not least because he wrestles with the canonical implications of Habakkuk's message. Historical-critical explorations, he warns, fail to access the heart of the book. Rather the tensions in the final form of the book present a theological presentation of history in which God's purposes cannot be thwarted: the evil will be punished and God's glory will be manifest throughout the world. Second, Childs sees that Habakkuk provides a model for faithful life in the face of suffering.[152]

Daniel Berrigan's commentary on the Minor Prophets aims at hearing God's address from that corpus for the church, particularly with a word of pacifism and antiwar policies. The gift of Habakkuk for the church in Berrigan's view is the prophet's ability to name injustice and terror in his day. Prayer is key here. The prophet faithfully recognizes and raises the issues of injustice in his day. As he has done, so must the church do as well.[153] As the church names evil, she fights against it, and with the hope that evil and death will not have the last word.[154]

Recently, Ntamushobora finds in Habakkuk a powerful model of faithfulness to God for the anguish of the African church. Among other poignant and relevant lessons, the book models a theology of suffering that the church can embody as they face serial corruption, war, violence, and famine. Ntamushobora provocatively suggests that from Habakkuk, African Christians may discover that they too may be freed to wrestle over the gritty relationship between God's justice and human suffering—in the Congo, Nigeria, Uganda, or wherever.[155]

---

151. Gowan, *Triumph of Faith*.

152. Childs, *Introduction to the Old Testament*, 452–55; for the influence of Childs, see G. Michael O'Neal, *Interpreting Habakkuk as Scripture: An Application of the Canonical Approach of Brevard S. Childs*, StBibLit 9 (New York: Peter Lang, 2007).

153. Daniel Berrigan, *Minor Prophets, Major Themes* (Eugene, OR: Wipf & Stock, 2009), 277–90.

154. Berrigan, *Minor Prophets, Major Themes*, 311.

155. Faustin Ntamushobora, *From Trials to Triumphs: The Voice of Habakkuk to the Suffering African Christian* (Eugene, OR: Wipf & Stock, 2009), 34.

Grace Ko reads Habakkuk to discover its resolution to the problem of theodicy. She employs a close rhetorical reading of the book (rather than a strict historical-critical investigation). She finds that Habakkuk presents four major themes: theodicy, the righteous shall live by his faithfulness, reap what you sow, and the sovereignty of God. Ko argues that Habakkuk stands on the side of the suffering people, challenging God's punishment of them. God's response in Hab 2:2–5 is the "resolution" to the theodicy question in the book; God *would* punish the wicked and he would deliver the righteous. What is needed is faithfulness to him in the face of pain. Habakkuk 3, with its cosmic reversal of the wicked and divine deliverance, gives surety to God's promise in Hab 2:2–5. Habakkuk's transformation and his teaching on theodicy become a paradigm for the faithful for generations after him.[156]

Increased interest in theological interpretation has given rise to new commentary series that will wrestle with Habakkuk theologically, namely, the International Theological Commentary Series and the Brazos Theological Commentary on the Bible. A recent contribution to Habakkuk comes from the Transformative Word commentary series.[157] The series is designed to bring to bear, in brief compass, the messages of individual books of Scripture for the church. As such, Thomas links Habakkuk and prayer, and connects Habakkuk to the life and ministry of Jesus:

> It is entirely appropriate to understand Jesus as the ultimate demonstration of God's faithfulness to his people anticipated in Habakkuk 2. . . . God is worthy of our fidelity precisely because of his extraordinary divine faithfulness, both in guaranteeing the vision of Habakkuk (2:2–3) and in guaranteeing the coming of Christ the Lord.[158]

## Conclusion

This brief overview of Habakkuk's reception reminds us that the life-topics that emerge in the book are not unique to human history. Faith in the faithful God remains vital for a healthy spirituality, especially in the face of horrors. This was true in Habakkuk's day, and it holds true today. People do horrible things to other people, and often in the name of God. As John Collins has noted, colonists in America wielded the Bible and the name of God to kill and dispossess

---

156. Ko, *Theodicy in Habakkuk.*
157. Thomas, *Faith amid the Ruins.*
158. Thomas, *Faith amid the Ruins,* 87.

Native Americans upon their conquest of the New World.[159] More current to the present day, various manifestations of the abuse and exploitation of parishioners at the hands of ministers is an all-too-common reality which the church must own. When such abuse occurs, it is indicative of an abandonment of the vital word of the Lord and an active disfigurement of the beauty and integrity of God's good creation.

Other instances of abuse may sit closer to the situation that Habakkuk saw. It is not uncommon to witness nations rise to power, with power-hungry leaders bent upon their own benefit (at the expense of others). Such was Babylon, as will be explored in this volume; and such is the case in human history. As I write in the state of Oklahoma in America, I am acutely aware of American policy toward Cherokee Indians among other Indian nations during the Jacksonian presidency that effectively sought to displace and relocate these peoples through a variety of exploitative tactics. The forced migration effectively severed roots of tribal social identity and eventuated into the great "Trail of Tears" that saw thousands upon thousands of Native Americans perish. American policy was motivated by several factors, not least the need of land for the white populace as well as an imperialist and colonizing mind-set that believed the Native Americans needed to be cultured and assimilated into a civil society.[160] This policy reverberates where I live and work at present, which has the highest concentration of Native Americans in the United States. Their concentration in Oklahoma is a result of unjust and forced migration policy.

The hubris of the policy effectively exposes the proclivity of human beings to satisfy themselves and their perceived needs while exploiting, subjugating, or even killing other humans to achieve that satisfaction and perceived need. History sees analogues to such policies outside the confines of American politics, and the power-grabs of Stalin in Russia or Pol Pot in Cambodia need not be rehearsed here. Sadly, this is an all-too-typical feature of the human experience, as recent history in the Sudan, Liberia, and the Balkan states illustrates.

When confronted with this set of traumas, neither is it unique to call upon God. People commonly ask God, "How long?" and "Why?" During the first crusade in the eleventh century CE, Christians massacred Jews brutally in the name of God (and money). Out of this context Rabbi David bar Meshullam of Speyer wrote his "Elohim: al domi ledami" ("God: Be Not Silent to My Blood"), in which he cries to God for protection and response in light of the crusaders'

---

159. John J. Collins, "The Zeal of Phinehas: The Bible and the Legitimation of Violence," *JBL* 122 (2003): 3–21, esp. 13–14. See also Conrad Cherry, ed., *God's New Israel: Religious Interpretations of American Destiny* (Englewood Cliffs, NJ: Prentice-Hall, 1971).

160. See Ronald N. Satz, *American Indian Policy in the Jacksonian Era* (Norman: University of Oklahoma Press, 2002).

slaughter. In the poem Meshullam presents the Jews as martyrs, as pregnant women are cut open by marauders and schoolchildren are slaughtered like sacrificial animals. The poet cries out: "After this, O Exalted and Triumphant Lord, will You hold back?"

The tone of martyrdom does not arise in the same way in Uri Zvi Greenberg's *Streets of the River*, but pleas to God remain. These cries arise out of the horror of Jewish decimation in Europe from the beginning of the twentieth century to the Shoah at the hands of the Nazi regime.[161] The tone of Greenberg's poetry is direct and strident, querying why the reality of Jewish suffering persists, and how one negotiates its horrors.

"Why, God?" is a persistent question amid horrors. As bombs fell and fighting persisted in Sarajevo, Zlata Filipović struggled to come to terms with bitter onslaught. She writes in her diary, "All around Vodoprivreda there were cars burning, people dying, and nobody could help them. God, why is this happening?"[162] Zlata's question "God, why?" is never fully answered in her diary.

When read alongside these questions that people offer to God, the ancient text of Habakkuk carries with it a currency not to be missed. Yet if the Bible is God's word of life given by God for his people to "eat" and energize them to love him and serve others, then Habakkuk may prove to be a word that turns bitter in our mouths.[163] This commentary argues that while it is a word that may stick in our throats, Habakkuk remains a feast for those who will take the time to dine at the table. As we read slowly and intentionally, Habakkuk helps us taste the Bread of Life. For her faithful witness to God, the church must learn to listen and to respond to the cadence of this relevant voice in the symphony of Scripture.

161. Cf. Alan Mintz, *Ḥurban: Responses to Catastrophe in Hebrew Literature* (Syracuse, NY: Syracuse University Press, 1996), 94–101, 165–202.

162. Zlata Filipović, *Zlata's Diary: A Child's Life in Sarajevo* (New York: Penguin, 1995), 44.

163. The metaphor of "eating" Scripture comes from Ezekiel and Revelation, but in popular imagination as well. See Eugene Peterson, *Eat This Book: A Conversation in the Art of Spiritual Reading* (Grand Rapids: Eerdmans, 2006).

# Habakkuk 1

## Translation

<sup>1:1</sup>The oracle that Habakkuk the prophet saw:

(Habakkuk's First Complaint)

<sup>1:2</sup>"How long, O Yahweh, have I cried out for help,
    But you will not listen?
I cry out, 'Violence!'

But you do not save?

<sup>1:3</sup>Why do you make me look upon iniquity,
    While you gaze upon trouble?
For devastation and violence are before me;
    And there is dispute, and contention arises.

<sup>1:4</sup>Therefore torah is ineffective,
    And justice never goes forth.
For the wicked surround the righteous;
    Therefore crooked justice goes forth."

(The First Divine Response)

<sup>1:5</sup>"Look among the nations and gaze:
    Be astounded; be amazed!
For I am doing a deed in your days;
    You would not believe it if it were recounted.

<sup></sup>¹⁶Behold! I am raising up the Chaldeans,
 The bitter and hasty nation,
The one who walks through expanses of earth
 To seize dwellings that do not belong to him.

¹⁷He is terrible and fearsome;
 His justice and his loftiness proceed from himself.

¹⁸His horses will be swifter than leopards;
 And they will be keener than evening wolves.
And his horsemen will spring about,
 And his horsemen will come from afar.
They will fly like an eagle hurrying to eat.

¹⁹Each and every one comes for violence;
 Their faces are full of the east wind.
 And he gathers his captives like sand.

¹:¹⁰He scoffs at kings,
 And rulers are a laughingstock to him.
He mocks every fortress,
 And he heaps up earth and takes it.

¹:¹¹Then a wind passes and moves over,
 And he will be guilty whose strength is his god."

(Habakkuk's Second Complaint)

¹:¹²"Are you not from old, O Yahweh?
 My God, my Holy One: will we not die?
O Yahweh, did you place him for judgment;
 And, O Rock, did you not establish him to reprove?

¹:¹³You are too pure of eyes to look upon evil,
 And you are not able to gaze upon trouble.
Why do you consider the treacherous?
 (Why) do you keep silent,
When the wicked swallow up (one) more righteous than he?

¹:¹⁴Have you made humanity like the fishes of the sea,
 Like a creeping thing, not having dominion over it?

¹:¹⁵He brings each one up with a fishhook;
    He will drag him away in his dragnet.
And he will gather him in his fishnet;
    Therefore he will be glad and rejoice.

¹:¹⁶Therefore he will sacrifice to his dragnet,
    And he will sacrifice to his fishnet.
For with them fat is his portion;
    And his food is rich.

¹:¹⁷Therefore shall he empty out his dragnet,
    And continually slaughter nations he does not pity.

## Summary

All encounter pain in life. Pain can be self-inflicted, but many times it comes because of grave injustice perpetrated against another. Habakkuk's pain is a result of the wickedness of his own community—the people of God. They ought to have known better but neglected fidelity to their God. Habakkuk 1 introduces the plight of the prophet and his community. He talks to God about his confusion and hurt, and then he waits for God's reply. When God does answer, the divine response leads the prophet to ask another series of questions. God then responds to the second set.

This "give-and-take" interaction is distinctive when compared with the remainder of the Old Testament. The Psalms use communal and individual voices to address Israel's God (e.g., Pss 22; 44; 74; 88), and Lamentations employs several voices in a similar way. In neither case, however, does God interact with the protagonist as he does with Habakkuk. The book of Job is closer to what emerges in Habakkuk's dialogue. In Job, a few speakers appear and interact, and only Job prays to God out of his pain (Job 9:28–31; 10:2–22; 13:17–28; 14:1–22; 17:4; 30:20–31:40). God speaks as well, though only once in the "whirlwind speeches" (Job 38–41). The closest text example to what one finds to Habakkuk's dialogue with God comes in Jeremiah's so-called confessions (Jer 11–20). Still, in the confessions, the tone is different and the dialogue between the prophet and God is not as concentrated or closely connected as it is in Habakkuk. So, Habakkuk's interchange with God is unique.

Habakkuk's interchange with God is pastorally relevant, because it clarifies the special way that *suffering* and *prayer* can and should sit closely together. It is natural for people to cry out to their God amid their pain. Understanding the relationship between pain and prayer in Habakkuk, in turn, informs the book's theology.

Habakkuk 1:2–4 comprises the prophet's complaint to God while Hab 1:5–11 marks God's response. The prophet then replies with another complaint in Hab 1:12–17 that continues through Hab 2:1. God then answers this second complaint in 2:2–5. Habakkuk 2:6–20 displays a different form of prophetic speech than what precedes it (woe oracles), but in the final arrangement of the book these verses still may be understood as part of God's response to Habakkuk. Chapter 3, then, provides Habakkuk's final reply to God. A progression of thought advances through the dialogue, which is identifiable through the poetic use of repetition. Repetition will be discussed in the commentary where it occurs. In summary, however, note figure 1 below.

**Figure 1: Repetition of Language in Habakkuk 1**

| Repeated Terms/Roots | Habakkuk Speaks | God Speaks |
| --- | --- | --- |
| יהוה/Yahweh | Hab 1:2, 12 | _____ |
| ראה/r'h | Hab 1:3, 13 | Hab 1:5 |
| נבט/nbṭ | Hab 1:3, 13 | Hab 1:5 |
| חמס/ḥms | Hab 1:2, 3 | Hab 1:9 |
| עמל/'ml | Hab 1:3, 13 | _____ |
| רע/עון/r'/ 'wn | Hab 1:3, 13 | |
| רשע/rš' | Hab 1:4, 13 | |
| צדק/ṣdk | Hab 1:4, 13 | (cf. Hab 2:4) |
| שפט/יצא/špṭ/yṣ' | Hab 1:4 (1:12, שפט/špṭ) | Hab 1:7 |
| אֱלוֹהַ/'ĕlôah | Hab 1:12 | Hab 1:11 |

## Commentary

**1:1** The title "the prophet" (הנביא/*hannābî*') first occurs here in the Minor Prophets as an introductory formula. It appears also in Hab 3:1; Hag 1:1, 3, 13; and Zech 1:1, 7, but in these latter four texts, the title is coupled with a date formula as well. The date is lacking in Hab 1:1, as well as in Joel, Obadiah, and Jonah. Using the title "the prophet" (הנביא/*hannābî*') *without* the date formula in Hab 1:1 is unique in the Minor Prophets.

The introduction also describes Habakkuk's succeeding speech as an "oracle" (משא/*maśśā'*). This description for prophetic vision occurs only eighteen times in the Old Testament. Other introductory oracular language is "word of Yahweh" (דבר־יהוה/*dĕbar-Yahweh*) or "vision" (חזון/*ḥāzôn*; see Hab 2:2). The term "oracle" (משא/*maśśā'*) can be translated as "burden" and then interpreted in such a way as to reinforce the terrible weight of God's message to Habakkuk—a word of judgment against God's people. After all, the noun derives from the root that means "to lift, bear," which would lend credence to this translation, at least from an etymological perspective. Typical of the interpretative practice of the church fathers, "oracle" (משא/*massā'*) was understood in this way: a "burden" of the prophet. But the meaning of words is not solely based on etymology.

Weis demonstrates that the משא/*maśśā'* oracle in prophetic superscriptions is a generic term for a divine revelation given to a prophet. Such oracles achieve two things: (1) they identify and reveal God's intentions in human affairs, and (2) they provide direction for human response in the light of God's revelation.[1] Weis's presentation of the meaning of משא/*maśśā'* fits well with Hab 1:1. The term is a descriptor of what will follow in the book of Habakkuk, both God's intentions in human affairs (raising up the Babylonians for judgment) and the appropriate human response in light of God's revelation (faithfulness to the faithful God). More specifically, God's revelation of what he is doing in human affairs is found in 1:5–11 and 2:6–20, balanced by Habakkuk's questions in Hab 1:2–4 and 1:12–17. The response that God expects from the faithful in the light of his revelation is found in Hab 2:2–5. As such, the oracle (משא/*maśśā'*) mentioned in the superscription gives a summary of the first two chapters of the book.

**1:2–4** After the superscription, Hab 1:2–4 introduces the substance of Habakkuk's laments as well as God's response. "How long?" (עד־אנה/*'ad-'ānâ*) and "why?" (למה/*lāmmâ*) are interrogatives often used in complaints to God, and are typical of prayers of lament.[2] Questions like these in the Old Testament quite often carry with them a rhetorical purpose—they are used to draw God's attention to the situation so that he might respond out of his goodness. Habakkuk uses these forms to address God in vv. 2–3. The motivations that underlie the questions appear after the questions themselves. Questions to God are not wrong. In fact, questions are *natural* human responses. Jesus requested that

---

1. Richard D. Weis, "A Definition of the Genre *Massa'* in the Hebrew Bible" (PhD diss., Emory University, 1986).

2. Cf. Exod 16:28; Num 14:11; Pss 13:1–2; 62:4; Jer 47:6. Variations are: "How long?" (עד־מתי/*'ad-mātay*; cf. Pss 6:3[H 4]; 74:10[H 9]; 80:4[H 5]; 82:2; 90:13; 94:3; Isa 6:11; Jer 4:14, 21; 47:5) and "How long?" (עד־מה/*'ad-mâ*; Pss 79:5; 89:46[H 7]). See the discussion of Claus Westermann, *Praise and Lament in the Psalms*, trans. Keith R. Crim and Richard N. Soulen (Atlanta: John Knox, 1981), 176–79.

the cup of the cross be taken from him in the garden of Gethsemane. Asking God questions is typically human, and this practice reveals a deep and utter dependence upon the Creator.

1. "How long?"—the prophet sees the world out of joint and wonders whether or when God will set it right. The issue here is the *duration* of injustice. Surely the prophet's experience of injustice will be an affront to God and he will respond! And yet the prophet deems God to be aloof, disconnected, and indifferent to the situation. This temporal interrogative "how long," however, shows that Habakkuk does not think that God will be this way indefinitely. Why could this be the case?

Often in the Old Testament, when God's people face injustice, God acts to deliver them because of his love for them. This is typified in Exod 2:23-25. As the Israelites face oppression under Pharaoh, they cry out to God for help. After this happens, God sees their situation, remembers his covenant with the patriarchs, and then determines to deliver them. The number of repeated terms between Exod 2:23-25 and Hab 1:2-3 is striking, revealing a similar pattern of call and response between petitioner and God:

> "their cry for help" (Exod 2:23) // "have I cried out" (Hab 1:2)
> "And they cried out" (Exod 2:23) // "I cry out" (Hab 1:2)
> "And he heard" (Exod 2:24) // "but you do not listen" (Hab 1:2)
> "And he saw" (Exod 2:25) // "You make me look" (Hab 1:3)

Yet these contexts are not identical. Exodus narrates God's hearing (Exod 2:24) the cries of his people, of seeing (Exod 2:25) their affliction, of knowing (Exod 2:25) of their suffering, and then *acting on their behalf*. The pattern of deliverance is inverted in Habakkuk's lament—God will *not* "hear" (Hab 1:3) the prophet. Instead of "seeing" his people's plight, God makes Habakkuk "look upon" (Hab 1:3) iniquity, while God seems to idly "gaze upon" (Hab 1:2) trouble. In light of what God has done in the past to deliver his people, especially in the exodus experience, how can his silence and idleness persist? Surely this is not who God is!

A similar cry to Habakkuk's is found on the lips of Job, as he faces the persistent divine silence in Job 19. In v. 1 Job wonders "how long?" (עַד־אָנָה/'ad-'ānâ) his adverse situation will go on, while in v. 7 Job exclaims: "See, I cry out, 'Violence!' But he does not answer. I cry out for help, but there is no justice." The similarities between this verse and the prophet's complaint in Hab 1:2-4 are evident. How long will the Lord be deaf to the cries of his people for justice?

2. "Why?"—coupled with the prophet's concern over the duration of injustice, Habakkuk simply does not understand *why* things are the way they

are. There is a cognitive dissonance between what Habakkuk knows of God and what his situation reveals. How can God *make* the prophet look upon iniquity (note the *hiphil* construction of the verb with a suffixed pronoun in Hebrew)? Why would God make the prophet look upon sin? The prophet does not engage a silent or aloof God as v. 2 intimates, but rather one who *causes* the prophet to observe iniquity and trouble. Further, Habakkuk wonders not why God would *do* this, but rather how could God *himself* "tolerate"[3] this injustice?

The world that Habakkuk describes is topsy-turvy. Habakkuk's complaint draws together a theological conundrum. God *actively makes the prophet see iniquity*, and yet also he *passively sits by and does not counteract sin*. For the prophet, both divine actions seem to be fundamentally opposed to who God is. What he perceives to be God's passivity *and* activity leads to a loss of order for his world, leading him to pray. This is hinted at in vv. 2–3, but will be explicitly brought to the prophet's argument in 1:14. From the perspective of the prophet, this upside-down world surely cannot be the kind of reality that God authorizes: chaos rises up, and this disorder comes as a result of God's passivity toward the injustice and inequity that was mentioned in the first lines.

Habakkuk names various kinds of injustice in vv. 2–3 (see also Hab 1:9; 2:17). His language depicts a world that God surely does not endorse: "violence" (חמס/*ḥāmās*); "iniquity" (און/*ʾāwen*); "trouble" (עמל/*ʿāmāl*); "devastation" (שׁד/*šôd*); "dispute" (ריב/*rîb*); and "contention" (מדון/*mādôn*). The general and negative term "violence" (חמס/*ḥāmās*) is used in v. 2. This is a theological term that indicates unjust action against God or other people. For example, in Genesis God judges his creation with a flood because of pervasive human violence (חמס/*ḥāmās*; cf. Gen 6:11, 13). By enacting violence in whatever form, humans reject the goodness of God's authority and harmonious design in creation.

J. J. M. Roberts says the term "violence" (חמס/*ḥāmās*), when coupled with "devastation" (שׁוד/*šôd*), could indicate something more specific. Namely, it could connote property that the government took by force. The word pair can be used for the oppression of a people by its officials and government (so Amos 3:10; Ezek 45:9). The word pair also appears in Jer 6:7 and 20:8, signifying the general oppression and injustice that condemns God's people for judgment. Roberts rightly notes that Jehoiakim and his administration certainly were guilty of oppression, and this may have been part of it. As Jer 22:13 reveals, Jehoiakim was guilty of driving his people into forced labor. The king also "shed the blood of the innocent" as well in his reign, as remembered by Jeremiah (Jer 22:17) and the writer of Kings (2 Kgs 24:4). He also tried to kill the prophet Jeremiah and

---

3. For this translation of תַּבִּיט /*tabbîṭ*, see O'Neal, *Interpreting Habakkuk*, 80.

killed the prophet Shemaiah (Jer 26:20–24). This commentary suggests reading the prophecy of Habakkuk in the reign of Jehoiakim, so Roberts's approach is instructive. He goes on to say, "How can God idly watch, the prophet wants to know, while these things are done before Habakkuk's very eyes?"[4]

The terms "dispute" (ריב/*rîb*) and "contention" (מדון/*mādôn*) derive from the legal sphere and indicate a breach of justice in the judicial processes in Judah. This may mean a perversion of justice on the one hand, or on the other hand it may indicate that disputes in the land are not even adjudicated by judges. In this latter case, proper administration of justice is not given. Contention and strife is the order of the day because the courts are not doing what they should be doing (see Jer 15:10 as a cotext to this idea). Modern analogues to this ancient lament are, sadly, all too common.

"Iniquity" (און/*ʾāwen*) and "trouble" (עמל/*ʿāmāl*) are used in a variety of ways in the Old Testament. Mária Eszenyei Szeles suggests that "iniquity" (און/*ʾāwen*) indicates "human wickedness in the form of deceit, misrepresentation, deliberate misleading of someone to do harm or cause him to suffer" (Isa 10:1; 59:4; Num 23:21; Job 5:6).[5] Of course, the term also connotes general human wickedness (cf. Gen 15:16; Exod 20:5; 34:7–9; Num 14:18–34). Further, she rightly notes that "trouble" (עמל/*ʿāmāl*) depicts "weariness, exhaustion, enervation, a loss of vitality, collapse, caused not by physical tiredness but by the hostile behavior of one's fellows that produces spiritual torture (cf. Ps 73:16; Isa 10:1; Hab 1:13)."[6] As language of horrific human experience piles on top of one another in 1:2–3, the poetry displays a generalized portrait of chaos, strife, and disharmony. Considering this situation, the prophet cries out—"Why?"—but God stands silent.

Habakkuk offers lament over the shattered and violent world he experiences. To be sure, it is a world where sin and its effects are evident. But Habakkuk refuses to resign himself to the present order of things. Instead, the prophet implicates God as acting against his good creation: "you do not save" (v. 2)! What does one make of Habakkuk's rather strident complaint? One response in the Christian tradition is to recognize Habakkuk's situation but encourage a different kind of faith than one finds in Habakkuk's prayer, one that embraces suffering rather than resisting it. Such was the position of Jerome, who wrote the first full commentary on Habakkuk, as we saw under the heading "Prayer, Divine Justice, and the Future Hope" in the introduction.

---

4. Roberts, *Nahum, Habakkuk, and Zephaniah*, 88–90 (quotation on p. 89).

5. Mária Eszenyei Szeles, *Wrath and Mercy: A Commentary on the Books of Zephaniah and Habakkuk*, ITC (Grand Rapids: Eerdmans, 1987), 18.

6. Eszenyei Szeles, *Wrath and Mercy*, 18.

It is true that suffering produces things in us. But this fact may also lead us to the conclusion that it is better not to pray to God about one's suffering. Habakkuk thought differently.

Although his prayers appear impious, it is not the case. The prophet's complaint against God is *persuasive*, attempting to *mobilize* God to act. An analogue to Habakkuk's prayer is Jesus's teaching on the parable of the persistent widow. In the face of injustice and sin, prayers enable the sufferer to address the God of justice. Like the persistent widow in Jesus's parable (Luke 18), the prophet goes to the Judge and cries for justice in his day. Only the Judge can give a just verdict. As will be discussed in "Centering Shalom: Habakkuk and Prayer," below, the prayer of Habakkuk exposes a radical piety before God. In a world where the rainbows of paradise lie shattered on the ground, where sin and violence abound, Habakkuk imagines a better world, one in which God will eradicate the devastation, sin, and strife in the present order. This is the persistent hope in lament prayer.

---

EXCURSUS: THE POWER OF LAMENT PRAYER

Lament is a resource for God's people who negotiate pain and suffering. Amid all the kinds of prayer that one finds in Scripture and the Christian life (petition, intercession, praise, confession of sin, meditation, etc.), lament is distinctive prayer because it enables God's people to plead for divine help and deliverance from distress, suffering, and pain. Although different definitions of lament emerge among scholars, I define lament as follows: *lament is a kind of prayer that voices a complaint to God about distress, and it is uttered to persuade God to act on the sufferer's behalf.* From Scripture, we see over and over again that lament is constitutive of the life of faith. The major literary contexts of lament lie in the Psalter, Job, Jeremiah, and Lamentations, though it is interspersed throughout the rest of the Bible (including our present text of Habakkuk). Notice some examples of lament:

> Arise, O Yahweh, in your anger; rise up against the rage of my enemies.
> Awake, my God; decree justice! (Ps 7:6)

> Hear, O Yahweh, my righteous plea; listen to my cry.
> Give ear to my prayer—it does not rise from deceitful lips. (Ps 17:1)

> My God! My God! Why have you forsaken me? (Ps 22:1; Matt 27:46;
> Mark 15:34)

Awake, O Yahweh! Why do you sleep? Rouse yourself!
Do not reject us forever! (Ps 44:23)

Rise up, O judge of the earth;
Pay back to the proud what they deserve! (Ps 94:2)

"Do not declare me guilty! Let me know why you prosecute me!" (Job
    10:2)

"Why do you hide your face and consider me your enemy?" (Job 13:24)

"I cry out to you for help, but you do not answer me;
when I stand up, you look at me.
You have turned against me with cruelty;
you harass me with your strong hand." (Job 30:20–21)

We have transgressed and rebelled—you have not forgiven! (Lam 3:39)

"O Lord, holy and true, how long until you judge and avenge our blood
from those who live on the earth?" (Rev 6:10)

One might also note Jesus's teaching on prayer in Luke 18 in his parable about the persistent widow. His description of the widow going to the judge to receive justice bears the marks of lament prayer.

In each of the prayers identified above, the lament is firmly rooted in a strong sense of divine justice. God is always and ever the One with whom the sufferer appeals, the One the sufferer believes is listening, powerful and just to give an appropriate response. The sources of pain in lament prayer are various. Pain emerges from the activity of enemies, from one's own sin, and one even sees the lamenter's pain emerging from the activity of God.[7] Notice that the pain expressed in the verses cited above, and in Habakkuk, surfaces not as petty complaints, but as serious issues of justice about which the lamenter cannot keep silent. Lament positions issues of justice that were *formerly* experienced—but are not experienced now—firmly in view before God *presently* (see especially Ps 74).

When compared with praise to God in Scripture, it is apparent that lament is situated a bit differently in the life of faith. Normally, praise looks *back* at what

---

7. Self (and sin), enemies, and God are all potential sources of pain in laments, and thereby the substance of the prayer to God, as Westermann has ably shown (*Praise and Lament in the Psalms*, 169).

God justly has done in the *past* in salvation, but lament looks forward to what God will do in the *present* and the *future* in salvation. Lament is constitutive to the life of faith because God can and does answer prayer, including lament prayer, based on the Lord's justice. Lament is peeking around the corner, anticipating the mercies and justice of God; and the just God does respond to lament. As Jesus's teaching in Luke 18 indicates, God the Father is a just judge, who can and will hear the cries of the afflicted and respond in righteousness.

Prayer, including lament, is vital to the life and history of the church. One sees that in the way Christian forebears have written about prayer since the days of Origen's famous and still important work on the subject in the late second to early third century CE.[8] Modern biblical scholarship clarified the nature of lament for the history of God's people. Hermann Gunkel and the scholarship that received his work understood lament (or, in the German, *Klage*) to mean *direct address to the Lord about distress.*[9] He labeled prayers such as we have in Hab 1:2-4 "communal complaint songs" or "individual complaint songs." The German term he used, *Klage*, could mean either "complaint" or "lament" when rendered in other languages (especially English!). But, due to differences (and imprecision) in the English language, this distinction can be confused with a simple expression of grief in times of distress. It is one thing to say, "Oh, God!" as a cathartic expression of pain, and another thing to say, earnestly, "Oh, God, help me in this time of trouble! You are God and I am not. Save me!" The difference is profound.

Lament does *more* than simply express a feeling. Confusion on this point may be a result of uncritical reflection on what is going on in the biblical material or a result of simple terminological confusion, but lament is more than an expression of grief, or something people do when they are sad, or depressed, or upset.[10] Lament is *prayer to God* about a distress.[11] To be sure, uttering lament can be cathartic and healing. It can ameliorate suffering through its very vo-

8. Origen, *Prayer/Exhortation to Martyrdom*, trans. and annotated by John J. O'Meara, ACW 19 (New York: Newman Press, 1954), 15-140. See also Alistair Stewart-Sykes, ed., *On the Lord's Prayer: Tertullian, Cyprian, and Origen*, PPS 29 (Crestwood, NY: St. Vladimir's Seminary Press, 2004).

9. Hermann Gunkel and Joachim Begrich, *An Introduction to the Psalms: The Genres of the Religious Lyric of Israel*, trans. James D. Nogalski, MLBS (Macon, GA: Mercer University Press, 1998).

10. One English dictionary defines lament: "to express sorrow or mourning often demonstratively: mourn; to regret strongly; a crying out in grief: wailing; dirge, elegy, complaint." See *Webster's New Collegiate Dictionary*, 8th ed., s.v. "lament." This is not a definition of biblical lament!

11. Westermann, *Praise and Lament in the Psalms*; Soulen notes the problems with, and takes great care to avoid, terminological confusion between English and German usage of lament language in his translator's note on 170 n. 15.

calization. Some psychological understandings of (and applications of) lament speech advocate this.[12] But biblical lament prayer is not aimed *primarily* (or only) at catharsis, healing, or self-actualization.[13] Lament's primary motivation is to take whatever distress before the throne of God, as Habakkuk does, and await his response.

This point about the *direction* of lament prayer remains important, because it reveals lament to be a kind of petitionary prayer.[14] It asks God something to get him to act; normally, this is suffering or pain. Now, whether he will answer the request or not (or how he will do so), however, is out of the lamenter's hands. God is not a glorified gumball machine. Lamenters pray to their only hope, God himself, in hopes that he will respond to the prayers based on his character: covenant love, mercy, and justice. Patrick Miller says: "[The] fundamental ground of prayer, that is, the responsiveness of God to the cry of human need, is lifted up. All the description of the plight of the afflicted, wherever it occurs in prayer, assumes God's care and compassion, especially for those in distress."[15]

The *tone* and *style* of lament prayer vary. It may appear argumentative in style or in a humble tone. Because of this, different terms touch upon different nuances to lament prayer.[16] So, for instance, penitential prayer confesses sin and

---

12. Without determining lament as a form of cathartic speech, Patricia Huff Byrne does move in this direction in "'Give Sorrow Words': Lament—Contemporary Need for Job's Old Time Religion," *Journal for Pastoral Care & Counseling* 56 (2002): 255–64. See the tendency of Walter Brueggemann, "Psalms and the Life of Faith: A Typology of Function," *JSOT* 17 (1980): 3–32; Brueggemann, *The Message of the Psalms: A Theological Commentary* (Minneapolis: Augsburg, 1984).

13. Note the nuanced and useful discussion of Kristin M. Swenson, *Living through Pain: Psalms and the Search for Wholeness* (Waco, TX: Baylor University Press, 2005), esp. 221–56.

14. See especially distinctions between petitionary prayer and meditation in Heath A. Thomas, "Relating Prayer and Pain: Pyschological Analysis and Lamentation Research," *TynBul* 61 (2010): 197–206. Although God is often the primary addressee in laments, he is not the *only* addressee in laments. See W. Derek Suderman, "Are Individual Complaint Psalms Really Prayers? Recognizing Social Address as Characteristic of Individual Complaints," in *The Bible as a Human Witness to Divine Revelation: Hearing the Word of God through Historically Dissimilar Traditions,* ed. Randall Heskett and Brian Irwin, LHBOTS 469 (London: T&T Clark, 2010), 153–70.

15. Patrick D. Miller, "Prayer as Persuasion: The Rhetoric and Intention of Prayer," *Word & World* 13 (1993): 359.

16. Craig C. Broyles calls lament "protest prayer"; *The Conflict of Faith and Experience in the Psalms: A Form-Critical and Theological Study,* JSOTSup 52 (Sheffield: JSOT Press, 1989). Anson Laytner identifies lament as arguing with God; *Arguing with God: A Jewish Tradition* (Lanham, MD: Rowman and Littlefield, 1990). Carleen Mandolfo identifies lament as "grievance" speech in that it brings a grievance to God for his adjudication; *God in the Dock: Dialogic Tension in the Psalms of Lament,* JSOTSup 357 (London: Sheffield Academic, 2002). John Day identifies lament speech as "complaint"; *Psalms,* OTG (Sheffield: JSOT Press, 1992). William S. Morrow prefers

reveals one kind of distress that needs relief: namely, forgiveness from sin. Other forms of lament prayer present to God different kinds of distress, where there is no confession of sin. These include suffering over sickness, being oppressed by enemies, or even suffering because of God's actions. In both penitence and general lament prayer, the hope is that God would see and respond to prayer.[17] So despite its variety in tone and style, such prayer remains fundamentally *rhetorical speech*.[18] To ignore this reality is to fundamentally misconstrue lament's purpose and effects. Some misconceptions should be exposed.

Despite the discussion above, Christians perennially have trouble with lament prayer. What are some of the challenges, practically speaking? Lament can be characterized as irritating complaint, or worse, adolescent whining: moaning about hardships in life instead of facing them head-on, bravely. Lament can be considered speech for the weak when one should put on a brave face during trouble. After all, suffering and trial *produce* something in the life of the believer: patience, perseverance, and other good traits. For this reason, one should not whine about suffering but rather embrace it as a good gift from God! In this way, Christians construe all suffering as "soul-building." No time to whine . . . God is doing something in the church! Finally, Christians may characterize lament prayer as "impoverished of faith." In this vein of thought, lament prayer is equated to rebellious protest where the petitioner, in effect, turns away from the Lord. Jerome takes this tack in his commentary on Habakkuk. Imagine an angry person striking out at God, upbraiding him over perceived failures

---

"argumentative prayer" for lament speech because God is not always the source of distress which breeds the argumentation *with* God (contra Laytner); *Protest against God: The Eclipse of a Biblical Tradition*, HBM 4 (Sheffield: Sheffield Phoenix, 2006).

17. I am breaking traditional form-critical boundaries to highlight the deeper similarity between lament and penitential prayer. See the very useful work that addresses these issues as well as "fuzzy" generic boundaries: Mark J. Boda, Daniel F. Falk, and Rodney A. Werline, eds., *Seeking the Favor of God: Volume 1, The Origins of Penitential Prayer in Second Temple Judaism*, EJL (Atlanta: Society of Biblical Literature, 2006); especially Samuel E. Balentine's afterword in the same volume, 193–204.

18. This still holds true regardless of whether one follows, with Morrow, that the actual complaint to God *about* God varies in the history of lament tradition. Whether the complaint (or protest) against God appears or disappears in literary tradition does not negate the reality that, e.g., penitential prayer, a form of prayer perhaps seen to be at odds with protest prayer, displays a similar *function* to protest prayer: both are grounded upon a logic that God will hear and respond to the situation of distress (in the case of penitential prayer, sin) experienced by the lamenter. This primary function of lament neither exhausts its ancillary functions nor negates the differences that really lie between conceptions of the world present (or questioned) within, say, lament speech versus penitential prayer. But the foundational issue between two forms of speech that scholars have generally set opposed to one another (lament vs. penitential prayer) is the supposition that God will hear the prayer and respond positively. This is different in function, for instance, than praise.

or decrying God's inability to meet one's needs. After the emotional outburst, the petitioner walks away, justified that he or she has successfully vented some steam. This way of thinking equates lament prayer with the advice of Mrs. Job: "Curse God and die!" (Job 2:9). These views may arise out of certain biases against lament speech, whether they are cultural or religious. I often encounter students who, when faced with the lament psalms in a class, tend to think that the petitioner is a bit off the mark and impious—followers of God ought not speak to the Lord that way!

In terms of systematic theology in the Christian tradition, it has been challenging to address lament as well. Bernd Janowski provocatively says that lament goes virtually unnoticed in dogmatic or systematic theology, and Old Testament scholars have noted this for years![19] Its neglect in Christian theology has led Eva Harasta and Brian Brock to edit a systematic theological exploration of lament in the Christian life in the delightful work *Evoking Lament*.[20] They endeavor to resituate lament within dogmatic and practical theology precisely *because* of its great value as a viable way of being before God in the life of many Christians and because of its neglect, especially in the Western Church. Harasta and Brock maintain that the church today is "beset by practical and theoretical difficulties that make it hard for us to picture Christian lament."[21]

In *Evoking Lament*, Matthias Wüthrich explores how particular views of theodicy (or the relationship between evil, human suffering, and divine justice) can cultivate a theological environment unhospitable to lament within systematic theology.[22] He addresses three views: (1) an Augustinian theodicy; (2) modern "suffering God" theologies; and (3) Barth's "Christological" theodicy. In his view, each of these in its own way undermines or suppresses lament in the life of faith.

(1) *An Augustinian theodicy and lament.* Wüthrich says that from Augustine to the present, theologians used theodicy as a means to exonerate God and incriminate humanity when it comes to human suffering and divine justice. He uses the works of John Hick and Walter Gross and Karl-Josef Kuschel as exemplars that find the theodicy tradition from Augustine into the present day. In this kind of theodicy, theologians tend to incriminate

---

19. Bernd Janowski, *Konfliktgespräche mit Gott: Eine Anthropologie der Psalmen* (Neukirchen-Vluyn: Neukirchener Verlag, 2003), 36.

20. Eva Harasta and Brian Brock, eds., *Evoking Lament: A Theological Discussion* (London: T&T Clark, 2009).

21. Harasta and Brock, *Evoking Lament*, 1.

22. Matthias D. Wüthrich, "Lament for Naught? An Inquiry into the Suppression of Lament in Systematic Theology: On the Example of Karl Barth," in Harasta and Brock, *Evoking Lament*, 60–76.

humanity for suffering, because suffering is a result of human free will and sin, and thereby God stands exonerated (or at least distanced) from the problem of evil and suffering because it is rooted not in God but in human sinfulness.[23] Attempts to pray for divine justice to be enacted on the lamenter's behalf, for instance, are unlikely in an environment where such a theodicy is predominant; crying out for justice would imply that divine justice is not real in the real world. Or as Wüthrich says, the Augustinian theodicy "systematically invalidates the existing theological right of asking the theodicy *question*," namely, is God right to do this or that action?[24] The Augustinian-type theodicy cannot deal sufficiently with the challenges of human suffering in the real world, instead silencing from the outset protests or questions that arise in lament.

(2) *"Suffering God" theodicy and lament.* Another way to negotiate the question of theodicy is to invoke a kind of suffering God, as modern theology has done in the work of Paul Fiddes, Jürgen Moltmann, and others.[25] This is a theology of the cross and a theology *from* the cross, or *Kreuzestheologie* as Fiddes describes it. In this approach, suffering is faced and the question of divine justice is properly raised, but it is answered with a God who suffers with his people. God takes the form of one who suffers with those who are oppressed and bears pain alongside humanity. But this approach raises a question, as Wüthrich rightly understands, about the power of God to be redemptive in *overcoming* situations of pain if he is suffering alongside suffering and oppressed humanity.[26] The power of lament prayer is the appeal that God would counteract experiences of distress and pain, which the biblical witness testifies again and again that he does! So can a God who suffers alongside the sufferer adequately respond to the sufferer in salvation? Wüthrich thinks this view does not adequately foster lament in the life of faith.

---

23. For Hick's explanation of Augustinian theodicy, and how it differs from Irenaean theodicies, see John Hick, *Evil and the God of Love*, 2nd ed. (San Francisco: Harper-Collins, 1977). For Gross and Kuschel, see Walter Gross and Karl-Josef Kuschel, *'Ich schaffe Finsternis und Unheil!' Ist Gott verantwortlich für das Übel?*, 2nd ed. (Mainz: Grunewald, 1995).

24. Wüthrich, "Lament for Naught?," 64.

25. Paul S. Fiddes, *The Creative Suffering of God* (Oxford: Oxford University Press, 1988), esp. 140–43; Fiddes, *Participating in God: A Pastoral Doctrine of the Trinity* (Louisville: Westminster John Knox, 2000), 115–51, 167–70. The changeable and suffering God is pictured as well in process thought (A. N. Whitehead) as well as in the eschatological orientation of Jürgen Moltmann's theology. Fiddes deals with both in his *Creative Suffering of God*. Jürgen Moltmann, *The Crucified God: The Cross of Christ as the Foundation and Criticism of Christian Theology*, trans. R. A. Wilson and J. Bowden (Minneapolis: Fortress, 1993).

26. Wüthrich, "Lament for Naught?," 65.

(3) **Barth's "Christological" theodicy.** Barth addresses the relationship of God, evil, divine justice, and "nothingness" (*das Nichtige*) in *Church Dogmatics* under the heading "God and Nothingness."[27] For Barth, nothingness (*das Nichtige*) is that which is opposed to God and his purposes in Jesus Christ: "There is opposition and resistance to God's world-dominion. . . . This opposition and resistance, this stubborn element and alien factor, may be provisionally defined as nothingness [*das Nichtige*]."[28] This includes evil, sin, the devil, death, demons, and so on. But if nothingness (*das Nichtige*) is opposed to God, then we see that nothingness (*das Nichtige*) sits in relation to God. The question for Barth becomes the nature of that relation. Barth insists that nothingness (*das Nichtige*) finds its place in the relation to God in terms of God's overcoming and victory over nothingness in Jesus. For Barth, then, nothingness (*das Nichtige*) is revealed in its opposition to God precisely because God has overcome it in Jesus Christ. Because Jesus defeats nothingness (*das Nichtige*), nothingness (*das Nichtige*) is revealed as powerless in its opposition to God and eternally weak before God's might. In his providence, God allows nothingness (*das Nichtige*), but only so that it might be overcome in the revelation of Jesus Christ. Despite this formulation, Wüthrich sees a problem in Barth's theodicy. Barth intensifies the problem of God's complicity in evil and suffering because nothingness (*das Nichtige*) has the basis of its very existence in its being overcome in the concrete history of Jesus Christ. If this is so for Barth, then "God's negation of nothingness, his repudiation of it, must be interpreted as the reason, the ground, for its existence in the first place."[29] Wüthrich believes the kind of theodicy Barth advances prevents lament because the very act of lament cannot find legitimation "if the problem of nothingness has already been 'authentically answered,' if nothingness is only allowed to have an illusionary status, if nothingness can only be recognized, even, in the light of God's self-justification in Jesus Christ."[30] Evidence of Wüthrich's critique is found in Barth's treatment of Job in *Church Dogmatics*. He says that Barth is "unwilling to concede any theological legitimacy to lament in his interpretation of the book of Job. Lament as such belongs to the realm of sin; it is *nichtig*, a matter of

---

27. *CD* III.3: §50, 289–368. Of course, the concept of "nothingness" (*das Nichtige*) in Barth is difficult. For an extended discussion, see Matthias Wüthrich, *Gott und das Nichtige: Eine Untersuchung zur Rede vom Nichtigen ausgehend von §50 der Kirchlichen Dogmatik Karl Barths* (Zurich: TVZ, 2006).

28. *CD* III.3: §50, 289.

29. Wüthrich, "Lament for Naught?," 68–69.

30. Wüthrich, "Lament for Naught?," 72–73.

nothingness. Its legitimacy is gained only *ex post*, in the course of Job's justification."[31]

In each of the three theodicies identified above, Wüthrich demonstrates the ways in which theological systems create an environment inhospitable to lament. However, as we take our cue from the book of Habakkuk, lament becomes *essential* for a healthy spirituality. How, then, can we embrace lament?

Practical difficulties can emerge from a theology of prayer that complicates lament in the life of faith. Garrett identifies five of them in the form of questions, from which I focus upon three: (1) If God is wise and good, why bother him with prayers of impertinence? (2) In the light of God's perfect foreknowledge, is not prayer pointless? (3) Does prayer in any way change the will of God?[32] The connections between these questions and their application of lament are readily apparent.

Adequate response would drive us too far afield, but at this stage it is worth responding briefly to each. God is wise and good, and it is on this basis that the lamenter recognizes disjunction between God's goodness and the present order of things. God's goodness, then, becomes a motivation for, rather than a detriment to, lament. On the second point, one should not be fatalistic about God's foreknowledge. God is free to respond to prayer because his foreknowledge actually encompasses all prayer as well. On the third point, God's eternal and salvific will in Jesus Christ is unalterable, and so lament could not change and does not change God's will in that sense. However, within that scope, there are many specific points and circumstances to which God is responsive to human prayer. Affirming the responsiveness of God to human prayer neither makes God a puppet to our whims nor makes humans divine, with coercive power over God. God's responsiveness to prayer, including lament, reveals a relational God. He is immutable in his justice, love, mercy, and goodness and yet responsive to those who cry out to him in distress.[33]

The Scriptures reveal God sufficiently, but not exhaustively; and on the scriptural witness, it is apparent that prayers go to God, who has the power and authority to change states of affairs. While prayer certainly may change *us*, as is commonly argued, it is apparent that lament prayers are designed to move *God* to act, which he does in the biblical testimony. The internal workings of how or why that might be the case do not fall so neatly into the purview of biblical

---

31. Wüthrich, "Lament for Naught?," 73.

32. Garrett, *Systematic Theology*, 408–9.

33. On this see especially Michael Widmer, *Standing in the Breach: An Old Testament Theology and Spirituality of Intercessory Prayer*, Siphrut 13 (Winona Lake, IN: Eisenbrauns, 2015).

reasoning. God *does* respond to the persistent cries for "help!" or "justice!" of those who are suffering or oppressed (Luke 18:1–6). But his response, as we shall see in Habakkuk, follows his own logic and design rather than being hemmed in by our requests.

Habakkuk, among other texts, shows that followers of God indeed *must* speak to God with the unfettered speech of lament. Lament speech is inherently relational and creaturely. Humans possess neither the mind of God nor the perspective of God (as he sees all, knows all, and is all in all). As a result, we must go to God when we are confused, or when we see injustice, or when we experience pain. Lament prayer is not God-denying language but God-affirming language that reveals a radical faith in God and a firm understanding of our dependence upon him for all things.

---

Verse 4 reinforces Habakkuk's complaint, even though it raises other theological and historical questions as well. As argued in the introduction to this volume, there are two antagonists in the poem: wicked Judahites that live during the reign of Jehoiakim (Hab 1:2–4) and wicked Babylonians whom God raises up (Hab 1:13). The wicked Judahites are rebellious and exhibit no fear of the Lord. They surround the righteous, by enacting violence among God's own people.

Eszenyei Szeles offers a more precise referent to the identity of the wicked in v. 4. She rightly demurs to the notion that these are the Babylonians. Nor could they be correlated with the Assyrians, because by Habakkuk's day the Assyrians were no longer a world power that would be a military threat. In fact, 627–610 BCE marked the period of collapse for Assyria. Ashurbanipal II died in 627 BCE, and Asshur was sacked in 614 BCE. Finally, Haran fell in 610 BCE. After this point, Assyria no longer functioned as the world player it once had been. Egypt's ascendancy was due in part to this. Northern campaigns are littered throughout Egypt's military history, and Psamtek I and Neco II made such an expedition. Eszenyei Szeles thinks the wicked represent Jehoiakim and his royal retinue. Neco defeated Josiah in 609 BCE and established Jehoiakim as his vassal king. Jehoiakim oppressed his people to pay tribute to Egypt and maintain peace in his country. His priests, top viziers, and courtiers were "beholden to Egyptian influence" and therefore neglected God's law and, therefore, the well-being of the society.[34] This is possible. But whether focused upon the broad Judahite populace or upon the royal retinue of Jehoiakim, surely the violence and twisted justice that proceed cannot be all right in God's world! The prophet is confused and unsure, and wonders what God will do to respond.

34. Eszenyei Szeles, *Wrath and Mercy*, 19–20.

Verse 4 presents the reader with the delicate phrase "torah is ineffective," which helps the reader see that the wicked are Judahites, not Babylonians.[35] Methodologically, first we will deal with the verb (תָּפוּג/*tāpûg*) and then address the subject of the verb, "torah"; תָּפוּג/*tāpûg* is a verb that does not need a direct object in the sentence (it is intransitive). Because of this fact, it could mean a couple of things. It may mean that the prophet admits (1) that the torah has some inherent defect in it—it cannot change the hearts of God's covenant people toward faithfulness to God—and so "is numb" or "ineffective."[36] Alternatively, the verb may mean that (2) the people are unable to keep the torah because of their unfaithfulness to God. In this way, the people have made the torah ineffective because of their sin.

It is best to follow (2) above and interpret the verse as not admitting an internal defect *of the law* but rather as a failure *of the people* to adhere to the law. This interpretation is more attractive when one takes account of the prominent conjunction "therefore" (עַל־כֵּן/*'al-kēn*) that precedes the verb.

If the prophet wanted to say that there is a problem with the law (its ineffectiveness in changing the hearts of the people) *so that* justice never goes forth, then the conjunction "therefore" would likely follow the verb. The text would read: "The law is ineffective; *therefore* justice never goes forth" (emphasis added). This, however, is not how the text reads. Instead, the syntax of the line presents something different.

The syntax affirms that the prophet envisions sin among God's people (vv. 2–3), which therefore (עַל־כֵּן/*'al-kēn*) will effect a paralysis (תָּפוּג/*tāpûg*), an ineffectiveness, of torah in them: "*Therefore*, the law is ineffective; justice never goes forth" (v. 4, emphasis added). The meaning of the line, then, is that prophet laments that the wicked hearts of God's own people are set on evil, and so their wickedness prevents the torah from permeating their lives. As a result, injustice is the order of the day and justice can never go forth.

With the understanding of the verbal clause in place, one must ask how to understand the noun, "torah." This term is often translated as "the law." Some view the very concept of torah or law in theology with a negative outlook:

1. Torah represents Israel's devolution into religious legalism because the codification of torah is a late development in the history of Israel's religion. Therefore, torah is a legalistic imposition upon God's people.

---

35. This clause is overlooked by those who see the wicked as referring to the Babylonians: Johnson, "Paralysis"; Sweeney, "Structure," 66; Sweeney, *Twelve Prophets*, 2:463–64.

36. Samuel Balentine, *Prayer in the Hebrew Bible: The Drama of Divine-Human Dialogue*, OBT (Minneapolis: Fortress, 1993), 184–85.

2.  Alternatively, torah may be understood as a lofty standard that is too high for Israel to attain. Because of this, God's torah is designed intentionally to reveal Israel's failure in sin, paving the way for God's gospel of grace.
3.  Finally, some view torah as a form of works-based righteousness which is opposed to the gospel as a free gift of grace.

On these models, torah proposes what *Israel does* to be distinguished from what *the Lord does*. These models, even if popular at different points in the history of Christian theology, are not fully accurate to the theology of torah in the Bible or Christian tradition. A productive understanding of torah in the Old Testament is not founded upon a dichotomy between legalism (human response) and grace (divine initiative). Rather, an appropriate understanding of the theology of torah may be understood ideally as a process in which:

1.  God demonstrates his grace by giving his torah,
2.  Israel's recognition of God's grace engenders faithful obedience to God's torah,
3.  Israel's faithful response to God in obedience to *torah* perpetuates divine blessing,
4.  God's divine blessing then leads his people to deeper appreciation of divine grace.[37]

Note, however, that this process represents the ideal. Although God maintains his participation in the giving of torah, Israel fails in their fidelity and sin shatters this process. Because of their sin, the beauty of torah—the very grace of God—is not embraced in the life of Israel. Instead of experiencing blessings, Israel experiences curse and contention. The persistence of sin in the face of God's grace and his torah remains central in the teaching, for example, of Deuteronomy.[38] It is also important to remember that the Scripture (both Old and New Testament) communicates that torah is in no way salvific, if one means that it offers life and forgiveness of sin. Only God saves. Only God gives life. Only God gives grace. Only God forgives. And only God gives the gift of torah. For those already rightly related to God, torah remains instructive for his chosen people. As Michael Williams says, "The law [torah] tells Israel how to

---

37. See the discussion of J. Gordon McConville, *Law and Theology in Deuteronomy*, JSOTSup 33 (Sheffield: JSOT Press, 1984), 16–18.

38. Heath A. Thomas, "Life and Death in Deuteronomy," in *Interpreting Deuteronomy: Issues and Approaches*, ed. David G. Firth and Philip S. Johnston (Nottingham: Apollos, 2012), 183–88.

live as God's image-bearers, what it means to be a kingdom of priests and a holy nation."[39]

This torah is given by God as a gift to be received by Israel.[40] When one overlooks the Israelite focus of torah, then one can overgeneralize the place and function of God's law in theological discussions. The Old Testament affirms that God's gift of torah was intentionally offered to Israel to distinguish them from other nations. Their obedience to God's law would differentiate Israel so that those nations might come to know who Israel's God is, what he values, and what his purposes are in his world (cf. Deut 4:6–7). We could call this the missional purpose of the torah. God gives Israel the torah so that this already chosen and already redeemed people might answer the question, "How then shall we live among the nations?" God's torah provides an answer.

With this broader theological understanding of torah in view, is it possible to define further the meaning of God's torah in Habakkuk? The Hebrew word "torah" certainly implies, for instance, the legal code of Deut 12–26 (what many think of in terms of "law/legal code"), but this term also correctly identifies the *entire set of instruction* given in the book of Deuteronomy.[41] The term also can connote a parent's instruction in wisdom books like Proverbs (e.g., Prov 1:8). So simply to assume that the term "torah" intends a mere list of rules would be an oversimplification.

As it relates to Habakkuk's use of the term in v. 4, Marshall restricts the content of torah to be God's promises for life and blessing identified in Deut 28. In Marshall's account, Habakkuk complains that the promises of covenant blessing (or torah) have become "paralyzed." The torah-promise of blessing has proved ineffective in at least three ways: King Josiah has died, Josiah's great reform movement has disintegrated in the waning days of the Judahite monarchy, and the Babylonians are coming in judgment against Judah. In the face of these realities, Marshall suggests that v. 4 means that the torah (promise of blessing) is ineffective (v. 4a) and the wicked Babylonians surround the righteous Judahites

---

39. Michael D. Williams, *Far as the Curse Is Found: The Covenant Story of Redemption* (Phillipsburg, NJ: P&R Publishing, 2005), 149.

40. So torah primarily is a gift for Israel and only in a secondary sense general instruction for the other nations. This is true even in wisdom material. Torah in Proverbs and Ecclesiastes, for instance, may be translated with the somewhat generic term "instruction," but this does not then lead one to conclude that wisdom instruction as secular teaching is on the same level as Israel's non-Yahwistic neighbors. Rather "instruction-torah" and "law-torah" remain associated concepts that derive from the Lord in the canonical presentation of the OT. See the discussion of Michael V. Fox, *Proverbs 10–31*, AB 18B (New Haven: Yale University Press, 2009), 951–62.

41. For further discussion on the meaning of torah in Deuteronomy, see Thomas W. Mann, *The Book of the Torah: The Narrative Integrity of the Pentateuch* (Atlanta: John Knox, 1988), 146–47; J. Gordon McConville, *Deuteronomy*, ApOTC 5 (Leicester: Apollos, 2002), 42–44.

(v. 4b).[42] Still, there is no real need to restrict the meaning of torah to promises of blessing as Marshall has done.

Another way of understanding the term, however, is to equate it with the Mosaic law *in general*, rather than focusing upon the specific blessing-cursing material in Deut 28–30. When one understands torah in this way, then it is possible to understand the torah's paralysis as an internal defect of the law itself. Balentine treats the meaning of torah in v. 4 in this way.[43] The law did not produce blessing as it said it would do, and so the Babylonians are coming to destroy Judah.

If we understand the torah of v. 4 as being internally deficient, it is possible to suggest further that its *deficiency* lay in the fact that it is impotent to change the hearts of God's people or did not do what it was supposed to do. The law did not create internal transformation of the people, but God's grace in the gospel did effect such change. This view fits well with what some scholars think the apostle Paul teaches in Gal 3–4, 2 Cor 3, and Rom 10, for example.[44] Thus there is something *wrong* in the law: it is impotent to effect God's grace. In this way, God's law is fundamentally opposed to God's gospel and represents a failed project.

But for this to be true, one must in fact prove that God's law *was indeed potent* to secure such internal (heart) change. Does the Old Testament teach that the law is, in fact, *potent* to secure faith? The short answer is no, and one cannot appeal to Lev 18:5 as the proof text: "The one who shall do these things [the statutes and judgments of law] will live by them." This is not a descriptor on how one can achieve eternal life or how the law is effective for heart change. In no way does this verse connote that the law was *salvific* or that it effected faith. Rather, this text reveals how God's *already* saved, *already* chosen, *already* covenanted people shall live missionally in God's world, as his ambassadors among the nations. If they live according to God's torah, then they would live— particularly in the land of Israel—as a missional people among the nations. This reading better fits the context of Lev 18:5. If Israel obeyed God's law, they would live in the land that God has given them. Did Israel embrace his law well, as indicated by the presentation of the Old Testament? No, and they were disciplined through exile. But that was not an internal problem of the torah, revealing it to be defective. Rather the problem lay in Israel's lack of faith, as indicated in Israel's songs (see Ps 78:22, 32).

42. Johnson, "Paralysis," 257–66.

43. Balentine, *Prayer*, 184–85. He follows Johnson, "Paralysis," 257–66.

44. See Ben Witherington III, *The Collective Witness*, vol. 2 of *The Indelible Image: The Theological and Ethical Thought World of the New Testament* (Downers Grove, IL: InterVarsity Press, 2010), 803–4.

To say that the torah is defective in either its intent or its effects has the unfortunate consequence of suggesting that in giving the law, God has given his people *stones* rather than *bread*. Nothing in the Old Testament supports this view. Even Ezek 20:25, where God states that he gave "not good" laws to the people by which they "could not live," does not support the idea that God gave Israel defective law. The point in this text is to reinforce Israel's failure in *obeying* God's law rather than to support the idea that there is something internally wrong with the law itself.[45] Charles Feinberg rightly says of Hab 1:4 that the prophet complains that torah

> came to be looked upon as being without force or authority. Because of unrighteous judges the Law was set to nought. Since the forms of judgment were corrupted, both life and property were insecure. Justice could not prevail because the wicked knew how to hem the righteous in on all sides, so that he could not receive his just due. Miscarriage of justice was the order of the day. Ensnaring the righteous by fraud, the ungodly perverted all right and honesty.[46]

Based on the syntax of the line as indicated above, it is best to understand the meaning of v. 4 as signifying that the torah is ineffective *because* God's people are rebellious against his law. This is not a statement about a problem with the law as much as it is an exposé on the problem of rebellious human hearts.

God's law was never intended to change the hearts of God's people, so of course it was *impotent* to effect such change. But if the theological argument begins with the idea that the law is impotent to change the hearts of people, one begins on the wrong theological foot, so to speak. Faith is secured not by law but by hearts that are changed by a gracious and loving God, by a God who first loved and *who gave the torah as a gift*. In this way, God's law cannot be called a failed project. Rather, hearts of men and women who reject God's torah are the real problem, which is Habakkuk's point. If God's people display a disposition of faith and fidelity to the Lord, then appropriate righteous actions follow. Through divine grace, God counts the inner disposition of faith in his follower as righteousness.[47] A righteous person will live in accordance to God's torah.

This discussion remains theologically significant. If one views the law as fundamentally opposed to grace, then a theological tension emerges. This is a

---

45. See the illuminating discussion of Daniel I. Block, *The Book of Ezekiel: Chapters 1–24*, NICOT (Grand Rapids: Eerdmans, 1997), 636–41; Daniel I. Block, "Preaching Old Testament Law to New Testament Christians," *STR* 3 (2012): 195–221.

46. Charles L. Feinberg, *The Minor Prophets* (Chicago: Moody Press, 1990), 207.

47. See Block, "Preaching Old Testament Law," 217.

view often attributed (wrongly) to Martin Luther's law-gospel hermeneutic. But even Luther does not present the law as *fundamentally* opposed to the gospel of grace, so that one effectively neuters the other. His view sets law and gospel in dialectic with one another. For Luther, the law teaches God's judgment that effectively *opens* the sinner to the gospel of Jesus Christ. The necessarily dialectical relationship between law and gospel identifies the law to be not a *failed project* but a *forward-looking project*. The law renders judgment against sinners and delivers them to the door of God's grace, which comes in Jesus Christ in the fullness of time. For Luther, God's law and God's grace remain complementary rather than contradictory. Preaching or teaching that opposes God's law and God's gospel runs the risk of dividing what should never be set asunder.

A different nuance of torah in v. 4 arises by reading it through the lens of wisdom theology. Scholarship has readily shown that wisdom language and themes permeate Habakkuk. So, it is possible to think of torah as a broader concept like "instruction" that comports with the "fear of Yahweh" that emerges in biblical wisdom literature (cf. Prov 13:14//Prov 14:27).[48] The "fear of Yahweh" is parallel to torah; both keep one "from deadly snares." Both the fear of Yahweh and torah come from God.

If one applies this thinking to Habakkuk's understanding of torah in v. 4, then a wisdom trajectory emerges. In light of the people's wickedness, the prophet admits that the fear of Yahweh fails among God's people. By their lack of fear of Yahweh, Habakkuk's own wicked Israelites are caught in the deadly snares of living as fools. As a result, injustice and strife are the norm rather than the exception.

Both options are possible, and it is unnecessary to be atomistic about what is intended by torah in v. 4. Both the "instruction of the Mosaic torah" and "wisdom instruction" remain coherent with the message of v. 4. David Daube pointed out long ago, and Ryan O'Dowd reinforces, the fact that law and wisdom are complementary concepts that should not be pulled apart from one another too readily, especially in theological interpretation.[49] Wisdom is rooted in the general order of creation (Prov 8), and the Mosaic law can be understood as an application of wisdom in the context of God's covenant relationship with

---

48. Cf. Ps 78:1; Prov 1:8; 3:1; 4:2; 6:20, 23; 7:2; 13:14; 14:27. For discussion on wisdom influence in Habakkuk, see Donald E. Gowan, "Habakkuk and Wisdom," *Perspective* 9 (1968): 157–66; Gert T. M. Prinsloo, "Life for the Righteous, Doom for the Wicked: Reading Habakkuk from a Wisdom Perspective," *SK* 23 (2000): 621–40; Antonius H. J. Gunneweg, "Habakkuk und das Problem des leidenden צדיק," *ZAW* 98 (1986): 400–415.

49. David Daube, *Law and Wisdom in the Bible: David Daube's Gifford Lectures*, vol. 2, ed. Calum Carmichael (Conshohocken, PA: Templeton, 2010); Ryan P. O'Dowd, *The Wisdom of Torah: Epistemology in Deuteronomy and the Wisdom Literature*, FRLANT 225 (Göttingen: Vandenhoeck & Ruprecht, 2009).

Israel.[50] What Israel needs is deep-seated faith in God that generates proper love toward God and neighbor. It is this faithfulness problem that is an inner defect among some of Habakkuk's contemporaries.

Through the ambiguity of the language "torah is ineffective," the reader is invited to reflect upon Habakkuk's complaint. His wicked people of Judah neither fear Yahweh (creation order) nor do they follow his decrees of law (covenant violation) (Deut 6:24; 10:12, 20; 31:12). The prophet, then, complains that because of their sin, God's "instruction is ineffective" among his people, which leads to "crooked justice" issuing forth. Habakkuk calls upon God to respond to their disobedience. Because of their rebellion, the prophet and his people must be delivered from their sin.

But what kind of change or deliverance exactly does the prophet envision in the divine response? Because of the remainder of the poem (vv. 5–12) as well as the prevalence of judgment in the prophetic literature (especially in the Minor Prophets), Habakkuk may anticipate *divine judgment* against his people's sin. From a canonical point of view, judgment can be understood in terms of the fulfillment of covenant stipulations in Deut 28:15–68. Habakkuk's contemporary, the prophet Jeremiah, also anticipated judgment because of Judah's sin. This vision also is taken up clearly in the teaching of Zephaniah that follows Habakkuk in the Minor Prophets. Zephaniah envisions divine judgment against Judah for sin and rebellion (cf. Zeph 1). Habakkuk expects divine judgment, particularly against the wicked Judahites.

Yet another option is possible, and it is the option that is preferred here. Habakkuk may have in mind not divine judgment but rather *divine deliverance*. Usually, when a lament is offered in the Old Testament, which we find in Hab 1:2–4, the one who prays petitions God for deliverance, not judgment! The psalmist prays: "Arise, O Yahweh, in your anger; rise up against the rage of my enemies. Awake, my God; decree justice!" (Ps 7:6).

One way that God brings deliverance in the Old Testament is by means of God's anointed king, sent to replace the old corrupt regime. Such a regime change took place in Habakkuk's times, with the appointment of Josiah to the throne reflected in 2 Kgs 21:23–24. This anointed figure may refer to the king that Habakkuk wants God to install, a king who will rule rightly and in accordance with God's torah (the kind of king envisioned in Deut 17:18–20). This is plausible but speculative.

What can be said clearly is that Habakkuk anticipates *change* in a world where only the Lord sets things right. It is reasonable to posit the change Habakkuk expects is not divine *judgment* but divine *deliverance*. This view makes

50. O'Dowd, *Wisdom of Torah*, 162–65.

sense of Habakkuk's use of complaint speech in vv. 2–4. Still, how should one evaluate Habakkuk's initial complaint in vv. 2–4?

*First, Habakkuk teaches a theology of God's fidelity to his creation.* God's devotion to his creation comes clearly into view in the prophet's complaint. The complaints in vv. 2–4 suppose that God *will* contravene violence and chaos because precisely it is *his* creation that is disordered. If the prophet did not think that God was a caring Lord over his creation, then it is sensible that he would give up, and the petition would never exist. But the prophet refuses to take this course. Rather, he believes God to be committed to the world that he has created. Because he fashioned this world with justice (Pss 33:5; 89:15), the experience of twisted justice (v. 4) in life is not justice at all in God's good world.

The tacit rationale in Habakkuk's complaint is grounded in a theology of divine commitment to creation. Notice that Habakkuk does not wish to be delivered *from* the world he inhabits. The interrogative "How long?" does not intend a deliverance *from* the corrupt world. Rather it speaks to God's redemption and healing *of* the violence of the world. Creation is that arena in which God's redemption might take place. More is said concerning this point in part two of this commentary, below.

*Second, Habakkuk vibrantly teaches a theology of God's fidelity to his covenant.* The rhetoric of Habakkuk's complaint works because it is directed to Yahweh, the God of Israel, with whom Israel is in covenant relationship (e.g., Exod 19–23; Deuteronomy; Josh 24). The prophet complains to God precisely because it is *Yahweh*, the covenant Lord, who is related to Habakkuk. As indicated above, the linguistic similarities between Exod 2:23–25 and Hab 1:2–3 are suggestive. Habakkuk calls upon the same Lord who heard the cries of Israel and delivered them from Egypt in the past (cf. Hab 3:3–12). Further, language of torah in v. 4 remains a fundamental link in this theological message. Habakkuk appeals to God's covenantal commitment precisely because the torah of God has been breached, whether in the general sense of wisdom instruction or the more specific Mosaic law. Based on the stipulations of the covenant, only God can engender change in the hearts of the people and deliver them from their own sin (cf. Deut 10:16; 30:6–10). Habakkuk's complaint aims at mobilizing God to act because of his divine commitment to the covenant.

*Third, Habakkuk's complaint teaches the importance of a loving and committed response to God.* Humanity's appropriate response to God should not be construed as a duty-bound obedience as much as a *loving response* to the God who has already demonstrated his grace. On this account, Habakkuk cries out to the covenant Lord because *it is this God* whom the prophet *knows*. It is *this God* who has created both the prophet and the world he inhabits. Habakkuk responds to this God in faith, he responds in prayer to the God who has given the covenant as a gift for communion with him. This communion is marked by, and intended for, peace and rest with God in his good creation. Considering the chaos that he experiences, Habakkuk petitions God for deliverance from violence and pleads for peace. The prophet refuses to sit idly by, because he does not imagine God to be an idle, passive, aloof, or dispassionate deity when it comes to his world.

Yet this focus upon appropriate human response is not just related to the prophet. It also takes God's rebellious people into account. Their relationship with God, administered through torah, demands right adherence for thriving and peace in the land. Through his complaint, Habakkuk acknowledges his people's failure in their obligation to God through the torah. Sin, violence, and injustice abound precisely because God's people have not followed the gracious parameters of life before their Lord. On this account, the prophet looks to God for deliverance from his own people's sin. Only God can effect a change that deals with sin.

**1:5–11** Habakkuk's complaints are not lost in silence. The creator God hears and responds to his covenant-bound prophet. In so doing, the Lord unearths for Habakkuk treasures in the darkness he experiences. This is made clear through the poetic repetition of language in the verses. Repetition of language effects a call-and-response format between Habakkuk and God.[51] Where Habakkuk complains that God has made him "look upon" iniquity and calls upon God to "observe" violence in v. 3, God responds by calling Habakkuk in v. 5 to "look and consider" what he is doing. Habakkuk complains of a lack of "justice" and the perpetuation of "violence" in vv. 2–4, to which God responds by expounding upon his work of raising up the Babylonians, who nonetheless are bound by their own vision of "justice" in v. 7 and who come forth set on "violence" in v. 9.

Now these verses, and God's response, have been understood as a problem in need of a solution. For at the very least, God does not seem interested in answering Habakkuk's complaint adequately. Instead of God ending violence, he uses a nation that enacts violence, which is their own form of justice. The poetic technique of repetition binds vv. 2–4 and 5–11 together:

**Lexical Repetition in Verses 2–4 and 5–11**

| Habakkuk's Complaint (1:2–4) | God's Response (1:5–11) |
|---|---|
| Look and observe (v. 3) | Look and observe (v. 5) |
| Justice does not proceed (v. 4) | Justice proceeds (v. 7) |
| Violence (vv. 2, 3) | Violence (v. 9) |

51. See fig. 1, above.

As a result, poetry invites the reader to regard God's and Habakkuk's interaction as an integrated whole. God replies to the prophet, employing Habakkuk's very own complaint language. Yet God's response takes an unexpected turn. His words do not provide the healing balm to comfort the prophet. Nor do his words resolve Habakkuk's complaint. Rather, Yahweh's response *redirects* the complaint in a different direction altogether.

Even though this kind of theological redirection remains (perhaps) frustrating for the reader, it is a technique not unknown in the Old Testament. Something similar appears in the book of Job, just after Job complains that God has unjustly afflicted him. He, like Habakkuk, sees something fundamentally wrong in creation—injustice is the order of the day (cf. esp. Job 3; 9:21–24; 19:7–8; 16:18–22). When God does respond to Job, he *redirects* Job's complaints in the whirlwind speeches (Job 38–40). Essentially, God does not answer Job's complaints, but he does affirm a divine order in creation even if it is hidden to Job. This *redirection* confirms for Job that there are things beyond his understanding and thereby hidden from him, but nonetheless that God is faithful to reveal himself during his suffering.

Similarly, in Habakkuk, God's response takes Habakkuk in another direction. But the point of this is not to frustrate Habakkuk (any more than it was to frustrate Job), but rather to draw him into the process of spiritual formation. Will Habakkuk allow himself to be challenged and expanded in vision? Of course, there are things in life beyond human reasoning or apprehension—as creatures who have been made by an infinitely other creator, could it not be any other way? Although the prophet sees his world "through a glass darkly," God draws his prophet to a place of trust. The question for Habakkuk remains for those who follow God in the present world: When the world is upside down, will those who follow God trust him and press toward his presence, or not?

God's words for Habakkuk are not for him alone. It is evident that God speaks to the whole of his people as well. A close reading of the text reveals that there is a curious and abrupt shift from singular verbs in vv. 2–4 to (second-person) plural verbs in v. 5. If God were only responding to the prophet, then one would expect singular, rather than plural, verbs in vv. 2–5. This problem has led some to think this section belongs somewhere else, comes from a different hand, or was written for a different audience. Perhaps it was written in a different period, or was originally a message given by the prophet to his contemporaries and only later set in its current literary position.[52] These options are possible, but the repetition of language between the sections serves

---

52. See discussion of Floyd, *Minor Prophets*, 84–88, 105–7.

as a literary tie that binds them together. For this reason, they are intended to be read together.

The plural form in v. 5 draws together not just the prophet, but all who are faithful to God in the time of violence. On this understanding the wicked and righteous in v. 4 are corporate groups of people even though they are designated with singular nouns. This corporate representation by an individual term is so common in biblical literature that it hardly needs mention, especially regarding the terms "wicked" and "righteous." God's response with the plural imperatives in v. 5 is directed to the prophet and all those righteous who suffer with him.

But what does God say to the prophet and his people? He draws their gaze not to Judah's wickedness, but rather to his work among the nations: Yahweh will raise up the Chaldeans for judgment. God describes this nation using abhorrent, violent, and oppressive language. They are "bitter and hasty," and they go about the earth literally to steal ("to seize dwellings that do not belong to him," v. 6) and oppress ("he gathers captives like sand," v. 9). They are like a terrifying beast (v. 7) that is ruthlessly efficient at destruction (v. 8).[53] God responds to Habakkuk's complaint about "violence" (חמס/ḥāmās) in v. 3 with a seemingly horrible proposal: God will raise a nation that comes for "violence" (חמס/ḥāmās) in v. 9! They are terrible, dreadful, fierce, and impetuous (vv. 6–7). This nation scoffs at other kings and princes (v. 10). The Babylonians are the masters of the universe, at least on their own reckoning.

These verses heighten the horrific reality of the Babylonian threat. Language stretches to the limit to grasp hold of the destructive power and psychological terror that typify the predator-nation. Rousing metaphors of threat emerge in vv. 8–10. These enemies are like "evening wolves," "leopards," or "eagles" flying to a feast (v. 8). They gather their captives in their hands like one does the sand of the seashore (v. 9). They are wolves on the prowl, giant cats bent on stalking their prey, and birds of prey swooping in to gorge themselves on carnage. They are prideful kings that scoop up nations in their iron fists. *In short, they are those whose notion of justice proceeds not from God, but from themselves.* The metaphors of predation and imperial power relate the ominous tone of God's "answer" to the prophet as well as the terrifying reality for those who live in the prophet's day: God is bringing a nation for judgment. Invasion and war march toward the small kingdom of Judah.

The repetition of this language between vv. 2–4 and vv. 5–11 stands out. The repeated language drives Habakkuk and the reader into (another) theo-

---

53. Notice the repetition of the phrase "evening wolves" in v. 8 and in Zeph 3:3, the only two occurrences of this collocation in the Old Testament. The phrase indicates the rapacious appetite of the predators: in Habakkuk, the Babylonians, and in Zephaniah, the princes of Israel.

logical quandary. How can God use a nation whose version of justice (מִשְׁפָּט/
*mišpāṭ*) is, in the final analysis, violence (חָמָס/*ḥāmās*)? To add insult to injury,
v. 11 reveals that this nation not only is bent on violence but is also idolatrous.
God's response seems to raise theological problems rather than providing answers to them!

Of course, on a biblical-theological reckoning, the Lord is not averse to
using a foreign nation to achieve his own aims. He does so with the foreign
prophet Balaam in Num 22–27. He does so with various foreign oppressors
in Judges (Judg 2:11–22). He uses the Assyrians and Persians in Isaiah (Isa 10;
44–45). He uses the Babylonians in Jeremiah (Jer 5:14–17). The reason why God
can raise up foreign nations for his purposes derives from his authority as God
over *all* nations.

The Old Testament testifies to the fact that Israel has a connection with
the Lord through the covenant, but this fact neither provides them exclusive
access to God nor affords them protection from foreign nations when Israel
rebels against their Lord. This point is proved germane by a cotext in the Minor Prophets. Amos 9:7 proclaims God's authority over all nations (here he
mentions Nubia, Philistia, and Aramaea) as well as Israel. Amos rhetorically
reinforces the point that *all* nations are God's and each of them has a responsibility for justice and righteousness before him. If God has prerogative over
all nations and is not particularly hemmed in by his covenant with Israel, why
could he not employ one of his (even rebellious) nations to perform a "wonder"
in the world (Hab 1:5)?

Following on the logic that Judah is the subject of the wicked in v. 4, it is
sensible to mark God's establishment of Babylon as judgment against his people's sin. This is how Jeremiah understands the role of Babylon in God's plans
(cf. Jer 20–21). Being a contemporary of Jeremiah, Habakkuk may understand
the situation this way as well. That God would use a nation to discipline his
own people is not uncommon in the Old Testament, as the cycle of sin and
judgment in the book of Judges testifies: Israel rebels against God, God raises
up an oppressor (a foreign, even idolatrous, nation), Israel cries out to God,
God raises up a deliverer/judge to rescue the people (see Judg 2:11–19). In Isa
10, Assyria is the rod of God's wrath against his people, to discipline them.
Thus, on a biblical-theological reckoning, Israel's God uses foreign nations to
discipline his people in judgment, "For whom Yahweh loves, he rebukes, as a
father the son (in whom) he favors" (Prov 3:12; see also Heb 12:6). If vv. 5–6
are understood in this way, then Habakkuk's initial complaint is answered.
The prophet's faithful response, then, would be to embrace judgment as a kind
discipline from the Lord.

This kind of theological gap-filling based on a whole-Bible theology is not so much wrong at this point as it is ill-timed. It may provide a theological rationale as to how and why God can do what he says he will do with the Babylonians in vv. 5–6. But simultaneously one may be led prematurely away from the poetry and the interpretative journey through which it carries the reader. Habakkuk's message does not stop at v. 6. It is important to follow the dialogue between prophet and God in vv. 5–17 to see where it goes. Any other route to answer the problem of God using a foreign nation prematurely limits interpretation and circumvents the process of spiritual formation that the interpretative journey *through* the book invites.

For whatever reason(s) God uses Babylon, v. 11 makes it plain that the violence with which they plunder the earth will not last. This verse is notoriously difficult, with the textual traditions reading portions of the verse differently.[54] Three options are possible for the phrase "then a wind passes and moves over":

1. The phrase may mean that Babylon will change its mind so that it is no longer bent on violence.
2. Alternatively, it may mean that God's intentions will change about using Babylon as an instrument of judgment.
3. The phrase may be simply an image that depicts the temporality and brevity of Bayblon's rule.

I prefer the third option. The collocation of the Hebrew words רוּחַ/*rûaḥ* and חָלף/*ḥālap* appears in Ps 78:39 in a similar way: "Then he remembered that they were but flesh, a wind [רוּחַ/*rûaḥ*] passing by [חָלף/*ḥālap*] and it does not return." In this way, the phrase may just be an idiom for the temporary nature of Babylon's tyranny.

Further my translation, "and he will be guilty whose strength is his god," generally follows the Hebrew sense of the line, but the LXX, Vulgate, and Qumran's Habakkuk Pesher all treat it differently. Each rendering has in common, however, a temporal break with the order of violence that Babylon has perpetuated. As I have translated the line, this change will come because Babylon will be found guilty of idolatry and violence.[55] In short, Babylon's violent power remains potent, but passing.

---

54. See Anthony Gelston, ed., *The Twelve Minor Prophets*, BHQ 13 (Stuttgart: Deutsche Bibelgesellschaft, 2010), 93, 116*–17* for the most up-to-date discussion.

55. The phrase "he will be guilty" may be understood as a *weqatal* 3ms, "And he will be guilty." Or it could be read as an adjective masc. sg., "guilty." The Habakkuk Pesher at Qumran reads the word as a *yiqtol* 3ms, "And he will place." LXX apparently reads a text and interprets it that the king will repent and make propitiation for his sins. The Vulgate, however, implies that the spirit of the king will pass, fail from him, and he will fall. Roberts emends the text, "And I was astonished" (*Nahum, Habakkuk, and Zephaniah*, 100). The first option is the most sensible following the logic and rhetoric of the poetry.

The temporality of the Babylonians' campaign is due to their idolatry. The last line of v. 11 uses a legal pronouncement, "he is guilty" (אשם/'*šm*), to identify the one who finds his strength (כחו/*kōḥô*) in a deity other than Yahweh. The notion of the God of Israel being the source of strength (כח/*kōaḥ*) for the faithful is well attested throughout the Psalter especially (cf. Pss 18:1–2; 19:4; 22:19; 27:1; 28:7; 73:26; 140:7), but in the larger canon of the Old Testament as well. By contrast, the notion that a foreign deity provides this kind of strength is unknown in the Old Testament. The sense of v. 11, then, is clear—by trusting in another deity for strength, the Babylonians have condemned themselves as guilty before the true God. Any nation that places their strength in a deity other than the Lord of Israel is guilty of idolatry, and that nation opens itself to divine punishment. The unique transcendence of Yahweh extends throughout the world, to all nations. All nations, then, are to worship the God of Israel. He is the strength (כח/*kōaḥ*) of Israel and the nations.

**1:12–17** The fact that God would employ this idolatrous nation—for *any* period of time—drives the prophet toward his second complaint. The repetition of the interrogative form in vv. 12, 13, 16 coupled with the repetition of language across speaking sections (cf. fig. 1) makes us think that the dialogue ensues.[56] But rather than providing solace for Habakkuk, God's response in vv. 5–11 has effectively made things more confusing for him. Verses 12 and 17 open with interrogative particles (הלוא/*hălô'*) that function as bookend questions to the prophet's speech and set the tone for the entire section: the prophet remains confused as to how God's *actions* cohere with his *character*.

Confusion concerning God's character and ways is not uncommon for people of faith. In fact, this is one of the issues that can drive believers to the brink of despair. Several interrelated questions emerge. "If God is good, then why does he do this thing, or at the very least, let this thing happen?" This question addresses the character of God and his actions. However, this very question raises another one: "*Is* God good, and if so, then how do we reconcile his actions in the world?" And another: "Can we attribute the 'things that happen' to God in terms of direct causation (and should we)?" And finally: "If we can attribute things that happen to the work of a good God, then how do we *measure* that causation . . . can mortals divine the things of God?"

Questions are natural in the life of faith, and questioning God is not a faithless action but rather a radically faithful response by those who know and

---

56. Note especially the repetition of ראה/*r'h*; נבט/*nbṭ*; חמס/*ḥāmās*; משפט/*mišpāṭ*; and אל/*'ēl*.

love God. Note the faithfulness of Habakkuk even as he offers his questions. The effusion of divine titles in v. 12 reaffirms Habakkuk's trust in God, even if he is nonplussed by the Lord's actions identified in vv. 5–11. Note the progression of divine titles: "Yahweh," "my God," and "my Holy One." Habakkuk first lodges his complaint with "Yahweh," the covenant God of Israel. This covenant title prepares the reader for the second appellation, "my God," which directly links back to v. 11. The poetic linkage between the divine titles אלהו/*'ĕlōhô*, "(the idolater's) god" (v. 11), and אלהי/*'ĕlōhāy*, "my God" (v. 12), rhetorically distinguishes the prophet from the idolatrous nation of Babylon. Contrasted against the idolater, Habakkuk, even in complaint, places his trust in his God—Yahweh, the Holy One. The first-person pronoun "my" that accompanies the other titles for Yahweh reaffirms the prophet's trust in the Lord alone. But nonetheless, Habakkuk cannot understand how *his covenant God* raises up the Babylonians for his purposes.

Habakkuk's confusion takes two forms in vv. 12–13. The first contrasts God's eternal nature against Israel's temporal nature. "Are you not from old, O Yahweh?" speaks to his eternal nature. The prophet contrasts God, who is "from ancient times" (מקדם/*miqqedem*) against his people, who are transitory—"Will we not die?"[57]

What is translated here as an interrogative could also be rendered as an indicative, "we will not die," or a modal, "we shall not die."[58] Although the indicative and modal statements are possible, both are unlikely. If indicative or modal, then this statement is an affirmation of trust in the Lord: in spite of the judgment God has prescribed for Judah, the faithful of God "will not die."

It is better, however, to follow a poetic reading of the phrase through the ellipsis of the interrogative. Even though used only in the first verset, the interrogative particle (הֲלוֹא/*hălô'*) serves a double-duty for both the first and second

---

57. With McCarthy, I am not convinced this verb (לֹא נָמוּת/*lō' nāmût*) is an example of *tiqqune sopherim*, in which scribes changed the supposed original from "you (Yahweh) will not die" (לֹא תָמוּת/*lō' tāmût*) to "we will not die" (לֹא נָמוּת/*lō' nāmût*) for theological reasons. There is no compelling evidence to suggest that "will we not die?" לֹא נָמוּת represents a scribal alteration. See Carmel McCarthy, *The Tiqqune Sopherim and Other Theological Corrections in the Masoretic Text of the Old Testament*, OBO 36 (Fribourg: Presses Universitaires; Göttingen: Vandenhoeck & Ruprecht, 1981), 105–11. Andersen rightly thinks לֹא נָמוּת is meaningful here but cannot fully understand the logic of the line, at least not as an indicative statement (*Habakkuk*, 169–77). If, however, the phrase is an unmarked interrogative, the logic of the line is sensible.

58. Indicative: O'Neal, *Interpreting Habakkuk*, 39–40; Roberts, *Nahum, Habakkuk, Zephaniah*; modal: A. J. O. van der Wal, "*Lo' namut* in Habakkuk I 12: A Suggestion," *VT* 38 (1988): 480–83; interrogative, but following the supposed *tiqqune sopherim*: Roberts, *Nahum, Habakkuk, and Zephaniah*, 100–103, and Andersen, *Habakkuk*, 169–77.

versets in the poetic line, marking the entire verse as a series of questions.[59] Habakkuk's questions are grounded upon faith in God, even if of a different order. In Habakkuk's complaint from v. 12, Israel's temporal nature contrasts against God's eternal nature in and through divine judgment. So why would God enact this judgment?

In v. 13 Habakkuk's confusion takes on another form. Here the prophet wonders how God, being pure and holy, can use a sinful nation to enact his judgment: they are idolaters! The judgment (מִשְׁפָּט/*mišpāṭ*) in v. 12 of which Habakkuk speaks is likely a God-ordained judgment for sin, which serves as a kind of reproof (from the Hebrew root יכח/*ykḥ*) meant to reconcile God's wayward people back to himself.[60]

It is not this *process* of reconciliation that the prophet demurs but rather the *person* whom the Lord uses to achieve it. The downside to this decimation of God's people is, of course, that God has destroyed his worshipers. The remaining Babylonians are idolatrous—they will not live to give glory to the living God in their worship.

In the rhetoric of the prophet, God's enacted judgment leads to the perpetuation of idolatry and an absence of proper worship. Again the problem of God seeing and gazing upon wickedness and trouble arises in v. 13. Through repetition of language, the prophet carries forward the complaint from vv. 3–4. So, the prophet in v. 13 says that God is too pure to "look upon" (מראות/*mēr'ôt*, cf. v. 3) evil and unable "to countenance" (or "gaze upon") (והביט/*wĕhabbîṭ*, cf. v. 3) trouble (עמל/*'āmāl*, cf. v. 3). Why, then, can God be silent when the wicked (רשע/*rāšā'*, cf. v. 4) idolaters swallow those more righteous (צדיק/*ṣāddîq*, cf. v. 4)—and at God's command and by his design?

Much has been said about the wicked (רשע/*rāšā'*) who swallow those more righteous (צדיק/*ṣāddîq*). The wordplay on the same roots from vv. 2–4 is too conspicuous to be accidental.[61] The prophet effectively uses language from the previous interaction to carry the dialogue forward. God is doing a wonder, but how can he do so with this idolatrous nation? The prophet's question is clearly a comparison based on the syntax of the line. The righteous, the prophet argues, are more righteous than the wicked. So how can God use the wicked to reprove the righteous?

If one interprets the text in terms of broad systematic theological lines of

---

59. So Roberts, *Nahum, Habakkuk, and Zephaniah*, 101.

60. God's judgment is not, then, an end in and of itself. Rather it is a disciplinary measure aimed at restoring a broken covenant relationship. See the helpful discussion on the concept and purpose of divine judgment in J. Gordon McConville, "The Judgment of God in the Old Testament," *ExAud* 20 (2004): 25–42.

61. See fig. 1, above.

thought, one may object that in fact the prophet has made a faulty comparison. How can anyone distinguish the righteous (either Judah or faithful Judahites like the prophet) from the wicked (Babylon) when all humans are sinners before God, none being righteous before him (cf. Pss 14:1–3; 53:1–3; Eccl 7:20; Rom 3:9–20)? Surely the prophet is asking a question that theologically misfires!

Calvin notes the difficulty with the prophet's speech in v. 13. He believes that it borders on blasphemy and is both full of doubt and impetuosity. The prophet is almost profane because he implies God has not ruled well and not acted justly in creation. As such, he does not affirm with faith that God rules well despite all other appearances.

Calvin thinks Habakkuk's problem is due to his loss of piety. He should have focused upon the glory and justice of God instead of human trouble. Calvin characterizes the prophet's speech as an internal struggle with the nature of human suffering more than grappling with the injustice of God, his creator.[62] Calvin's theological move, however, does not ameliorate the complaint but rather presses it home even more.

The reason is because of v. 14, in which the text draws attention to creation language in the prophet's complaint to God, particularly, the language of Gen 1:

> And God said, "Let us make man [אדם/*'ādām*] in our image, after our likeness. And let them rule over the fishes of the sea [בדגת הים/*bidgat hayyām*], and over the birds of the heavens, and over livestock and over all the earth, and over every creeping thing that creeps [ובכל־הרמש הרמש/*ûbĕkōl-hāremeś hārōmēś*] on the earth." So God created man [אדם/*'ādām*] in his own image. In the image of God he created him. Male and female he created them." (Gen 1:26–27)

> And did you make a man [אדם/*'ādām*] like fishes of the sea [כדגי הים/*kidgê hayyām*], like a creeping thing [כרמש/*kĕremeś*], not having dominion over it? (Hab 1:14)

The intertextual linkage remains conspicuous and reinforces the notion that Habakkuk affirms the Lord as creator—Yahweh has made humanity to exercise rule over creation. But the prophet also wonders if this order of creation has been overturned as the Lord raises up the Babylonians for judgment. Shall God's people, who are given the responsibility by God to exercise his dominion in the world, be replaced with a nation that does not adhere to God's order of things? The Babylonians are idolaters!

62. Calvin, *Commentaries on the Twelve*, 45–48.

The prophet pleads that God would not look upon the trouble that the Babylonians will bring. He begs that God will not keep silent and will act on behalf of some of the righteous among his wicked people (v. 4). He pleads that God will act on behalf of these righteous, oppressed by the wicked Babylonian idolaters (v. 13). Through poetic wordplay, the prophet draws together the complaint advocated in vv. 2–4 and couples it with the complaint of vv. 12–17. Habakkuk contends with God about his order of creation turned topsy-turvy. God's people will no longer be able to properly worship their God and exercise dominion in creation. Surely God will not wipe away the righteous with the wicked, and not least by way of an idolatrous nation!

Verses 15–17 build upon the inversion of the created order isolated in v. 14. In an ironic twist, the idolatrous nation of Babylon is the one exercising dominion in creation. But different than the righteous of Israel who would properly give God his proper worship in their exercise of dominion, this idolatrous nation (that God has raised up) pulls up the fishes (nations) from the seas (the kingdoms of the world) and gives worship to . . . his nets (v. 16). Habakkuk's clever complaint affirms the topsy-turvy order of creation. Would God use this nation for his purposes when this nation worships the *created thing* rather than the *creator* (cf. Rom 1:25)? Habakkuk concludes with a question: "Therefore shall he empty out his dragnet, and continually slaughter nations he does not pity?"

Habakkuk's selection of effective fishing tackle in vv. 15–17 is striking. Fishhooks (v. 15) catch one fish at a time on a line. As such, they are effective, but not as efficient as a fishnet. This second device is not mentioned once (as with fishhook) but twice in vv. 15 and 16. Fishnets are more efficient and effective than a single hook as they garner more fish while expending less time and labor for fishermen. These are round nets that are thrown out by one or two persons to attempt a greater catch of fish than could be accomplished with a hook or spear. But dragnets are the most efficient of all.

Dragnets appear three times in vv. 15, 16, and 17. A dragnet is wide netting made like a kind of wall and could be extremely long, 750–1000 feet in length, and 5 feet high on the ends and 25 feet high in the center, according to Janny de Moor. Large nets like these would require roughly fifteen to sixteen workers to set it out into the waters and gather it back together and harvest the catch. The goal was to scour the waters at every level, to empty the waters of their fish.[63] Through the imagery of fishing tackle in vv. 15–17, the prophet sets on display human ingenuity, rational design, communal cooperation, and labor

---

63. Janny de Moor, "In the Beginning Was Fish: Fish in the Ancient Near East," in *Fish: Food from the Waters; Proceedings of the Oxford Symposium on Food and Cookery 1997*, ed. Harlan Walker (Totnes: Prospect Books, 1998), 85–86.

to highlight the massive yield that derives from technological advancement. As a technological advance, fishing is a good thing, for it brings the maximum amount of food for a maximum amount of people for a minimum amount of labor.

But we must remember that in Habakkuk's image, Babylon's technology of fishing is not fishing at all. Fishing is a literary vehicle that confronts the hearer with the reality of warfare. Fishing becomes an ironic metaphor to introduce the technology of *death* instead of *life*. As a technological tool, fishing ironically displays how efficient human warfare can be. Presenting fishing implements as devices of Babylon's warfare is to juxtapose image against reality. Fishing is (in theory) life giving, but in Babylon's hands this technological advance is death-dealing because it serves as an efficient way to slaughter nations and peoples. Note the parallels between the metaphor of fishing and the reality of warfare (where the sign // stands for "parallel to"):

**Parallels in the Literary Presentation of Fishing**

> Fishing//Warfare
> Fishermen//Babylon
> Fish//nations & peoples
> Hooks, fishnet, dragnets = technology that sustains human life// implements of the Babylonian war machine = technology that ends human life

As one can see, the prophet's use of fishing imagery stimulates and provokes. The utensils fishhook (v. 15), fishnet (vv. 15–16), and dragnet (vv. 15, 16, 17) represent the productivity of Babylon's war machine, but it remains vital to recognize these utensils properly as *technology*.

Jacques Ellul identifies technology as *technique,* or "the totality of methods rationally arrived at and having absolute efficiency . . . in every field of human activity."[64] For Ellul, technology is any method or practice which humans rationally enact to maximize efficiency. For the enterprise of fishing, efficiency means exercising the technology of hooks and nets. Scooping the rivers and seas with nets indicates an advanced level of technology beyond that of fishing with spears or harpoons precisely because of their efficiency, according to de Moor.[65] Fishermen belonged to special guilds in Egypt and Mesopotamia, and

---

64. Jacques Ellul, *The Technological Society*, trans. John Wilkinson (New York: Knopf, 1964), xxv; see also 73–74.

65. De Moor, "In the Beginning," 85–86.

de Moor provocatively asserts that fishing techniques were known technological advances prior to the invention of writing.[66] So fishing with implements (beyond one's bare hands) represents a great technological advance. This is more significant because fishing was not a major industry in Judah at the time of Habakkuk's prophecy. The prophet employs a technological advance from Babylonia to make a point about the horror of the Babylonian war machine.

In Habakkuk's image, Babylon's great failure is that their use of technology is death-dealing and does not accord with God's order of creation. It is fascinating, and no doubt intentional, that the prophet immediately links Babylon's misdirection of technology toward death with idolatry: "Therefore he will sacrifice to his dragnet, and he will sacrifice to his fishnet" (v. 16). Upon closer inspection, Babylon's worship is not to their nets as much as what these fishing tools represent: the technology of war and the devastation that it yields.

Habakkuk's critique of technology in his day becomes a resource for us to reflect upon technology, and its use, in our day. Technology can be productive or destructive. Habakkuk recognizes the benefits of technology even while using it to launch his critique, and this is why the discordance between fishing and fighting is so palpable in the image of Babylon as fishermen. Habakkuk's image does not allow the interpreter to long for a return to a pristine, technologically free society. Fishing brings good: food, and life! But technology *misdirected* in destructive and sinful ways is surely death. The image of Babylon as fishermen draws us to reflect upon how humans ought to deliberate (as much as we can) on the technologies we employ so we can direct them toward vitality and human flourishing. Without adequate reflection or adequate care, in the normal order of things technology can go the way of Babylon.

It would be tempting to shift the prophet's critique to focus solely upon war and the horrors of technological advances of war. Daniel Berrigan does just that as he explores vv. 15–17. He argues that the poet shifts his gaze to the true sin that marks Babylon: "Uncontrollable crime, evil that is even rendered virtuous 'for reasons of the state,' (crimes of war that is, liable as they are in principle to international law, but falling cunningly through the interstices of the net)—such crimes biblically understood, invariably imply—idolatry."[67] Berrigan sees in Habakkuk's complaint a critique of war. I do not disagree, but I see the prophet opening a critique against a much deeper root: the misdirection of technology. Babylon's war machine is a perversion and misdirection of technology, as Habakkuk's trenchant critique of technology in his day speaks to the use of technology today as well.

---

66. De Moor, "In the Beginning," 85.
67. Berrigan, *Minor Prophets*, 288.

# Habakkuk 2

## Translation

(Habakkuk's Response, continued)

2:1I will stand upon my watchpost;
    And I will station myself upon a tower.
And I will look out to see what he will say to me;
    And what I will return concerning my reproof.

(The Second Divine Response)

2:2And Yahweh replied:
"Write a vision, and make it plain on tablets,
    So that the one reading may run into it.

2:3For (the) vision is a witness for the appointed time;
    And it is a witness for the end — it will not lie.
If it delays, wait for it;
    For surely it *will* come — it will not dawdle.

2:4Behold! — the one who faints before it,[1]
    His soul is not upright in him.
        But the righteous one shall live in its faithfulness.

2:5Yet indeed, the wine is treacherous,
    The strongman (is) proud, and he will not remain.

---

1. "It," i.e., the "vision" of vv. 2–3.

(The one) who enlarges his life like Sheol;
  And like death — he is not satisfied.
He gathers for himself all the nations,
  And he collects for himself all the peoples."

(Woe Oracles)

2:6Will not these — each one of them — lift up a proverb over him,
  And a satire, an epigram, for him? And (each one) will say:
"Woe to the one who heaps up what does not belong to him!
  How long? And who makes himself heavy with pledges."

2:7Will not your debtors arise suddenly;
  Will not those who violently shake you awaken?
    Then you will be the spoils of war for him.

2:8Because you plundered many nations;
  All of the remnant of the nations will plunder you.
(On account of) the blood of humanity
  And the violence of the land of the city,
    And all its inhabitants.

2:9Woe to the one who makes an evil profit for his house.
  To place his nest in the heights, to be safe from the hand of evil.

2:10You have devised shame for your house —
  To make an end of many peoples —
    But your own soul is wronged.

2:11For a stone from a wall will cry out,
  And a beam of woodwork will respond:

2:12"Woe to the one building a city with bloodshed,
  And establishing a city with injustice."

2:13Is it not from Yahweh of the Armies:
  That peoples have worked without profit,
    And nations weary themselves for nothing?

2:14For the earth will be filled,
  To know the glory of Yahweh
    Like the waters cover the sea.

²:¹⁵Woe to the one causing his friend to drink from the bowl of his wrath
   Even to drunkenness, in order to gaze upon their nakedness!

²:¹⁶You shall be satisfied with shame rather than glory,
   Drink! And now, stagger!
The cup of the right hand of Yahweh shall go around to you,
   And disgrace shall be yours rather than your glory.

²:¹⁷For the violence against Lebanon will cover you.
   And the destruction of beasts will shatter (you).
   From the blood of humanity,
   And the violence of the ground of the city,
      And all the inhabitants in her.²

²:¹⁸What has a graven image profited? For a graven image is his own image.
   A cast image – and a lying teacher!
For the one who engraved the image trusts in his very own image
   (but only) makes dumb idols.

²:¹⁹ Woe to the one saying to the wood,
   "Wake up!" (or) "Awaken!" to a dumb stone.
Is it a teacher? Look! It has been encased in gold and silver,
   And there is no breath inside it.

²:²⁰ But Yahweh is in his holy temple.
   Be silent before him, all the earth!

## Summary

Habakkuk 2 carries forward the dialogic interaction between God and the prophet that began in the previous chapter. The progression of thought is identifiable through the poetic use of repetition (note fig. 2, below). Habakkuk 2:1 continues Habakkuk's complaint from 1:12–17, and God answers Habakkuk in 2:2–5. The woe oracles in Hab 2:6–20 do not appear in any other portion of the book, but they can be understood as part of God's response to Habakkuk and they continue the divine speech begun in 2:2.

---

2. Cf. v. 8.

## Figure 2: Repetition of Language in Habakkuk 2

| REPEATED TERMS/ ROOTS | HABAKKUK SPEAKS | GOD SPEAKS |
|---|---|---|
| ראה/*r'h* | Hab 2:1 (cf. Hab 1:3, 13) | (cf. Hab 1:5) |
| יכח/*ykḥ* | Hab 2:1 (cf. Hab 1:12) | _____ |
| יהוה/Yahweh | Hab 2:2 (cf. Hab 1:2, 12) | Hab 2:13, 14, 16, 20 |
| נפש/*npš* | _____ | Hab 2:4, 5, 10 |
| גוי/עם/*gôy*/*'am* | (cf. Hab 1:5, 17) | Hab 2:5, 8, 10, 13 |
| מות/*mwt* | (cf. Hab 1:12) | Hab 2:5 |
| צדק/*ṣdk* | (cf. Hab 1:4, 13) | Hab 2:4 |
| משל/*mšl* | (cf. Hab 1:14) | Hab 2:6 |
| חמס/*ḥms* | (cf. Hab 1:2, 3) | Hab 2:8, 17 (cf. Hab 1:9) |
| רע/עון/*'wn*/*r'* | (cf. Hab 1:3, 13) | Hab 2:9 |
| נבט/*nbṭ* | (cf. Hab 1:3, 13) | Hab 2:15 |
| שד/*šōd* | (cf. Hab 1:3) | Hab 2:17 |
| אמן/*'mn* | _____ | Hab 2:4b (cf. Hab 1:5b) |

## Commentary

**2:1** Verse 1 may be an internal monologue spoken by the prophet. He prepares himself for divine response (as God has done in 1:5–11), but also hypothetically prepares an answer to return to the Lord (as the prophet did in 1:12–17) *after* God responds. Up to this point in the dialogue between God and Habakkuk, divine responses to the prophet have raised more questions than offered answers, and so there is little surprise that the prophet expects the same, steeling himself to once again respond.

The use of the root שׁוב/*šwb* in v. 1 to depict an answer in a conversation is unique in the Minor Prophets and more suited to narrative contexts. An interesting intertext to this usage exists in Job 31:14, where Job asks what he shall answer (שׁוב/*šwb*) to God if the deity engages him. Here an afflicted petitioner hypothetically braces himself to answer the Lord if addressed by the divine. It appears that this is the situation for Habakkuk as well, as reflected in Hab 2:1. So the use of שׁוּב/*šwb* in Hab 2:1 is exceptional in the Minor Prophets, but not entirely without exception in the Old Testament.[3]

The prophet has concluded his complaint to God, as is evident from the shift from the interrogative form in 1:17 to the indicative report in 2:1. Habakkuk takes his position at his post to await God's response to his "reproof" (תּוֹכַחָה/*tôkaḥâ*). The reproof is Habakkuk's, and this is clear based on the first-person common suffix "my" on the noun. There is some discussion as to the meaning of reproof (תּוֹכַחָה/*tôkaḥâ*); the options are listed below:

1. It may connote a legal dispute against God that Habakkuk begins in the preceding complaint of Hab 1:12–17.
2. It could be an indicator of a contrarian argument that suggests God's raising of the Babylonians for judgment is not acceptable.[4]
3. It may be a summary statement that defines the complaints of 1:2–4 as well as 1:12–17.[5]
4. The reproof (תּוֹכַחָה/*tôkaḥâ*) term may not connote forensic language against God at all but rather is language that anticipates God's response to the prophet through an oracle in Hab 2:2–5. As such, reproof (תּוֹכַחָה/*tôkaḥâ*) belongs to the realm of oracular enquiry at the temple rather than forensic dispute.

It is difficult to pin down exactly, but there is evidence that reproof (תּוֹכַחָה/*tôkaḥâ*) is used in texts that complain against God rather than specifically indicating oracular enquiry.[6] Still, it is not out of the question that the term might be oracular in nature, as Habakkuk has positioned himself possibly in the temple, where oracles were transmitted. The watchpost and tower in v. 1 may be located in the Jerusalem shrine. But, as I have argued in the introduction, the evidence is not as strong as one might wish. We can firmly state that whether the reproof (תּוֹכַחָה/*tôkaḥâ*) indicates an oracular enquiry or indicates a response to his previous complaints, the prophet uses this language anticipating divine

3. See the helpful discussion on *šwb* in Habakkuk by Jason LeCureux, "The Thematic Unity of the Book of the Twelve: The Call to Return and the Nature of the Minor Prophets" (PhD diss., University of Gloucestershire, 2010), 163.

4. This is a suggestion proffered by David Vanderhooft, "The תוכחת, 'Disputation' of Habakkuk as a Contrarian Argument in the Book of the Twelve" (paper presented at the Annual Meeting of the Society of Biblical Literature, Atlanta, GA, 20 November, 2010).

5. Andersen, *Habakkuk*, 116–18, 194.

6. Michael H. Floyd, "Prophetic Complaints about the Fulfillment of Oracles in Habakkuk 1:2–17 and Jeremiah 15:10–18," *JBL* 110 (1991): 399–401.

response. On both interpretations, it is unclear to the prophet how God will respond; the prophet only wishes for some sort of divine rejoinder and prepares himself to answer.

The rich intertextuality in Habakkuk (see fig. 2) has been underdeveloped in scholarship on Habakkuk, yet remains significant for theological interpretation. The word ראה/*r'h* in 2:1 draws together Habakkuk's first and second complaints with his anticipation for God to respond to him. Yet, true to the view that God is the just judge to whom all complaints can go, the prophet unabashedly presents his case before the Almighty to "see" (לְרְאוֹת/*lir'ôt*; cf. Hab 1:3, 5, 13) what will be God's good response. Further, the root יכח/*ykḥ* plays upon Habakkuk's recognition that God has raised up the Babylonians for judgment (לְהוֹכִיחַ/*lĕhôkîaḥ*) against his people in Hab 1:12. The repetition of this root heightens the interplay between divine and human action in Hab 1: God raises the Babylonians for judgment (לְהוֹכִיחַ/*lĕhôkîaḥ*), but Habakkuk questions God's instrument of judgment through his reproof (תּוֹכַחָה/*tôkaḥâ*) and awaits God's response to it.

Even if one thinks that Hab 2:1 represents a statement somewhat removed historically from the complaints in Hab 1, at some stage the poetry has been brought together intentionally. When brought together, the meaning of תּוֹכַחָה/ *tôkaḥâ* combines Habakkuk's first and second complaints in the context of the book. Considering how closely they work together in the logic of the first poem as discussed in the previous chapter, the reproof can be understood as a dispute brought before God, awaiting his response. Similar constructions can be found in Ps 38:15; Job 13:6; 23:4.[7]

As such, prayer (and what counts as legitimate prayer) once again comes to the forefront in the book. How should the prophet pray to God, and how should followers of the Lord in future generations pray? Hayyim Angel describes a midrash on Hab 2:1 that wrestles with the issue of Habakkuk's prayer, his reproof. The midrash is uncomfortable with the tone of Habakkuk in the verse:

> *Keep your mouth from being rash* (Eccl. 5:1). . . . When Habakkuk said *I will stand on my watch, take up my station at the post* (Hab 2:1). . . . This teaches that he drew a form [*tzar tzurah*], and stood in its midst. He said "I will not move from here until You answer me." . . . God replied, "You are not an ignoramus, but rather a Torah scholar!" . . . When Habakkuk heard this, he fell on his face and supplicated. He said, "Master of the Universe! Do not judge me as a willful transgressor, but rather as an inadvertent sinner

7. Vanderhooft, "'Disputation' of Habakkuk."

[*shogeg*]." This is what is written, *A prayer of the Prophet Habakkuk. In the mode of Shigionnoth* (Hab 3:1). (Midr. Psalms 7:17)[8]

In this case, the prophet is impudent and rash for praying the way that he does. Other rabbinic responses have been offered as well: from suggesting that although Habakkuk prayed this way, his spirituality is unique and should not be a model for the rest of us mere mortals; to a fully orbed embrace of strident prayer in the mode of the lament psalms.[9]

Different from this rabbinic view, I suggest that the prophet's strident protest is not *impudent*, but *typically human*; this is what humans do when they are confused and grasping for God's ways! How could we do other than go to the God that made us? In confusion, we pray. When we don't understand, we pray. When we are angry, we pray. The prayers all go to the Lord and await his response . . . whatever it may be. This kind of prayer looks to God in faith.

A great deal of effort has been exerted to clarify the meaning of the watchpost (מִשְׁמָר/*mišmār*). In popular thinking, the watchpost image here may relate to the watchman image in Ezekiel (3:16–27; 33:1–20). Both Habakkuk and Ezekiel are often linked with the priesthood or cultic spheres, so the connection is understandable. However, the terminology between the two texts remains different. Habakkuk's watchpost (מִשְׁמָר/*mišmār*) refers to the place where the prophet waits to hear from God. The watchpost and tower may be technical terms for the place of received oracles from God at the temple (cf. Isa 21:8).[10] But then again, the language simply may reflect Habakkuk's knowledge of temple activity and instead be indicating through metaphorical use of language that the prophet will take his stand and wait for God's response, in the fashion of a prophet waiting for God's response in an oracle at the temple. It is probably too vague to say with certainty that the prophet went straight up to a particular watchtower at the temple and waited for God's response to his complaint. Habakkuk could have done so, but this is not finally necessary to understand the sense of the verse.[11] Ezekiel's watchman (צֹפֶה/*ṣōpeh*) imagery, by contrast, is different and refers not to receiving a vision from God. Rather, it denotes a watchful prophet, speaking God's word to a rebellious people.

**2:2–5** Without a doubt, these are some of the most complicated verses in the book. However, it is possible to uncover some of the riches that are available

---

8. Quoted in Hayyim Angel, "Biblical Prayers and Rabbinic Responses: Balancing Truthfulness and Respect before God," *JBQ* 38 (2010): 4.

9. Angel, "Biblical Prayers and Rabbinic Responses," 4.

10. Floyd, "Prophetic Complaints."

11. Roberts, *Nahum, Habakkuk, and Zephaniah*, 108.

to those who would patiently work through them, and indeed they provide the key to unlocking the book. These words constitute God's response to Habakkuk introduced by a typical syntactical formula that indicates as much: ענה√/ʿnh +אמר√/ʾmr.

God's words are not described as an oracle as in Hab 1:1, but rather as a "vision" (חָזוֹן/ḥāzôn). The meaning of the vision, why it is written down, and the expected response to it are all challenging yet stimulating issues to be addressed from v. 2. We shall deal with these in that order.

### *The Meaning of the Vision*

First, in the Old Testament, a vision (חָזוֹן/ḥāzôn) appears in a variety of contexts. 1 Samuel 3:1 describes a time when the "word of Yahweh" (דְּבַר־יהוה/dĕbar-Yahweh) was rare and there was no vision (חָזוֹן/ḥāzôn) being spread about the land. The parallel between the word of Yahweh (דְּבַר־יהוה/dĕbar-Yahweh) and vision (חָזוֹן/ḥāzôn) is striking. In this example, a vision (חָזוֹן/ḥāzôn) is not a *visual manifestation* given by God, but it is first and foremost a divine *word*. For this reason, it is not surprising that the term "vision" (חָזוֹן/ḥāzôn) is often associated with prophetic speech in the Old Testament. Without God's word, God's world goes into chaos. This language is not only rooted in prophetic literature, however, as Prov 29:18 attests: "When there is no vision [חָזוֹן/ḥāzôn], people run wild." In this way, a vision (חָזוֹן/ḥāzôn) provides divine guidance and instruction for God's people. It is often associated with divine correction of his people (Ezek 7:13, 26; 12:22–25).

The term "vision" (חָזוֹן/ḥāzôn) also appears in the context of either a visual manifestation (Dan 9; 10; 11) or a dream (Dan 8:1). Indeed, at the beginning of Daniel, the text informs the reader that Daniel is given the ability to interpret "every vision and dreams" (Dan 1:17). In the context of Daniel, the vision (חָזוֹן/ḥāzôn) represents more than a word from God. It is a kind of visionary experience the prophet undergoes. There is other evidence from the Old Testament that parallels the use of "vision" (חָזוֹן/ḥāzôn) in Daniel, but it is less pervasive than the term as associated with a divine message.[12]

The semantics of vision (חָזוֹן/ḥāzôn) in Hab 2:2 is a *word* given by God, particularly a word of judgment that is close to being fulfilled. The great irony in this statement, of course, is that it *confirms* God's message to the prophet in Hab 1:5–11, and this was the impetus for his complaint in vv. 12–17. Habakkuk awaits response that would counteract his confusion, but God's vision

---

12. See A. Jepsen, "חָזָה," *TDOT* 4:288.

reaffirms the very thing that confused the prophet. The vision confirms Habakkuk's fears: God *is* going to use the "bitter and hasty" nation of Babylon to enact judgment.

## Why the Vision Was Written

God commands the prophet to write the vision down plainly "upon tablets." The tablets could have been made of either wood or stone. Both are mentioned in the biblical material, with the same word used (לוּחַ/*lûaḥ*). Whichever of the two is meant, that God would command the vision to be written on tablets of wood or stone indicates that the message of the vision was to be remembered by the people. Yet the content on the tablets is a bit more difficult to determine.

It is apparent that the message was written down as a testimony of God's action, but that this action was to be fulfilled in a future time. The first half of v. 3 could also be rendered "For (the) vision is a *witness* for the appointed time," as opposed to "For (the) vision is yet for the appointed time," if one emends the particle "yet," עוֹד/*ʿôd*, to the noun "witness," עֵד/*ʿēd*. When one emends in this way, parallelism ensues from the first line to the second line in v. 3a: "For (the) vision is a *witness* for the appointed time; and it is a witness for the end." I follow this emendation and translation, as it finds a parallel in various texts from Proverbs, as will be demonstrated below. Still, the emendation is not essential for understanding the meaning of the verse.[13] The appointed time is the future time in which the vision will come to pass. Its certainty is without question: "It will not lie . . . for surely it will come—it will not tarry." An interesting cotext that illuminates our text in Habakkuk is Isa 30:8. Here, God instructs the prophet Isaiah to write down a prophecy on a tablet (לוּחַ/*lûaḥ*) that will be fulfilled in a future day. The tablet, then, serves as a witness and confirmation of God's word of judgment. This is the sense that is found in God's message to Habakkuk, as well.

Translating the phrase from v. 3 as I have done here, "it is a witness for the end," deserves comment, not only for the linguistic challenges of the clause but also because of the theological import that arises from the translation. The verb וְיָפֵחַ/*wĕyāpēaḥ* has long been considered a translation challenge, but new light was shed on this difficulty with insight from both wisdom material and the Ugaritic language (which is a sister language of Hebrew). The Ugaritic root *yph* is used in that language to connote "wit-

13. See Andersen, *Habakkuk*, 206–7.

nessing" or "testifying."[14] This is also picked up in wisdom teaching from Proverbs:[15]

A truthful witness (יָפִיחַ/*yāpîaḥ*) will report righteousness,
But a false witness (עֵד/*'ēd*) (will report) deceit. (Prov 12:17)

A truthful witness (עֵד/*'ēd*) does not lie,
But a lying witness (יָפִיחַ/*yāpîaḥ*) is a false witness. (Prov 14:5)

A truthful witness (עֵד/*'ēd*) preserves lives,
But a lying witness (וְיָפִיחַ/*wĕyāpîaḥ*) (preserves) deceit. (Prov 14:25)

A false witness (עֵד/*'ēd*) will not go unpunished,
And a lying witness (וְיָפִיחַ/*wĕyāpîaḥ*) will not escape. (Prov 19:5)

A false witness (עֵד/*'ēd*) will not go unpunished,
And a lying witness (וְיָפִיחַ/*wĕyāpîaḥ*) will perish. (Prov 19:9)

If one follows the pattern above, then the verb of Hab 2:3a (וְיָפֵחַ/*wĕyāpîaḥ*) could be repointed to a substantive (וְיָפֵחַ/*wĕyāpiaḥ*) with defective spelling. This is how I have understood it here.[16] In any case, whether one keeps the pointing for the verb or the substantive, the meaning of the line is clear: God's vision to the prophet will serve as a witness that is faithful and true. In short, it "will not lie" (וְלֹא יְכַזֵּב/*wĕlō' yĕkazzēb*) (v. 3a). The parallelism between the terms עֵד/*'ēd* and וְיָפֵחַ/*wĕyāpiaḥ* becomes apparent.

Once the linguistic meaning of these words is understood, one can appropriately wrestle with their theological content. Although the usage of the root יפח/*yph* is confined to economic contexts in extant Ugaritic texts, in the contexts of Proverbs, the usage of the root connotes faithful and truthful testimony versus lying or deceitful testimony. The meaning of the line, then, is clear: God's vision comprises faithful and true testimony that does not lie or deceive. Because the vision is written down, it serves as inscribed testimony. It memorializes and consecrates the verity of God's vision.[17] God's world *is* ordered and

---

14. See the extensive discussion of Dennis Pardee, "*yph* 'Witness' in Hebrew and Ugaritic," *VT* 28 (1978): 204–13.

15. See also Ps 27:12.

16. Alternatively, one may retain the pointing for a verb and suggest that the text here reflects a very rare denominative use of the root יפח/*yph*, "to serve as a witness/to testify, to witness."

17. As will be shown in the exegesis below, the vision from vv. 4–20 reveals that the great reversal of the wicked and restoration of the righteous are certain.

*is* comprehensible. Therefore, the faithful who hear or read the vision can trust God, his word, and his world. They can rely on the message of God's vision.

But this point brings us to the question of what, precisely, is written down on the tablets. Several options are possible. The content of the vision inscribed on the tablets may be the message of Hab 2:4, "Behold! It is inflated—His soul is not upright in him. But the righteous one shall live in his/its faithfulness." In many ways, this message constitutes the heart of the teaching of Habakkuk as well as the divine response to the prophet's second complaint. Yet, given the size of the stone or wood tablets being used, would one really need more than one tablet to hold this message? After all, the "tablets" of v. 2 are plural: there is more than one of them. Unless the prophet was inscribing in very large letters (which is not likely), there is no reason that he would need more than one tablet (or even one scrap of material) to write such a message. It is probable that the tablets held a larger amount of material. With this in view, some have suggested that the message on the tablets is the theophany of Hab 3, or at least some portion of it.[18] This suggestion rightly takes account of the amount of material that is necessary to fill out the tablets, but it is not at all clear that Hab 3 is the best candidate for the content of the vision.

This commentary posits that the relationship between the oracle (מַשָּׂא/ *maśśāʾ*) from Hab 1:1 and the vision (חָזוֹן/*ḥāzôn*) from Hab 2:2–3 provides a context to consider the content of the vision. As indicated in the exegesis of Hab 1:1, the oracle (מַשָּׂא/*maśśāʾ*) is a revelation of God's actions that also includes human response in light of those actions. In our thinking, the vision (חָזוֹן/ *ḥāzôn*) comprises the missing piece of the full oracle (מַשָּׂא/*maśśāʾ*): namely, the vision presents the needed human response of the oracle. The best candidate for the content of the vision (חָזוֹן/*ḥāzôn*), then, is Hab 2:4–20.[19] There are several reasons for this:

1. This amount of material would be large enough to fit on a set of tablets.
2. The vision (חָזוֹן/*ḥāzôn*) provides the human response in the oracle (מַשָּׂא/ *maśśāʾ*) of the book, so Hab 2:4 stands out as the way that God's people should respond to his revelation.
3. The woe oracles in Hab 2:9–20 provide encouragement for the faithful. The woes present the great reversal of the Babylonians, where the retri-

---

18. See Roberts, *Nahum, Habakkuk, and Zephaniah*, 81; see the discussion of Michael H. Floyd, "Prophecy and Writing in Habakkuk 2,1–5," *ZAW* 105 (1993): 472.

19. See the discussion of Floyd, "Prophecy and Writing in Habakkuk 2,1–5," 472–73, who also suggests that at minimum Hab 2:4 is the content of the vision mentioned in vv. 2–3, but then in a footnote offers his view that Hab 2:4–20 is the whole of it.

bution principle that derives from wisdom thinking takes full swing: the wicked *will* reap what they have sown and the righteous will be vindicated.

So, the content of the vision advances a robust theodicy. God's people come to understand that his actions *do indeed* fit within his moral order. God's people *can* live before him in absolute faith and trust in God's faithfulness (Hab 2:4) precisely because chaos will not persist indefinitely. At an appointed time, God will set all things right (Hab 2:5–19). His reign is sure, and the world is rightly established from the temple in Hab 2:20. This message written on the tablets was available to those who would read them, encouraging them in faith despite the coming judgment at the hand of the Babylonians.

### The Expected Response to the Vision

Finally, the rationale for the vision arrives in the phrase "so that those reading may run into it" (v. 2). Admittedly, the line is difficult. A regular translation, "So that he who reads it may run," is possible, but then it is unclear what exactly is intended. Does it mean that God gave the tablets to remind the Judahites of divine judgment as they ran out of Jerusalem, fleeing destruction? If so, the tablets were an emblem of terror: divine judgment against the wicked Judahites has come to pass by the wicked Babylonians, whom God has raised up. The fact that an extended portion of Habakkuk's prophetic word likely existed on the tablets makes this interpretation less than likely. It takes some time to read the poetry; it is not well suited to reading on the run!

Andersen suggests that God gives the vision to Habakkuk so that he might write it on small, portable tablets. Habakkuk would transport the tablets (and their message) here and there, reading them aloud to the Judahites.[20] This is possible, but there is little indication that the vision is written down in order to sharpen Habakkuk's memory of God's message, or that the tablets were designed to be portable. The grammar of the line may not suggest this, either, as Roberts demonstrates.[21]

What is communicated is clarified by understanding the metaphor of running in the line. The Hebrew reads, "Write a vision and make it plain upon tablets, so that the one reading may run *into it* [יָרוּץ קוֹרֵא בוֹ/*yārûṣ qôrē' bô*]." A similar construction occurs in Prov 18:10, "the name of Yahweh is a strong tower, and the righteous one will run *into it* [בוֹ-יָרוּץ/*bô-yārûṣ*] and find security."

---

20. Andersen, *Habakkuk*, 204–5.
21. Roberts, *Nahum, Habakkuk, and Zephaniah*, 109.

The righteous will "run" into the name of Yahweh just as one who is oppressed would run into a tower for security.

In Hab 2:2, the only noun that fits the gender and number of the third-person masculine singular pronoun "it" is the antecedent "vision" (חָזוֹן/*ḥāzôn*). With this parallel from Proverbs in view, it becomes clear that the running in Hab 2:2 is *metaphorical*: those who read the tablets will "run" into the vision disclosed to them. The runner finds security and comfort in the message of the vision. The message of the vision, then, is one of encouragement and hope.

But it is important to note that the message is not one of deliverance *out of* judgment but rather a message of deliverance *after* judgment. God responds to the wickedness of Judah described by the prophet in Hab 1:2–4 by raising up the Babylonians. This message is confirmed in both Hab 1:5–11 and Hab 2:2a. Yet Babylon's pride and idolatry will likewise be judged, as the vision teaches. God will use this nation in judgment, but "a spirit will pass over and he will be guilty whose strength is his god" (Hab 1:11). In other words, God demonstrates that his judgment against wicked Judah is certain, but that the Babylonian threat will not persist indefinitely. In the end, the Lord will purify Judah through judgment *and* judge the wicked Babylonians for their sin. Nothing escapes the divine verdict.

For the readers of the vision, this message encourages them because it affirms a rich, if not complex, picture of divine justice. God's use of the Babylonians is not without cause, and he will not be put to shame by them. Yet in proclaiming the sure punishment of Babylon's pride, God demonstrates to his own faithful people that they will be vindicated and not put to shame, either. They can affirm God's world as ordered and good, even if the present Babylonian threat (an idolatrous nation!) will discipline them for Judah's sin.

Verse 3 indicates the time frame of the great reversal. It appears at an "appointed time" (לַמּוֹעֵד/*lammôʿēd*) and at the "end" (לַקֵּץ/*laqqēṣ*). This language is eschatological in the sense that it is for a time in the future when God will vindicate the righteous and judge the wicked. The Minor Prophets do not use this terminology except in Amos 8:2, and there it refers to the time of judgment against God's people for sin.

The collocation end (קֵץ/*qēṣ*) and appointed time (מוֹעֵד/*môʿēd*) occurs in Dan 8:19. It speaks of the time in which eschatological events unfold in Daniel's vision (see similar constructions in Dan 11:27, 29, 35). This time frame in Daniel does not concern itself merely with local judgment, but with cosmic judgment as well.

In Hab 2:3, the time frame of the end is unspecified, but its scope will involve the reversal of Babylon, to be sure, but the reversal of all those who defy God as well. Prinsloo says, "Through these verses the focus of attention is moved from the distress of the present to the intervention of Yahweh in the eschatological future."[22] If Hab 2:2–3 touches upon a similar concept though using specific eschatological language in end (קֵץ/*qēṣ*) and appointed time (מוֹעֵד/*mô'ēd*), then these verses reemphasize the divine sovereignty of Yahweh in all time, and over all nations. The readers of the vision, then, would find encouragement for faithfulness from its message.

A connection is made between particular and universal judgment in the Minor Prophets clearly in, for instance, Obadiah. There, God's judgment against Edom in Obadiah becomes a figure for divine judgment against *all* nations who sin against God: "For the Day of Yahweh draws near over all nations; just as you (Edom) have done it will be done to you" (Obad 15b; cf. v. 16).

Before proceeding to v. 4, however, we draw attention to the supposed delay attested in v. 3. Some ancient interpreters viewed the antecedent of v. 3 to be a "him": if *he* tarries, wait for *him*. The delay is that of a coming individual, a deliverer. This reading is possible from the Hebrew pronoun, as it is a third-person masculine singular pronoun. We have identified the antecedent as the vision, as argued above. But the Old Greek translators render the line with the sense of a coming individual as well. Cyril of Alexandria is reading from the Greek text, of course, so the reading of v. 3 is understandable. He says of the verse:

> As far as the historical account goes, then, it was Cyrus son of Cambyses to whom reference is made in the phrase, *If he is delayed, wait for him*; it was he who took Babylon, plundering other cities along with it. But as for a mystical treatment and spiritual account, I would say that the force of the expression would rightly be applied to Christ the Savior of all; he is the one "who is and who was and who is to come," and the word of the holy prophets foretold that he is to come in due time.[23]

For Cyril, the delay is explained as the time period between the fall of Jerusalem at the hands of the Babylonians and the coming deliverer Cyrus, whose edict in 539 BCE enabled the exiles to return to the land of Israel, as recorded in Ezra and 2 Chronicles. The spiritual meaning of the verse is prophetic testimony of the coming of Jesus, the deliverer and judge. We should note that this is the reading of Heb 10:36–39 as well, based on the Old Greek of the text, but with a significant difference. The delay in Heb 10:36–39 has to do with Jesus's second coming rather than his first. But the logic is similar.

---

22. Prinsloo, "Life for the Righteous," 627. Prinsloo goes further and rightly argues that "end" (קֵץ/*qēṣ*) and "appointed time" (מוֹעֵד/*mô'ēd*) terminologically mark the eschatological shift in the verses (630).

23. Cyril of Alexandria, *Commentary on the Twelve Prophets*, 349–50.

Cyril's reading was not unanimous. The most influential interpreter in ancient Christianity on Habakkuk is Jerome, and he clearly read the antecedent to be the vision mentioned in vv. 2–3. He says that the vision is that which is coming, rather than a person ("wait for *him*"). He has an extensive discussion on the differences in translation among the witnesses (Aquila, Symmachus, etc.), and he follows the Hebrew. Still, he does not disagree that the verse can be understood as a prophecy concerning Jesus, as mentioned in Cyril's reading, above.[24]

But whether one follows the Greek tradition or the Hebrew tradition (we have followed the Hebrew, reading the antecedent to be the vision that is delayed but surely coming), one notes a tension present in the verse. Gowan rightly says that the words of the vision "seem to contradict themselves; it is hastening but awaits its time! It will not delay but it seems slow and we must wait for it!"[25] Verse 4 anticipates a sense of doubt concerning the certainty of its message among those who would receive it, yet counteracts the very notion that delay is coming. Carroll rightly asserts, "Although there may be a long wait for the vision to be realized, there can be no question of its ultimate failure. It is therefore a word of reassurance which takes into account a general feeling about the question of delay but denies the ultimacy of such pessimism."[26]

Still, the exact timeline is not specified. Gowan is right to say that when God says he will do something, it is still up to him to decide when that will be. All of the speculation in the world cannot provide a firm timeline. "At this point we are frankly left with a mystery, because we cannot calculate the time, we do not understand why the time is not Now. Only God knows that. And that is where faith comes in."[27]

Faith means being faithful to God rather than relying upon a specific timeline. Temptation seduces believers when they begin to rely on God's *schedule* for security and hope rather than on God *himself*. This is a kind of disordered love, which will lead to disordered lives. A timeline may take our eyes away from the One who gave it.

Systematic theologian Adrio König, for instance, recognizes this tendency when it comes to Christians and their fascination with "end times" prophecy. He notes that the doctrine of the last things often addresses various issues, but the one on whom the last days center, namely Jesus Christ, "plays practically no role at all."[28] The desire for knowledge of God's timelines may also expose a

---

24. Jerome, *Commentaries on the Twelve Prophets*, 199–200.

25. Gowan, *Triumph of Faith*, 41.

26. Robert P. Carroll, "Eschatological Delay in the Prophetic Tradition?" *ZAW* 94 (2009): 52–53.

27. Gowan, *Triumph of Faith*, 41.

28. Adrio König, *The Eclipse of Christ in Eschatology: Toward a Christ-Centered Approach* (Grand Rapids: Eerdmans, 1989), 1.

deep idolatry: we want to know so that we have *power* to control our time. Such control makes us masters of the universe, even in the midst of impending trouble, and decenters God from his rightful throne. Yet God's insistence at leaving the timeline unclear places *him* at the center. Habakkuk 2:2–3 reminds believers that *God is always the treasure amid the darkness and uncertainty of life*. His time for salvation *will come*, but in the meantime, we are called to live in faithfulness before the Lord of time.

As this teaching relates to Hab 2:3, the point is that God *will* ensure the vindication of the righteous and punishment of the wicked at the appointed time and end. This is for certain, as this is his sovereign will. Meantime, even if God's timeline (the end) does not meet the standard of human planning, the vision calls God's people to trust in him all the same and wait.

Waiting is a spiritual discipline that cultivates the life of faith. Waiting in faith leaves it up to God to break open that future into the present. After all, the vision is a witness for "the end," and "it will not lie."

With the backdrop of Hab 2:2–3 established, it is possible to move to Hab 2:4. It almost goes without saying that this verse is a foundational theological text. Habakkuk 2:4 stands out for several reasons. In both Jewish and Christian traditions, this verse becomes an orienting point to the life of faith before God. For Jews, this text has been identified as the distillation of the entire law, while for Christians, especially the apostle Paul, it crystallizes the heart of the gospel. Rabbi Simlai in the third or fourth century CE suggested that all 613 precepts in the Torah had been reduced to 11 by King David (e.g., Ps 15), to 6 by Isaiah (Isa 33:15–16), to 3 by Micah (Mic 6:8), to 2 elsewhere by Isaiah (Isa 56:1), then to 1 by Amos (Amos 5:4). However, it is Habakkuk who based all the teaching of the torah into one principle: "The righteous shall live by his faith" (Hab 2:4; b. Mak. 23b–24a). As Beker programmatically states, "Hab. 2:4 is *the* crucial Old Testament text for Paul" as evidenced in Rom 1:17 and Gal 3:11.[29]

Further, Christian interpreters through the ages have leaned upon Hab 2:4 for inspiration, guidance, and encouragement since the early church. For example, Saint Augustine also deploys this verse in many writings, suggesting that the verse provides a paradigm for faithful living before God: Christians are those who live in the present world (often persecuted and oppressed) but are awaiting a new world, the heavenly city. Christians live, then, by faith in what is yet to be seen, and Christ makes this possible.[30] Incidentally, this is also the thrust of the use of this text in Heb 10:38–39.

---

29. J. Christiaan Beker, "Echoes and Intertextuality," in *Paul and the Scriptures of Israel*, ed. Craig A. Evans and James A. Sanders, JSNTSup 83 (Sheffield: JSOT Press, 1993), 68.

30. See the discussion of Coggins and Han, *Six Minor Prophets*, 71–73.

Yet the verse remains difficult for two reasons. The first has to do with the translation of Hab 2:4a, and the second reason has to do with the identity of the "faithful" in Hab 2:4b. Other challenges extend outward from these, but here we shall engage both difficulties and then move toward a theological understanding of the verse.

*Habakkuk 2:4a*: This line presents a tangle for interpretation. In the first place, the verb often translated "it is puffed up" or "it is inflated" (עֻפְּלָה/*'ūppĕlâ*) is difficult. The only other place where the root occurs is in Num 14:44, where the meaning of the verb is contested. It may mean something like "to be presumptuous or impudent," so that the Israelites "were impudent to ascend the hill" (Num 14:44). The root (עפל/*'pl*) also intends something that is raised when used as a substantive. This can either be a raised hill (Isa 32:14; Neh 3:26) or a boil (cf. Deut 28:17; 1 Sam 5:6). The ESV reads the verb with this meaning: "Behold, his soul is puffed up."

This may not be the root, however. Some emend to the Hebrew root עלף/*'lp* ("to be faint, to swoon, to diminish"), thinking that the final two letters of the root were switched somehow. If this is the case, then the line could read something like, "Behold, he whose soul is not upright within him shall fail" (RSV).[31] Alternatively, the consonantal text of the Hebrew is retained, but divided up. So instead of עֻפְּלָה/*'ūppĕlâ* some read עָף לֹה/*'āp lōh*, which would mean that the first word is a *qal* active participle from the root עוף/*'wp*, to fly away and the second word is a *lamed* preposition with a suffixed pronoun, third-person masculine singular (archaic form). This approach simply glosses over the problem of the *lamed* and *heh* that remain.[32]

Another way to solve it is by dividing עֻפְּלָה/*'ūppĕlâ* into עָף לֹה/*'āp lōh*, but treating the root as a II-*yod* root: עיף/*yp*, "to faint." In this case, the rendering of the line would be something like, "Behold, the one who faints before it, his soul is not upright in him."[33] Roberts translates the line in this way, thinking that the subject of the pronoun "it" is not the soul of the wicked one, but rather it is the vision mentioned in vv. 2–3. Therefore, the entire verse of Hab 2:4 contrasts the one who hears the vision and "faints before it" (and does not walk in the ways of the vision) against the one who hears the vision and responds in faithfulness.[34] I should note that this seems to be how the LXX has understood and translated Hab 2:4a. The present commentary recognizes the difficulty of the line, but believes that the LXX translation could well reflect an early (obscure) Hebrew text and wrestles with its meaning.

31. See the discussion by J. A. Emerton, "The Textual and Linguistic Problems of Habakkuk II.4–5," *JTS* 28 (1977): 15.

32. Emerton posits that these may be a corruption in the text and so deletes them; "Textual and Linguistic Problems of Habakkuk II.4–5," 16.

33. Roberts, *Nahum, Habakkuk, and Zephaniah*, 107.

34. Roberts, *Nahum, Habakkuk, and Zephaniah*, 107, 111–12.

Still, the majority view considers the subject of the verbs in v. 2:4a as "his soul," and thinks that the soul of the person who is "puffed up" or "faints" or "is wearied" or flies away is "not upright in him." As both verbs in Hab 2:4a are feminine singular, the most obvious subject (of both verbs) would be the feminine singular noun, "soul" (נֶפֶשׁ/*nepeš*). The ESV continues in Hab 2:4a, "Behold, his soul is puffed up; it is not upright within him." This translation may make some sense of the line, especially if we think that God is addressing the inner soul and uprightness of the moral disposition of the entity being described. Yet it is not at all clear that soul indicates the inner life of the person or that upright indicates the moral disposition of that person.

Considering the discussion above, the challenges of the line become apparent. I prefer to follow Roberts's emendation that divides עֻפְּלָה/*ʿuppělâ* into עָף לֹה/*ʿāp lōh* ("the one who faints before it"). This makes the best sense of the line, but the traditional reading ("Behold, his soul is puffed up") remains sensible. On both interpretations, Hab 2:4a establishes a contrast between two people. The possible identity of the two people is listed below:

1. *Babylonian king vs. faithful Israelite*: If we follow the reading that translates the inflated soul to be the Babylonian king (which is not upright within him), then that prideful king is contrasted against the righteous follower of Yahweh, who relies on God's vision and trusts its veracity. This follower of Yahweh responds in faith to God's faithful vision. Or:
2. *Faithful vs. faithless Israelite*: If we follow the emended text of Hab 2:4a, the one who hears the vision of God (from vv. 2–3) but whose soul faints within him is not established. This is to be contrasted against the righteous one who hears the vision (from vv. 2–3) and embraces God's fidelity with a life of faithfulness to God.

It remains a challenge to decide between these two options on the basis of the difficulty of the text, but the second is preferred here. *What is clear, however, in both, is that God provides assurance that the righteous will respond to God's faithful actions with faithfulness to him.*

If the soul of the Babylonian king is the subject of the verbs (option 1, above), then this is consistent with both Hab 1:14 and Isa 10, where one sees the frailty of human kings before the power of Yahweh. Those who work against Yahweh will pass away. Isaiah 10:5–15 especially demarcates the king of Assyria as the instrument of God's judgment. God describes Assyria as the rod of God's anger and the instrument of his wrath. Yet, this king is guilty of pride, for he thought that the work of taking up nations to himself was by his own hands rather than by God's hands. For this, the Lord says that he will punish the pride and arrogance of the Assyrian king (Isa 10:12–15). Likewise, it may be that Hab 2:4a is the prelude to the judgment that is coming upon the Babylonians, which is fully described in Hab 2:5–20. In this case, theologically, Hab 2:4a *confirms* the great reversal described in Hab 2:2–3, where the righteous are vindicated and the wicked judged. This reinforces the theology of divine justice depicted there.

However, if v. 4a envisions a contrast between the Judahite who hears God's vision and trembles/faints before it and the Judahite who hears God's vision and responds in faith (option 2, above), then the verse transitions to a clear call for perseverance. In this case, the admonition is to wait expectantly before the Lord's vision and live faithfully before him in the meantime. If it tarries, the person should not fall away from fidelity to God. Rather, the faithful should remain true to God against all odds. Calls for perseverance or affirmations of patience are common in the Minor Prophets, not least in Hab 2:2–3; 3:16, but this theme also appears in Hos 12:6; Mic 7:7; Zeph 3:8. Micah 7:7 depicts this well: "But I will look to Yahweh, I will wait for the God who saves me. My God will hear me." If the contrast between groups in Hab 2:4 is between those who hear the vision and respond in faith, and those who do not, then the verse crystallizes the call for perseverance mentioned in Hab 2:3.

*Habakkuk 2:4b*: As mentioned above, this text remains significant for Christian and Jewish interpretation. As a result, the interpreter should exercise great care and precision in delineating its meaning. I proceed by exploring three major questions that emerge from this verse:

1. Who is the "righteous"?
2. Whose "faithfulness" is in view?
3. What kind of life is in view?

Answering these questions will give purchase to the meaning of the line.

### 1. Who is the "righteous"?

The Hebrew term "righteous" (צדיק/*ṣaddîq*) is translated variously as "just" or "righteous" or even "right." The identity of the righteous is one who is faithful to Yahweh. But many scholars believe the term indicates something more specific, even a messianic title, "The Righteous One" (as the Old Greek may imply).

There is evidence for both views in the way the text was received in Judaism up to the second century CE. The Jewish targum on Habakkuk reflects a nonmessianic understanding of the righteous, going so far as to say "the righteous ones will live by their [i.e., the visions in vv. 2–3] truth." The Habakkuk

Pesher envisions the sectarians who are righteous by virtue of their obedience to God's law and obedience to the Teacher of Righteousness. In these Jewish renderings of the Hebrew text, there is not explicit messianic reading of the righteous from Hab 2:4b. The reception of Hab 2:4b in 2 Baruch clearly indicates a nonmessianic understanding of the righteous, emphasizing a contrast between those who are wicked and those who are righteous in their faith in God (2 Bar 54:16–18). But these indicators are not unanimous. Another Qumran text, 8Ḥev1, does read δίκαιος/*dikaios* as a messianic title, "Righteous One."

And there is some indication that the Hab 2:4b LXX employs translation techniques that betray a messianic expectation. Thus, the one who has faith in God's fidelity is none other than "The Righteous One," the messiah. He does not shrink back (Hab 2:4a) but stays true to his (undisclosed) calling. Richard Hays argues that in the New Testament, Paul employed an apocalyptic understanding of the messianic Righteous One from Hab 2:4b to identify Jesus. So, what is envisioned in the reception of Hab 2:4b in Rom 1:17 and Gal 3:11 (and Heb 10:38) is a prophecy concerning the Righteous One, Jesus Christ who was coming. Hays leans on the messianic expectations of Second Temple Judaism to show that Jesus is the only true righteous messiah in whom the New Testament calls people to believe.[35] Hays's suggestion, however, is not entirely persuasive, and will be discussed further in the chapter on biblical theology below.

For now, it is enough to state that the identity of the righteous in Habakkuk is the one who trusts in God and lives faithfully before him. Mulroney's extensive and close analysis of the Old Greek of Hab 2:4 indicates that although the verse *could be applied* to a messianic figure, in the original Greek text it is not necessary.[36] The text was appropriately applied to Jesus and the eschatological fulfillment that attended his incarnation, death, and resurrection.

But what is called for in Hab 2:4b is faithfulness to the Lord, which those who are righteous emulate. This call for faithfulness is also the note that is rung out in Rom 1:17 and Heb 10:38. God is worthy of trust and belief and obedience in the face of all obstacles precisely because of his extraordinary divine faithfulness, both in guaranteeing the vision (vv. 2–3) and in guaranteeing Christ the Lord (per the New Testament evidence). Placing faith in God's faithfulness exhibits the fitting or righteous behavior of the follower of God. But if this solves the question of the identity of the righteous, we are still left with broader questions that need to be resolved: Whose faithfulness is in view in Hab 2:4b, and what is life for Hab 2:4b?

---

35. Richard B. Hays, *The Conversion of the Imagination: Paul as Interpreter of Israel's Scripture* (Grand Rapids: Eerdmans, 2005), 119–42.

36. For a full discussion, see James A. E. Mulroney, "Revisiting Hab. 2:4 and Its Place in the New Testament Eschatological Vision," *STR* 6 (2015): 3–28.

### 2. Whose faithfulness is in view: God's or the people's?

The Old Greek translates this text differently from what one finds in the Hebrew reflected in the MT. Interpreters are divided as to the precise understanding of the verse. Does it indicate a kind of righteousness that derives from *faith* or *faithfulness*, as if these concepts can be pulled apart from one another? It should be said that the LXX wrestled with the whole of the verse. The Greek reads, "If he shrinks back, my soul is not pleased in him; but the righteous will live by my faithfulness" (or "will live by faith in me").[37] Note the Greek reads, "The righteous will live by my faithfulness" (ἐκ πίστεώς μου ζήσεται/*ek pisteōs mou zēsetai*), while the Hebrew reads, "The righteous will live by his faithfulness" (בֶּאֱמוּנָתוֹ יִחְיֶה/*be'ĕmûnātô yiḥyeh*). The difference between the two derives from the pronouns, obviously: "my (God's) faithfulness" (LXX) or "his (the righteous one's) faithfulness" (MT). The question turns on *whose* faithfulness is in view in these words. It is often thought that the Hebrew MT emphasizes the faithfulness *of the righteous follower of Yahweh*. In the LXX, the emphasis likely falls upon "God's faithfulness," because of the first-person singular pronoun given, "*my* faithfulness," and the speech is in the mouth of God.

The Greek rendering is a bit more complex as well, because the LXX version of Hab 2:4 ties closely with Hab 2:3. Rendered with explanatory glosses, the text translates roughly: "If (he) shrinks back [or rebuffs God's vision described in vv. 2–3], my soul [God himself] is not pleased in him. But the righteous one will live by my faithfulness [i.e., the righteous will trust in God's faithfulness to fulfill God's statements in vv. 2–3]."[38] The LXX version, then, establishes a distinction that is like the faithful vs. faithless Israelite contrast identified above.

But when we pose the question of whose faithfulness is in view, we must note that the very construction of the question needs reconsidering. In fact,

---

37. If one reads the genitive construction ἐκ πίστεώς μου/*ek pisteōs mou* as a subjective genitive, God's faithfulness is in view: "God's faithfulness" rather than "faith in God." But, if one reads the genitive construction ἐκ πίστεώς μου/*ek pisteōs mou* as an objective genitive, human faithfulness is in view: "faith in God" rather than "God's faithfulness." For an excellent discussion of the differences in the Greek versions, see Andersen, *Habakkuk*, 209–16.

38. In this, I follow the thought of Wolfgang Kraus without fully embracing all of his points. See Kraus, "Hab. 2:3–4 in the Hebrew Tradition and in the Septuagint, with Its Reception in the New Testament," in *Septuagint and Reception: Essays Prepared for the Association for the Study of the Septuagint in South Africa*, ed. Johann Cook, VTSup 127 (Leiden: Brill, 2009), 111–13, who views the contrast expressed in v. 4 (in the LXX) as a contrast between the faithful who hears God's vision and trusts in God's faithfulness (v. 4b) and the faithless one who hears the vision and shrinks back away from both its content and God himself. For a different approach, see the translation provided by George E. Howard, "The Twelve Prophets," in *A New English Translation of the Septuagint*, ed. Albert Pietersma and Benjamin E. Wright (Oxford: Oxford University Press, 2007), 808.

the faithfulness in view may refer neither to God nor to faithful people, at least according to the Hebrew text. What is trustworthy and faithful is the *vision* that God has mentioned in vv. 2–3: "*its* faithfulness." The grammar certainly allows this, and Haak says that the third masculine singular suffix on faithfulness (בֶּאֱמוּנָתוֹ/*be'ĕmûnātô*) actually refers to "the vision, since it is the reliability of the vision that is in question (cf. Hab 2:3a)."[39] He translates v. 4b: "but the righteous because of its fidelity [God's vision in vv. 2–3] will live."[40] It is certainly the case that the vision stands as the fundamental backdrop to v. 4, but it is difficult to distinguish the vision's faithfulness/fidelity from God's fidelity. Haak admits, "It is difficult, and probably not desirable, however, to draw too sharp a distinction between the vision, the content of the vision. . . , and the author of the vision (Yahweh). Their reliability is interdependent."[41]

Still, one must take seriously the contrast between the unfaithful person (either a faithless Israelite, which is preferred here, or the wicked Babylonian king) and the faithful Israelite in v. 4. I believe that the text presents a contrast between the one who embraces God's vision and its faithfulness and the one who does not. The one who faithfully lives in the light of the reliability of God and his vision stands as righteous.

There is an inbuilt human response to the vision of God's faithfulness. Righteous people *trust* in God's fidelity to enact justice and a faithful life of expectancy before him no matter the cost (so the injunction to "wait for it" in vv. 2–3). The Greek and Hebrew versions closely relate God's response to the prophet in vv. 2–4.

Both Greek and Hebrew versions present God's response to the prophet in vv. 2–3 as the *divine answer* to the prophet's questions concerning the enemy nation. God's response in these verses remains an indicator of his justice and salvation. Yahweh can be trusted; his vision can be trusted. This vindication of God (where the righteous will be delivered and the enemy will be defeated) is for the appointed time, *the end*. God's people should persevere in patience, and faith, waiting for this time to come. It will not delay. Habakkuk 2:4, then, in both the Greek and Hebrew versions, reiterates the point that God is faithful and those who are righteous will then respond in faith to God's faithfulness.

*The versions foreground one dimension or another, but in both, neither God's fidelity nor the Israelite's fidelity is completely out of view.* God's fidelity to bring about the end ensures that he will do what he says. This point, I believe, takes center stage in the verse. But be sure, Hab 2:4 suggests that Yahweh's fi-

---

39. Haak, *Habakkuk*, 59.
40. Haak, *Habakkuk*, 25.
41. Haak, *Habakkuk*, 59.

delity *demands* faithful response: his righteous followers can trust him and are encouraged to do so in v. 4b. These people are identified as righteous.

In this way, there remains a beautiful interplay between divine faithfulness and human response. One simply cannot tease apart the two. Divine faithfulness engenders faithful response from those who love him. As God demonstrates his fidelity to justice (especially in the case of the promised vindication in Hab 2:2–3), Yahweh is shown as righteous. As his followers respond with faithfulness to what Yahweh says he will do, Yahweh's people are shown to be righteous.

### 3. What kind of life is in view?

Another significant question that emerges from this verse is the meaning of the statement "the righteous will live" in Hab 2:4b. It is important to remember the dialogic nature of Habakkuk at this point, because in Hab 1:12 the prophet asked God, "O Yahweh, will we not die?" In the divine response of Hab 2:4b, God affirms that those who are faithful to God will *not* die, but in fact, they will *live*. For those who place their trust in God and live faithfully before him, life is guaranteed.

But does the text intend eternal life or heaven? When he exposits this verse in his 1526 commentary, Luther says: "If you wish to abide and be preserved, you must believe this inscription on the tablet [from Hab 2:2–3], which says that the Christ will come with His kingdom."[42] In this construction, eternal life in Christ's kingdom comes by belief or faith in God's promise. Can the idea that the text aims at in Hab 2:4b roughly be translated: "Those who are declared righteous in God's sight will go to heaven by faith in Jesus's justification which imputes Christ's righteousness upon the godless"? The next few paragraphs will explore this.

The exact nature of life envisioned in Hab 2:4b remains ill-defined. Regardless of how this verse relates to a Lutheran doctrine of justification, it is unlikely that the "life" in view means eternal life in heaven. In the first place, the text indicates that the righteous will not be swept away in the Babylonian onslaught but rather will be exiled and live in a foreign land. This understanding of life, then, would parallel the theological thinking of Habakkuk's contemporary, the prophet Jeremiah. In Jer 31:1–6, God affirms that he will exile God's people into the wilderness of Babylon, but God will bring them back to Zion. God has punished his people with the sword, but he says in Jer 31:4: "I will build you up

---

42. Luther, *Luther's Works*, 197.

again and you will be built, O Maiden Israel!" He will gather his people from the ends of the earth and resettle them in his place, under his rule, as his people. If this is a fertile cotext to help illumine the nature of life in Hab 2:4b, then it reveals that God will not utterly destroy his people in the face of their sin, but rather will preserve a remnant that is made pure through the fires of judgment. Life, then, is a grace of God as he preserves Israel in salvation *through* judgment.

As fertile as this understanding may be, it is possible to construe the view of life in this verse a bit more broadly. In light of the teaching on the vision in vv. 2–3 as being about the end, the meaning of life in Hab 2:4b may indicate a kind of resurrection. Of course such a claim remains contentious, and for a number of reasons. Is there not a difference between healing from sickness and resurrection from death? Can one attribute the concept of resurrection to so early a biblical text? Is it appropriate to think that life here has to do with another concept equated to eternal life? The list goes on.

It is true enough that a clear attestation of an afterlife appears in the prophecy of Daniel, but Jon Levenson persuasively argues that the concept of resurrection is apparent in the texts and traditions of Israel that precede Daniel's prophecies.[43] For example, already in Hos 6:1–2, God has taught his people that divine judgment against them will not be final. They will die in exile, but they will find God, and he will find them, amid their ruin and be revived. Or, more specifically: "In two days he will make us whole again, on the third day he will raise us and we shall *live* [חיה/*ḥyh*] before him" (Hos 6:2). Death in this text is real: Israel dies in the wilderness of exile, but God raises them back into vitality and returns them to the land. For our purposes with the connection to Habakkuk, in this verse, the root חיה/*ḥyh* is the same as one finds in "the righteous will *live* [חיה/*ḥyh*] in his faithfulness" in Hab 2:4b. A similar thought appears in Zech 10:9: "Though I sowed them among the nations, yet in far countries they shall remember me, and with their children they shall *live* [חיה/*ḥyh*] and return." The metaphor of God sowing his seed among the nations indicates that God's people have been scattered, have been broken open on the ground of the nations in death, and yet through their death they spring forth into new life. God revives them and they shall live. Within the Minor Prophets, the concept of God drawing life out of death for Israel stands at Habakkuk's front and rear guard. This is a corporate understanding of a life after exile and death for Israel.

---

43. Jon D. Levenson, *Resurrection and the Restoration of Israel: The Ultimate Victory of the God of Life* (New Haven: Yale University Press, 2006), esp. 201–13. See also the discussions of John Day, *Yahweh and the Gods and Goddesses of Canaan*, JSOTSup 265 (Sheffield: Sheffield Academic, 2002), 118–22.

Habakkuk teaches that as the faithful embrace God's vision, trust him, and live faithfully before him, they will experience life. This is true whether the nuance falls upon the focus of restoration through judgment or upon the focus of resurrection. God's vision will occur and God's people should not lose heart. In this way, this verse cannot be said to be a simple proof text to the doctrines of imputation or justification (gift-righteousness of God credited to sinners by faith in the Son, Jesus). This doctrine is true, but it is derived from other texts. Rather, the present verse speaks to those who have *already* experienced such salvation and reconciliation. It is a word of encouragement for those who believe God will do what he says he will do: have faith in God's faithfulness, because he will give life!

Of course, God's faithfulness is by no means *earned*. (Incidentally, this is clear in Paul's reception of this text in Gal 3:10.) God's grace is his divine prerogative. But nonetheless, he extends it to those who would trust him by faith. Habakkuk 2:4 encourages (and identifies) the righteous as those who exhibit their faith in God's faithfulness! God *will* give Israel life out of faithfulness to his word.

Still, when precisely will this restoration/resurrection life happen? The vision reminds God's people that it will happen at the appointed time—the end. Whenever it occurs, the faithful find hope in God's faithfulness: all will be set to rights and God's people will live, not die. Even if they experience the reality of judgment, Yahweh pronounces a verdict of "Yes!" to the life they will receive in their faithfulness to him and his vision.

We do not want to get too far ahead of ourselves in the commentary, but this second understanding of life (i.e., resurrection) gives some insight on the scale of Hab 3. There, God's work has cosmic effects: the heavens and the earth are affected by God's work. They bow, shudder, and worship God. In light of God's activity, Habakkuk (strangely) embraces death in Hab 3:16–19 rather than crying for life as he does in Hab 1: "I calmly wait for the day of distress, to come to a people who raid us" (Hab 3:16b). Habakkuk's prayer in chapter 3 does not *seek* death, but neither does it seek to *avoid* death. In the face of impending distress the prophet says, "I will rejoice in Yahweh, I will exult in the God of my salvation" (Hab 3:18). His embrace of distress/death is embedded in his knowledge of his restoration (resurrection) *through* death. His life becomes a model of faith, and it reveals a hope in the resurrection of *all* the faithful departed. Hosea has affirmed this point and Zechariah will again affirm it as well: resurrection and restoration are coming in the salvation of God. How does one live *into* such life? Through faith in God and his faithfulness.

In the Christian faith, a dying to self and rising to new life is indicative of the cruciform life. Paul's admonition in Rom 12:1–2 is instructive. In view of God's great mercy, it is reasonable for followers of Christ to lay their lives down as a "living sacrifice." The metaphor is mixed and incongruous. Sacrifices in the ancient world were bound for one thing: ritual slaughter. Yet Paul jarringly promotes a dying that brings life, a living sacrifice. As we die to ourselves, we do so as witnesses to God's plan in and through Messiah Jesus. Yet ironically in our death we do not die but are raised to new life in our Savior. Indeed, we can say with Paul: "I have been crucified with Christ. It is no longer I who live, but Christ who lives in me. And the life I now live in the flesh I live by faith in the Son of God, who loved me and gave himself for me" (Gal 2:20 ESV).

As we move to v. 5, we should bear in mind once again that Habakkuk is written in poetic form; and Hebrew poetry is, by design, terse and full of imagery. Indeed, it is this imagistic use of Hebrew words stripped down and made unfamiliar that marks Hebrew poetry *as* poetry. A feature of Hebrew poetry is what is called parataxis, or the way that Hebrew verse sets one image on top of and beside another image, so that at first blush, the sense of the line is unclear. However, it is the juxtaposition of the (seemingly discordant) imagery and language that *invites* the reader to slow down in the reading or hearing process and reflect upon the complexities of the imagery and language.[44] Indeed, although seemingly discordant at first, parataxis is used in Hebrew poetry to "hint subtly, to push the thought of [the] audience along certain lines" by using "motifs, images, key words, and ideas in such a way" that the audience figures out what ideas are most pertinent.[45] Such is the case in v. 5.

God's words move from the contrast between the faithless (whether Babylon or faithless Israelites) and the righteous (faithful Israelites) in v. 4 to a description of wine, death, and nations. The apparent stark shift in terms of subject has led a good number of commentators to suggest that a definite break exists at v. 4 and that v. 5 marks a new focus in Hab 2. However, we suggest that v. 5 follows upon v. 4 through parataxis, and that v. 5 focuses for the reader the reversal of the Babylonian power. The syntactical construction of the first couple of words in v. 5 remains a challenge. I have translated it "Yet, indeed," following Andersen and treating the Hebrew *waw* as a disjunctive ("yet") and אַף כִּי /*'ap kî* as an asseverative construction, meaning "indeed."

But how do we understand the following jarring words "wine is a traitor" (ESV) or "wine betrays the haughty man" (NASB)? Where does wine fit into the discussion up to this point in the poetry? Many scholars have suggested that it does not, and so follow the Qumran scroll of Habakkuk and emend to "wealth" rather than "wine." The words are similar when one looks at them (just the difference between a *waw* and a *yod*), and so the emendation is sensible.

---

44. For more on the effects of Hebrew poetry, see Thomas, *Poetry and Theology*, 74–95.

45. Alan J. Hauser, "Judges 5: Parataxis in Hebrew Poetry," *JBL* 99 (1980): 26 n. 9.

Still, it is true that wine is often pictured as the instrument of divine judgment in the Old Testament. Note Ps 75:8 [H 9]:

> There is a cup in the hand of Yahweh,
>> And foaming wine fully mixed.
>>> And he pours from this [cup].
> Surely, they will drain and drink down its dregs
>> All the wicked of the earth.

In this text, the cup of judgment is a foaming wine that God pours out on the wicked. They drink the wine of divine judgment down to the dregs. The whole of the verse, however, is a metaphor of judgment, and in the psalm, the metaphor of the wine is a way to show how God vindicates his justice in the world: "All of the horns of the wicked I will cut, (but) the horns of the righteous shall be exalted" (Ps 75:10 [H 11]).

Habakkuk's contemporary, Jeremiah, also used the metaphor of wine as a picture of judgment (Jer 25:15; 51:7). This may be what is in view in Hab 2:5, even though the image appears here for the first time in the book. The association of drinking and divine wrath appears again in Hab 2:15–16, so Andersen thinks that it is unwise to attempt to omit or emend the reference to wine in v. 5.[46] If this is correct, then v. 5 begins to confirm the reversal promised and anticipated in Hab 2:2–4. Judgment is coming and the cup of God's wrath is being poured out upon "the strongman."

The Hebrew word for this "strongman" is גֶּבֶר/*geber*. It has military connotations, and because of it, the term indicates the person in view is the Babylonian invader. This word "proud," יָהִיר/*yāhîr*, which is only found here and in Prov 21:24, connotes someone who is a scoffer and a presumptuous person. The outcome of the strongman's arrogance in Hab 2:5a is judged in the next line: "he will not remain." I have translated the line in this way in part because the root of the verb (נוה/*nwh*) may well be associated with the idea of "settling down" or "having rest." Although strength and war are his bids for security, the strongman nonetheless proves ephemeral in God's economy.

"Sheol" and the "grave/death" in the next lines reveal that the Babylonian exploits, for all their horrors, ultimately lead to death. The irony is apparent. His greed is as insatiable as death. His throat opens up as wide as Sheol as he collects nations and peoples to himself.[47] But his insatiable appetite is self-destructive.

---

46. Andersen, *Habakkuk*, 215–16.
47. See Hab 1:17 for the intertext of "nations" and "peoples" that are collected by Babylon.

In his lust to secure his own life at the expense of others, he sentences himself to the grave!

This great retributive principle that also appears in the wisdom materials of the Old Testament reveals, in the prophecy of Habakkuk, that God's vision is to be trusted. The faithful will experience salvation and not die (cf. Hab 1:12) at the hands of the Babylonians. God's reversal of the wicked and vindication of the righteous begins here and carries on through the woe oracles in vv. 6–20.

**2:6–20** This section expands upon the great reversal delineated in vv. 2–5. There are five woe oracles in this section, each introduced by the Hebrew particle הוֹי/*hôy*, which means "woe!" or "alas!" Yet this English rendering does not fully capture the tone of or intent of the oracles. They are mocking-songs intended to taunt the oppressor. So Gowan translates הוֹי/*hôy* as "Oh, ho!" with a scornful tone.[48] The oracles ridicule the folly of the Babylonians.

The oracles in vv. 6–20 reveal a reversal of fortunes that follows the character-consequence nexus in wisdom literature in the Old Testament. The nexus can be understood in this way: if a person or group demonstrates a life that exudes folly, then disaster overtakes them (generally speaking) because their character is exposed as wicked and foolish; alternatively, if a person or group lives a lifelong pursuit of fidelity to God and neighbor, then they are shown to be wise and to fear God, and this is the life that God blesses.[49] Babylon is a foolish nation because their character is shown to be prideful, violent, wicked, and idolatrous. The woe oracles expose and mock this character deficiency, revealing that this nation eats their bitter deserts.

Woe oracles such as these usually contain an introduction with an accusation against the offender, which is followed by an explication of the judgment against them. Isaiah 5, 10, and 28–31 depict woe oracles similar in form to what appears in Hab 2:6–20.[50] The five oracles proceed as follows:

1. "Woe to the one who heaps up what does not belong to him." (Hab 2:6)
2. "Woe to the one who makes an evil profit for his house." (Hab 2:9)
3. "Woe to the one building a city with bloodshed." (Hab 2:12)
4. "Woe to the one causing his friend to drink." (Hab 2:15)
5. "Woe to the one saying to the wood, 'Wake up!'" (Hab 2:19)

---

48. Gowan, *Triumph of Faith*, 55–67.

49. Bartholomew and O'Dowd, *Old Testament Wisdom Literature*, 270–75.

50. See the now classic discussion of Claus Westermann, *Basic Forms of Prophetic Speech*, trans. Hugh C. White (Cambridge: Lutterworth Press, 1991), 190–95.

### 1. *"Woe to the one who heaps up what does not belong to him." (Hab 2:6)*

Nations the Babylonians have captured in their nets of destruction (see Hab 1:17; 2:5) now mock the wicked invaders. Three words are used to describe the manner of their taunt songs in Hab 2:6: "proverb," "satire," and "epigram." Babylon's wicked ways are now a living example of the futility of sin: it comes back to haunt the sinner. In this case, the strongman or the warrior (v. 5), who collected the nations, now becomes a living proverb to all those who would act in a similar way.

Let the reader be advised! The example of the Babylonian demise becomes instructive for the life of wisdom. Folly turns back upon the foolish. Habakkuk 1:6 describes the Babylonians as a nation who seizes houses that are not their own. Habakkuk 2:6–7 affords the vanquished nation their own voice, and it is a speech of woe and reversal. The words "heavy with pledges" in v. 6 indicate the typical process in which an invading nation makes the conquered people their vassal. Goods from the land now go not to the people or to the conquered nation, but to their imperial overlord. In the rhetoric of the woe, the process of exploiting the conquered nation through these "pledges" (the unique Hebrew word עבטיט/*'abṭîṭ*) remains profoundly wrong. Andersen rightly suggests that this process reduces the conquered nation to bankruptcy.[51] He also accurately describes the debtors of v. 7 as the oppressed nations that Babylon vanquished. Babylon's reversal from glory to shame is foretold as the debtors now rise up against their oppressors: "Then you [Babylon] will be the spoils of war for *him* [the oppressed nation(s)]."[52]

Moreover, v. 8b, which is reiterated in v. 17, explains that the blood and violence that Babylon perpetrated against humanity and lands will now come back upon their heads. Verse 8a pronounces the reversal in poetic repetition: "Because you plundered [שלל/*šlk*] many nations; all of the remnant of the nations will plunder [שלל/*šlk*] you!" It is interesting that the Hebrew word "violence" (חמס/*ḥāmas*, Hab 1:2, 3; 2:4) now comes full circle in Hab 2:8. The prophet cries violence (Hab 1:2–3) and the Babylonians are judged for their violence (Hab 2:8, 17). Even if God uses this nation for Israel's reproof, their bloodshed will not last. Whether it is due to their heart of pride (as with Assyria in Isa 10) or to their injustice toward people and land, as the refrain in Hab 2:8 and 2:17 implies, the verse shows that Babylon is accountable to a holy God.

---

51. Andersen, *Habakkuk*, 236–37.
52. Andersen, *Habakkuk*, 237.

Tyranny against people and land has its natural consequences. In his commentary on the Minor Prophets, George Adam Smith comments on the first woe, saying of Babylon:

> Tyranny is intolerable. In the nature of things it cannot endure, but it works out its own penalties. By oppressing so many nations, the tyrant is preparing the instruments of his own destruction. As he treats them, so in time shall they treat him. He is like a debtor who increases the number of his creditors. Some day they shall rise up and exact from him the last penny. So that in cutting off others he is *but forfeiting his own life.* The very violence done to nature, the deforesting of Lebanon for instance, and the vast hunting of wild beasts, shall recoil on him . . . tyranny is suicide.[53]

And in a modern homily, the peace activist Daniel Berrigan notes concerning the fate of the Babylonians: "The blood of the victims condemns them; so (and this in a stroke of mystical insight) does the cry of the devastated earth. Behold then the emperor and his belikes, naked to the winds of heaven."[54]

### 2. "Woe to the one who makes an evil profit for his house." (Hab 2:9)

In vv. 9–11, the focus of the taunt centers upon the faulty thinking that the acquisition of profits will provide security from all harm. Seeking financial security is not an evil thing, to be sure, but such a search that leads to the unlawful exploitation of others is not only unjust, it is immoral. Babylon has made her "nest in the heights" like a lofty bird of prey. Thinking that she is safe from harm, she can go on with her life unimpeded by the worries of the world. But her profits for luxury and security derive from ill-gotten gains, and her understanding of progress and security is stunted by her own stupidity. A house built on the sands of injustice is doomed to ruin.

There is no high place that can avoid the long arm of God's justice, and so this woe mocks the depraved rationality of the Babylonians. The reversal motif—high to low, honor to shame, oppressor to oppressed—features here and reveals the inner corruption of the thought and actions of the Babylonian imperial power. Habakkuk 2:10 crystallizes the profound irony of Babylon's war machine: "You have devised shame for your house—to make an end of many

---

53. George A. Smith, *The Book of the Twelve Prophets, Commonly Called the Minor,* vol. 2 (New York: Armstrong and Son, 1902), 144 (emphasis original).

54. Berrigan, *Minor Prophets,* 298–99.

peoples—and your own soul is wronged." What seems to be profitable proves to be, in God's economy, profitless because it works on evil gains. What seems to secure safety is, in God's estimation, an exposed sanctuary destined for sacking. Babylon's line of thought on security and well-being is doomed to fail because it is founded on exploitation and greed.

### 3. "Woe to the one building a city with bloodshed." (Hab 2:12)

The phrase "building a city with bloodshed, and establishing a city with injustice" echoes a similar text in Mic 3:10, which condemns Jerusalem's leaders for "building Zion with blood and Jerusalem with injustice." These parallels are too significant to ignore. In both cases, peoples are indicted for crimes of building cities with blood and injustice. In Micah, it is the leaders of Jerusalem, while in Habakkuk, it is the leaders of Babylon. This shows the absolute ethical demand on all nations: God desires righteousness and justice for all peoples and all cities. Whoever acts unjustly is set for the divine verdict.

Yet our text in Habakkuk is unique because the speaker here, in fact, is not the oppressed nation but rather the *house* that has been defrauded and abused by Babylon. This is a powerful use of personification, where an inanimate object is given voice and personality for a particular reason. So v. 11 concludes, "For a stone from a wall will cry out, and a beam of woodwork will respond." The beleaguered house cries out against its oppressors. Genesis 4:10 witnesses the ground crying out from the blood that was spilled upon it, and here it is the stone and beam that cry out on behalf of the violence done against them. In this third taunt-song, the oppressed city cries out against the city of bloodshed, Babylon herself. The very stones cry out against the corrupt and immoral imperial power.

Habakkuk 2:13 expands upon the accusation of injustice in v. 12. In fact, the injustice/blood that permeates the city is, disgustingly, matched with public works designed to honor the city of bloodshed. The Hebrew phrase "people labor" in v. 13 connotes heavy toil under some sort of job. One such job could have been public works projects. So Elizabeth Achtemeier says of this woe: "That government which thinks to glorify itself by its own achievements— by establishing a city or putting up public buildings or instituting new laws or providing services—and which does so by forced and unjust measures is making its subjects labor for that which cannot last."[55] The beautification or embellishment of the city built on bloodshed is akin to beautifying a corpse; it

---

55. Elizabeth Achtemeier, *Nahum–Malachi*, IBC (Atlanta: John Knox, 1986), 50.

is dead and there is no amount of perfume to cover its stench. This labor is "for nothing," as v. 13b affirms.

The city of bloodshed is violent and vacuous, both in the ancient and modern age. George Steiner remarks that the twentieth century in no wise should be regarded as utopian. Despite the medical, social, scientific, and military advances in the age, for Europe and Russia the twentieth century was a time of bloodshed. Indeed, it could be identified as the age of bloodshed with cities of bloodshed. He somberly suggests:

> There have been no utopias, no communities of justice or forgiveness. . . . When, however, allowance is made for selective nostalgia and illusion, the truth persists: for the whole of Europe and Russia, this century became a time out of hell. Historians estimate at more than seventy million the number of men, women and children done to death by warfare, starvation, deportation, political murder and disease between August 1914 and "ethnic cleansing" in the Balkans.[56]

Well into the second decade of the twenty-first century, sadly, the realities are not reversed. "Hell on earth" is not only a title that could be given to the city in Habakkuk's text. It can be applied to the cities in the present world: from Europe and the Balkans, to the Americas, Africa, Asia, and wherever. We are people of unclean lips and live among peoples of unclean lips.

Yet despite their thirst for horrors, cities of death in ancient and modern times are not outside the control of God, as v. 13 reminds. God's power still reigns supreme. So this woe oracle exposes a great irrationality that lies at the heart of all these cities of bloodshed: they proceed in their own perceived permanence and inviolability, but their mode of operations remains vain, ephemeral, and ultimately broken! For all their deathly activity, they work for nothing (v. 13b), and they are doomed for the cup of God's wrath. They will not last, *unless* there is great repentance by the populace and a radical changing of ways. The king of Nineveh reminds us of this possibility in the book of Jonah: "Who knows? God may turn and relent, and he will turn from the heat of his wrath and we will not perish" (Jonah 3:9).

Indeed, Hab 2:14 contrasts the city of death doomed to fail with another city, a better one where death will be no more. Babylon's demise illustrates the justice of God, how it can be said that "the earth will be filled to know the glory of Yahweh as the waters cover the sea" (Hab 2:14). This verse is similar to Isa 11:9,

---

56. George Steiner, *Grammars of Creation: Originating in the Gifford Lectures of 1990* (London: Faber and Faber, 2001), 2–4.

which depicts an eschatological context. But for Habakkuk, the downfall of the wicked and the vindication of the righteous *equate to* God's glory revealed in the earth. Habakkuk's use of the phrase points in the direction of a better time, a better place, where the stain of sin will not mar God's world. Evil will be set to rights. This verse provides once again the surety that vindication *will* take place. If we connect this idea to Hab 2:2–3, then the *time* in which the God's glory will fill the earth is at the end and appointed time.

The Jesuit priest Berrigan provocatively suggests that the downfall of the city of bloodshed in Hab 2:13 opens the way to a *different* city in Hab 2:14. It depicts the heavenly city of God's glory and provides word of hope set at the tail end of the third woe:

> There is to be another "city" than the sinister glory of this or that imperial Disneyland. This city, forever new, shall be and be and be; a consortium of heaven and earth. It will stretch from end to end, of time, of the world. Borrow the old images to be sure, a "dwelling," a "city"; but all made new, marked at last by the holy stigmata of justice and peace.[57]

### 4. "Woe to the one causing his friend to drink." (Hab 2:15)

This woe oracle offers various levels of meaning as it compounds metaphor upon metaphor. Debauchery and drunkenness are clearly mentioned here, but these sins are offered as a springboard for yet another critique against Babylon. The woe mocks the one who makes his friend drunk in order to "gaze upon their nakedness," which is bad enough but may be a euphemism for illicit sexual contact. Genesis 9 is a useful intertext to compare the usage here. But it is not at all clear how a nation (if Babylon is in view, which makes sense in the context) can gaze upon another nation sexually. At any rate, the illicit sexual innuendo of the verse sets the tone: what is done is immoral and exploitative. If the point here is not to address questions among friends, but rather to address Babylon's depravity in seducing other nations to drink down the cup (which is shown to be the cup of God's wrath!), then it is clear that the sin that is identified is neither drunkenness nor illicit sexuality per se, but rather the sin of leading others astray. This eventuates into divine judgment. The cup that Babylon gives will turn back on them in God's wrath. Habakkuk 2:16 shows that they will be satisfied with "shame rather than glory." Again, this is a variation on the reversal theme present in the woes.

57. Berrigan, *Minor Prophets*, 300.

This word represents a powerful warning concerning unreflective or hasty human action in God's world, both for individuals and for communities. There is an inherent danger or risk present in any decision, but the wise will well consider the implications of any action and how it impacts others. Now, to be sure, the Babylonians expose themselves as fools and their character is willful against God in the woe oracles. In a way, it is unsurprising that they lead others away from the Lord. The fact that they draw others to sin and judgment is the major focus in the woe.

However, it is helpful to consider the danger of rash and unreflective action in the church as well, because Babylon's actions can too often look like those of God's people! We are reminded of James's warning to teachers, who hold a greater accountability precisely because they teach and lead others (Jas 3:1). And Jude warns against teachers in the church that lead God's people to sin in the world (Jude 3–16). This fourth woe of Habakkuk holds out a heavy but good word: the wise should be careful about which and what action taken, especially in regard to how one leads others. A wise teacher promotes life, but a foolish teacher facilitates death. A key to demarcating the difference between the two is how deeply they reflect upon the nature and outcomes of human action in God's world.

God's cup of wrath comes around to Babylon, leaving her drinking and staggering, moving from glory to shame (Hab 2:16). This nation, whose avarice is as "insatiable [שָׂבַע/*śbʿ*] as death" (Hab 2:5), is now "sated [שָׂבַע/*śbʿ*] with shame" (Hab 2:16). Babylon's reversal is complete, and for good reason: "For the violence against Lebanon will cover you, and the destruction of beasts will shatter (you). From the blood of humanity and the violence of the ground of the city, and all her inhabitants in her" (Hab 2:17). This repetition from Hab 2:8 brings out once again how the violence of Babylon (and all cities of bloodshed that act as she has done) turns back on the perpetrator. "Violence" and "destruction" is the same word pair that occurs in Hab 1:3. But there is a difference in the usage between the two verses. In Hab 1:3, these sinful acts by Judahites lead to divine judgment *by means of* Babylon. In Hab 2:17, the actors are different: not Judahites, but Babylonians. This wordplay reveals that *Babylon's various sins come back upon them*: violence against land, destruction of animals, killing people, and violence against city and inhabitant. These sins overwhelm and shatter the city of bloodshed. Like a flood that overflows the walls of a dam, the sins of its own making engulf the city of bloodshed and shatter its walls, leaving it in ruin.

### 5. *"Woe to the one saying to the wood, 'Wake up!'" (Hab 2:19)*

The final woe oracle in the series begins not with the accusation statement ("Woe to") but with a question: "What has a graven image profited?" (Hab 2:18). Because of this, the verse seems out of place, and vv. 18 and 19 need to be reversed to follow the normal pattern present in the other woes in the chapter. However, a variation like this alerts the reader that the woes are, in fact, coming to a close. The paradigmatic statement in Hab 2:20 provides the concluding statement upon the whole chapter, emphasizing the sovereignty and transcendent power of God. This final woe is important, because it addresses Habakkuk's second complaint about the idolatry of Babylon in Hab 1:14–17. God engages the idolater in this final woe, although we know from Hab 1:11 that he "whose strength is his god" is not bound to last.

Habakkuk 2:18–19 is, by all accounts, an idol polemic designed not only to taunt Babylon (by virtue of the woe oracle form) but also to denigrate the irrationality of idolatry (by virtue of the polemic). Similar polemics occur in Jer 10:2–10; Isa 40:19–20; 41:5–7; 44:9–20; and 46:5–7. The words of Isa 44:9–11 are instructive:

> Those who make an idol, all of them (are) nothing,
> > And their precious things will not do anything.
> And they are their witnesses: They see nothing and they know nothing
> > Therefore they will be shamed.
> Who would fashion a god or cast an image
> > That is unable to do anything?
> Surely all of his companions will be shamed!
> > And the craftsmen are humans.
> They all will assemble together and stand;
> > They all will be startled and put to shame.

Note as well Jer 10:14–15:

> Everyone is stupid and arrogant;
> > Every goldsmith is put to shame because of the idol.
> For his molten image is a lie [שקר/*šeqer*],
> > And there is no breath [רוח/*rûaḥ*] in them.
> They are vanity, a work of mockery.
> > At the time of their doom, they will perish.

Both prophets rail against the folly of idolatry, precisely because the idols are nothing . . . but God is everything! The woe is similar in Hab 2:18–19:

> "What has a carved image profited? For a graven image is his own image.
>    A cast image—and a lying [שקר/*šāqer*] teacher!
> For the one who engraved the image trusts in his very own image
>    (but only) makes dumb idols.
> Woe to the one saying to the wood,
>    'Wake up!' or 'Awaken!' to a dumb stone.
> Is it a teacher? Look! It has been encased in gold and silver,
>    and there is no breath [רוח/*rûaḥ*] inside it."

In Habakkuk's woe, the futility of the idol is contrasted against the potency of God and the surety of his vision given in Hab 2:2–4. God is trustworthy, but idols are not. Those who follow idols are fools, worshiping the created thing rather than the creator and trusting in emptiness rather than trusting in the one true God (Rom 1:22–25).

Idolatry remains a problem for humanity. In the late seventh century BCE in Judah, idolatry is a threat internal to God's people (as Jer 10:2–9 suggests) as well as external to God's people (as our woe in Habakkuk suggests). The apostle Paul identifies the sin of idolatry as endemic to the human heart in Rom 1. We are reminded that the challenge of cultural idolatry persists in the present as well: from the subtle seduction of worshiping one's retirement plan or savings account as the source of security in life to the overt idolatry that is present in a weekend football game or trip to the shopping mall. Our favorite pastime pleasures or consumer goods may be good gifts, but they are terrible gods.[58]

It should be borne in mind, however, that Israel's struggle with idolatry, like ours, is not a simple matter. We should not think that idolatry simply equates to the notion that a god is present in an idol, whether a graven image of wood, stone, or something else. This may be an accurate description of the beliefs and practices of ancient or modern peoples. However, theologically speaking, idolatry is broader than this.

Theologically, *idolatry is anything that replaces love for the Creator with the thing that he has given as a gift. Idolatry is, at root, misordered love—a love problem.* James Smith attempts to identify and redirect the problem of misordered love in his stimulating work *Desiring the Kingdom*, which is helpful. Misordered love is a kind of idolatry, and idolatry is a subtle seduction. Idolatry takes our

---

58. James K. A. Smith, *Desiring the Kingdom: Worship, Worldview, and Cultural Formation*, Cultural Liturgies 1 (Grand Rapids: Baker Academic, 2009).

vision down and away from God and his purposes with the world achieved through Jesus Christ (see Col 1:15–20). In the modern world, idolatry focuses upon the now of life instead of the now and not yet of the kingdom of God. But as the modern Christian considers what it means to live well before God, we will see that the whole of life—finances, security, relationships, leisure, food, clothes, work, family—are not *gods* but *gifts*! They all come from the hand of a loving heavenly Father. Embracing the gift of life from the Father of lights enables our idols to be smashed. When this happens, the now moments of each day become reordered within the now and not yet certainty of God's new creation.

### Habakkuk 2:20

Considering the idol polemic in the final woe oracle, it is fitting that the chapter concludes with God present in his holy temple. Although he has a temple like those graven images, the verse confirms that Yahweh is neither an idol nor a dumb piece of wood or stone!

The verse begins with a disjunctive *waw* "but" to contrast against the emptiness of the idols in v. 19. Idols offer neither oracles nor divine verdicts. They cannot do so because they are lifeless. By contrast, Yahweh remains vital, potent, and able to provide vision. Yahweh is in his holy temple. Calvin's analysis of this verse rightly contrasts the abode of Israel's God with the gods of the nations. Both Israel and the nations built temples for their deity(ies). Calvin, however, notes that the fundamental difference between pagan and true worship lies in the aniconic impulse present in Israel's faith.[59] Israel's God is not bound by a graven image, the work of human hands. God is present and active, and he pronounces judgment from his holy temple.

In the Old Testament, the temple is the place where Yahweh pronounces and performs the divine verdict. The phrase "holy temple" is used in a particular way in the Minor Prophets as well as the larger corpus of the Old Testament. Taking the closest parallel first, the opening half of Hab 2:20 virtually parallels Ps 11:4a:

> **Yahweh is in his holy temple;**
>> Yahweh's throne is in heaven.
> His eyes perceive,
>> His eyelids see the children of man. (Ps 11:4)

---

59. Calvin, *Commentaries on the Twelve*, 130–31.

"And **Yahweh is in his holy temple**;
>   Be silent, all the earth, before him!" (Hab 2:20)

The psalmic text reveals that the holy temple of Yahweh is the judgment seat where God authoritatively renders his holy judgment. In the Minor Prophets, the prophet Jonah longs for *this* place in his time of trouble; his petition goes up "into your holy temple" (Jon 2:4, 7). Jonah's prayer goes before Yahweh in the temple to receive the divine verdict. In Mic 1:2, it is from the holy temple that Yahweh is a witness against all the peoples and all the earth. As a witness against the lawlessness of his world, God then renders judgment from the temple against his people and land (Mic 1:3–7). It is the *temple* where Yahweh's faithful ones look because it is there that he will give his divine decree. This is the place where God vindicates the righteous and punishes the wicked.

The need for a just ruling from God drives Habakkuk to offer his prayers in Hab 1:4 and 1:13: "The wicked surround the righteous" and "the wicked swallow up (one) more righteous than he." Habakkuk 2:20 shows that God *will* vindicate the prayers of the righteous. We are reminded that God, the good judge, hears the cries of the faithful. Like a good judge and a loving heavenly father, he administers justice and righteousness. So, Jesus's teaching on faithful prayer in Luke 18:1–8 makes good sense. Faithful prayer is necessary, to be sure, but we can be confident that the good God hears, and responds. In Hab 2:20, the text delineates the *place* where God hears and responds: the temple.

Once this is understood, then the second half of the verse ("all the earth be silent before him!") needs unpacking. If God renders judgment from his holy temple, then why should "all the earth be silent"? The best explanation comes when one begins to see how the notion of silence before the Lord functions in the Minor Prophets. In fact, this phrasing is special, and occurs nowhere else exactly as it does in Hab 2:20, even though there are similar phrases in Zechariah and Zephaniah. The command for the earth to "be silent" before the Lord in Hab 2:20b is a way of calling creation to recognize the divine verdict of judgment: Babylon will undergo reversal and downfall, and as Babylon experiences their demise, God's faithful will then be saved.

Two cotexts reinforce our interpretation of Hab 2:20b: Zech 2:13 and Zeph 1:7. The closest of these to Hab 2:20 is Zech 2:13 [H 17]:

Be silent [הס/*has*], all flesh, before Yahweh.
>   For he is aroused from his holy place [קדשו/*qodšô*].

The language parallels our Habakkuk text: "Be silent [הס/*has*], all the earth [כל־הארץ/*kol-hā'āreṣ*], before him!" (Hab 2:20b). Zechariah 2:13 [H 17] is the culmination of God's verdict of judgment against Babylon and salvation for Zion (see Zech 2:1–12 [H 1–16]). The command for all flesh to be silent before Yahweh, then, is a call to hear this divine verdict of judgment/salvation, recognize it, and see that it is coming to pass: "For he is aroused from his holy place." This is the closing statement of judgment in Zech 2 and parallels what is found in Hab 2:20; this connection reveals that both verses function in a similar manner.

Further support comes in Zeph 1, where the command for silence is closely associated with the "day of Yahweh." The text reads:

> Be silent [הס/*has*] before my Lord Yahweh,
>   For the day of Yahweh approaches.
> For Yahweh has prepared a sacrifice
>   He has consecrated those he has bidden. (Zeph 1:7)

In this text, the command for "silence" (הס/*has*) stands as a summons to recognize the divine verdict of judgment that comes in the day of Yahweh. In this way, "be silent" is not a call to *avoid* speaking but rather a call to *recognize* God's verdict and then its subsequent enactment: judgment. It is a call to still oneself before the justice of God and to trust him.

Habakkuk 2:20, then, pictures the *locus* of the divine verdict (the holy temple), but also the *proper response* (*reverential recognition* of God's verdict and *anticipation* of its fulfillment). As Hab 2:20 closes the woes of vv. 6–19, the certainty of the great reversal described in those verses comes as a result of the sovereign word of God. He has judged Babylon worthy of judgment, and all of creation is called to recognize his word and anticipate their sure demise. The upside of the fall of Babylon, at least on a holistic reading of Hab 2, is that the faithful of Judah will be delivered. In other words, the eschatological vision of Hab 2:2–3 *will* come to pass. One needs only to wait patiently for it. The faithful can trust him because, unlike idols, Yahweh remains *the living God* who administers judgment.

---

Excursus: The Power of Silence

There is power in disciplining the mind and body to focused silence. Habakkuk 2:20 draws the hearer to silence and stillness before God as it commands one to rest in the Lord's sure justice. The wicked will indeed get their just deserts and the righteous will be vindicated. This theme appears in Habakkuk, to be sure, but also in the Minor Prophets.[60] In the book of Revelation, God's justice in and through Jesus Christ remains a glorious vision that draws the church to wonder and awe . . . to worship (see Rev 5). But can the church witness Habakkuk's vision break open into the present world? A cultivated habit of silence is necessary for the church to do so.

God's command for silence in Hab 2:20 is a call for his people to recognize his power to vindicate the righteous and judge the wicked. Although his salvation occurs in the future, the surety of it brings hope for today. Silence provides the space for the faithful to embrace his divine verdict. Although, as Hab 3 reminds, vindication occurs only *after* the invasion of the Babylonians; God still calls his people to silence—to embrace God's future salvation in the present. The kind of silence intended in Hab 2:20, as well as in this excursus, is more than the absence of words. Spiritual silence can be matched by physical silence, but not necessarily so. Contemplation upon God and his ways requires spiritual silence—rest—before the Lord, and often this comes by stilling oneself and preserving absolute quiet.

Martin Laird teaches such contemplation in his *Into the Silent Land*. Human beings have a hard time with this, but it remains an underdeveloped spiritual resource in the life of faith. He suggests that Christians rediscover its power by focusing in prayer upon one word: "Jesus." This kind of prayer centers the mind and body on the person of Christ without any distraction. "It is an ancient way of praying that disposes the one who prays to the open depths within by drawing to stillness the wandering mind that flits and skitters all over the place. . . . The Jesus Prayer, indeed any contemplative discipline, tries to interrupt this chatter."[61] As we embrace the silence in prayer, our world is met with Christ, or as Laird describes: "Our self-forgetful gaze on God is immersed in God's self-emptying gaze on us, and in this mutual meeting we find rest."[62] This is a kind of silence that stills the self before the awesome majesty of God.

Silence helps us set our own daily experiences of pain and toil into the larger economy of God's caring redemption of the world both now and in the future. Of course, the contemplative life is inherently relational: as one invests oneself in Christ, the Father begins to speak to his children and they hear him in the power of the Spirit. We find, amid the toils and anxieties of life, our place in God's life, in God's plan. This kind of reflection does not come easily, precisely

---

60. Thomas, "Hearing the Minor Prophets," 363–68, 374–76.
61. Martin Laird, *Into the Silent Land: A Guide to the Christian Practice of Contemplation* (Oxford: Oxford University Press, 2006), 48–49.
62. Laird, *Into the Silent Land*, 48–49.

because it demands quiet before the Lord, which is hard-won![63] Contemplation is the process of spiritual shaping where individuals and communities slow down, learn to be still and silent before the Father, and quiet the self. Communion with the Lord in this manner leads the church into her *true identity* and *relevant* action in God's world. Dangers appear on the horizon for the church when we abdicate the call for silence and reflection.

*One such danger is the overestimation of what we do in God's world.* Habakkuk 2:20 reminds us that God's justice, not human action, remains the final word on the world. His command for silence reminds us that God has *already* enacted justice in Christ, and he has already overcome the world. Christian action simply works in accord with what he has already accomplished. In this way, the world does not depend upon us. We respond to God's work in Christ, proclaiming and promoting the gospel of Jesus Christ. Yet Christian action in the world remains, always and ever, a sign in the rubble of a broken world that points back to King Jesus and his coming kingdom.[64] Our work is not the *culmination* of the kingdom, but *the sign* that the king has come and he will come again.

*The neglect of silence may lead the church toward explicit or implicit cultural compromise.* Silence gives space for the church to evaluate her work. The church should ask whether and how her service in God's world is, in fact, pleasing to him or accommodating sinful culture. Busy-ness and the chaotic desire to "do something—and quick, mind you!—for God" may lead the church toward compromise. Christian morality gives over to what works in the culture. The call for Christian suffering gives way to a health-wealth-prosperity gospel. Structure and sacraments become nothing more than things we do in the marketplace of the church. Silence, however, provides the space to allow God to speak his fresh word into a culturally compromised church, purge her, and purify her so she might be more faithful in her discipleship and more effective in her witness.

At its best, contemplation centers the church within God's life so that she might live authentically as the body of Christ, rather than being conformed to the idolatrous patterns of the present world. Helpful tools (idols?) in our culture—pragmatism, expediency, prosperity, and simplicity—can become misdirected in unhealthy ways. Instead of being bent *toward* the kingdom of God, these tools become monsters that lurk in the shadows, overtaking our practices and leading us away from the centrality of Christ and his gospel. The church's

---

63. For helpful entrees into spiritual theology and the practice of contemplation, see Laird, *Into the Silent Land*, 48–49; Eugene H. Peterson, *Christ Plays in Ten Thousand Places: A Conversation in Spiritual Theology* (Grand Rapids: Eerdmans, 2005).

64. See Lesslie Newbigin, *Signs amid the Rubble: The Purposes of God in Human History*, introduction by Geoffrey Wainwright (Grand Rapids: Eerdmans, 2003).

first question should not be "What works?" but rather "What is faithful to Christ and his coming kingdom?" The very actions and practices of the church must be considered and processed prayerfully. Stillness, contemplation, and reflection give the time and space to combat these tendencies and to see that our work matches the vision of the kingdom of God. Contemplation enables the church to "Be still, and know that I am God. I will be exalted among the nations, I will be exalted in the earth" (Ps 46:10). Or in the words of Habakkuk: "Let all the earth be silent before him" (Hab 2:20).

# Habakkuk 3

## Translation

<sup>3:1</sup>A prayer of Habakkuk the prophet. According to *Shigyonoth*.

(Programmatic Introduction)

<sup>3:2</sup>O Yahweh, I heard your report,
I feared, O Yahweh, your wondrous work.
In the midst of years, declare it
In the midst of years, make it known.
Though angry, may you remember compassion.

<sup>3:3</sup>Eloah came from Teman
And the Holy One (came) from Mount Paran.          *Selah*
His majesty covered the heavens
And his praise filled the earth.

<sup>3:4</sup>And (his) radiance was like the sun;[1]
Rays of light (came) from his hand,
And there (it was) a veil of his might.

---

1. This is a difficult line. I read with the LXX here, translating "and his brilliance was like (the) sun/light" (καὶ φέγγος αὐτοῦ ὡς φῶς/*kai phengos autou ōs phōs*). The Hebrew may be ונגתו כאור תהיה/*wěnōgātô kā'ôr tihyeh*, where the final *taw* and *ḥolem waw* in ונגתו/*wěnōgātô* were misread as a *he*. Alternatively, the 3ms suff. may be lost in the MT parent text and the Old Greek translator read a different manuscript with the suffix retained. Or, this may simply be an instance of poetic concision.

139

3:5Before him went pestilence
   And plague went forth before his feet.

3:6He stood and the earth shuddered.
   He looked, and the nations were startled.
And the age-old mountains were shattered.
   The ancient hills bowed down.
   The ancient paths (bowed down) before him.

3:7I saw the tents of Cushan under havoc,
   The pavilions of the land of Midian trembled.

3:8Was Yahweh angry with Neharim?
   Or was your anger against Neharim?
      Or was your rage against Yam?
   When you rode upon your horses,
   Your chariots of salvation?

3:9You have surely exposed[2] your bow,
      You will say (that) you have satisfied your bowstring.[3]   *Selah*
      You split the earth with streams.

3:10The mountains saw you, they trembled.
   A torrent of water passed over,
The deep gave its voice,
The heights lifted up its hands.

3:11Sun (and) moon stand in their lofty dwelling,
   They vanish[4] before the gleam of your arrows.
      (They vanish) before the radiance of the lightning of your spear.[5]

3:12With rage you trod the earth,
In anger you trampled nations.

---

2. Read עָרֹה תְעָרֶה/ʿārōh tĕʿāreh *piel* inf. abs. + *piel* impf. 2ms from ערה/ʿrh.

3. Reading שֹׁבַעְתָּ מֵיתָרְךָ תֹּאמֶר/śibbaʿtā mêtārekā tōʾmar.

4. This verse is difficult. I render the rare *piel* yiqtol form יְהַלֵּכוּ/yĕhallēkû, "they vanish," as serving double duty on both clauses, an instance of verbal ellipsis.

5. See v. 4, וְנֹגַהּ/wĕnōgah.

³:¹³You have gone out to save your people
　　To save your anointed.
You have smashed the head of the house of the wicked
You have uncovered (it), from foundation up to the top.　　　*Selah*

³:¹⁴You have cracked with his staff the head of his leader;
　　They were blown away like chaff,⁶
　　　Their throats⁷ consume misery in a secret place.

³:¹⁵You trod the sea (with) your horses,
The great waters foaming.

(Human Response)

³:¹⁶I heard and my bowels quaked,
　　At the sound my lips quivered.
Rot entered into my bone,
　　And I trembled in my place.
I will wait quietly for the day of distress,
　　To come to a nation that raids us.

³:¹⁷Although the fig tree will not blossom,
　　And there will be no fruit on the vines,
The olive production fails,
　　And fields make no food,
Sheep are cut off from the fold,
And there are no cattle in the pen.⁸

---

6. Following the emendation יְסֹעֲרוּ/*yĕsōʿărû pual* impf 3mp, סער/*sʿr*, "they were blown away." Instead of כְּמוֹ/*kĕmô* ("like him") read כְּמֹץ/ *kĕmōṣ* ("like chaff"), transposed and placed after יְסֹעֲרוּ/*yĕsōʿărû*. See Hos 13:3. כְּמוֹ/*kĕmô* ("like him") remains sensible. The difference lay in the development of the metaphor of harvest.

7. See G. R. Driver, "Hebrew Notes," *VT* 1 (1951): 247; John H. Eaton, "The Origin and Meaning of Habakkuk 3," *ZAW* 76 (1964): 155.

8. JPS offers the possible translation from v. 15: "You will make Your steeds tread the sea,/ Stirring the mighty waters,/That I may have rest on a day of distress,/When a people come up to attack us./But this report made my bowels quake,/These tidings made my lips quiver;/Rot entered into my bone,/I trembled where I stood:/That the fig tree does not bud,/And no yield is on the vine;/The olive crop has failed,/And the fields produce no grain;/The sheep have vanished from the fold,/And no cattle are in the pen." I do not read, however, כִּי/*kî* as causal in v. 17a. Rather, I read it as a concessive clause that concludes with the *waw* beginning in v. 18: "*Although* the fig tree will not blossom. . . . *Yet* I shall triumph in Yahweh."

³:¹⁸Yet I shall triumph in Yahweh,
I shall rejoice in the God of my salvation.

³:¹⁹My Lord Yahweh is my strength
  He makes my feet like the deer's (feet),
    And upon the heights he causes me to tread.

For the leader. With instruments.

## Summary

### Figure 3: Repetition of Language in Habakkuk 3

| Repeated Terms/Roots | Habakkuk Speaks | God Speaks |
|---|---|---|
| ראה/*r'h* | Hab 3:2, 6, 7 (cf. Hab 1:3, 13; 2:1) | (cf. Hab 1:5) |
| פעל/*p'l* | Hab 3:2 | (cf. Hab 1:5) |
| שמע/*šm'* | Hab 3:2, 16 (cf. Hab 1:2) | _____ |
| יהוה/YHWH | Hab 3:2, 8 (cf. Hab 1:2, 12; 2:2) | (cf. Hab 2:13, 14, 16, 20) |
| אֱלוֹהַ/*'ĕlôah* | Hab 3:3 (cf. Hab 1:12) | (cf. Hab 1:11) |
| חי/*ḥyh* | Hab 3:2 | (cf. Hab 2:4) |
| בוא/*bw'* | Hab 3:3 | (cf. Hab 1:8, 9; Hab 2:3) |
| קדש/*qdš* | Hab 3:3 (cf. Hab 1:12) | _____ |
| ישׁע/*yš'* | Hab 3:8, 13, 18 (cf. Hab 1:2) | _____ |

This poem is one of the most difficult in the Old Testament due to the prevalence of unique grammatical forms, archaic language, highly stylized poetry, succinctness, and cosmic symbolism that is, for many, shrouded in mystery. Each of these features makes the poem foreboding and challenging. The discussion that follows in this chapter engages critical issues as an avenue leading into theological discussion.

The reason for this is twofold. In the first place, the purpose of this commentary is to bridge exegesis and theology so that God's address might be heard. To this end, the goal of the commentary is not to rehearse exhaustively the spectrum of lexical, text-critical, or poetic issues that arise in the scholarship on the poem. For such analysis, I recommend Andersen's exemplary work or Hiebert's close research on the poem.[9] There is not enough space here to address the complexity of the poem in full. The helpful work of Andersen, once again, remains exemplary coupled with the close analysis of Avishur on Hab 3.[10] The challenges that arise in interpreting and translating this work afford monograph-level work just on the third poem alone! Nonetheless, the structure of the poem is straightforward and identifiable based on shifts in speech and repetition of language, as will be demonstrated below.

## Commentary

**3:1** After the prophet's encounter with Yahweh's response to his questions with a vision, the prophet then concludes with a psalm. This is a recital psalm that recounts the actions of God in the past, which then becomes a foundation for the praise that the poetry constructs. The psalm is unique in that it contains not only a superscription ("a prayer of Habakkuk the prophet, according to the *šigyōnôt*") but also a subscription at its close ("for the director of music with stringed instruments"). The former occurs in the superscription of Ps 7. Scholars generally identify Ps 7 as a lament psalm and thereby do so in Hab 3 as well. Therefore, Kraus thinks שִׁגְיֹנוֹת/*šigyōnôt* is a technical term for lament. If this is the case, then Hab 3 is a lament whose theme is praise. The closing words of the poem, "stringed instruments" (נְגִינוֹת/*něgînôt*), are more commonly found in the superscriptions of the psalms (e.g., Pss 4; 6; 54) and indicates that the poem was sung with music as a song. It is quite possible that the song was sung at the cultic site in formal worship practices, but as a text inscribed into the book of Habakkuk and then in the Minor Prophets, the psalm outstrips these potential originating circumstances. Certainly, the song was sung (and now *is sung*) by people of faith who anticipated the work of their God, who renewed their strength and set their feet on high places (Hab 3:19).

**3:2** Structurally, Hab 3:2 couples with Hab 3:16–19. This is apparent based on the first-person speech in Hab 3:2, 16–19 that is contrasted by the change to third-person reportage in vv. 3–15. Repeated Hebrew roots also conjoin vv. 2,

---

9. Andersen, *Habakkuk*, 259–355; Hiebert, *God of My Victory*.

10. See ch. 2 on Hab 3 in Yitzhak Avishur, *Studies in Hebrew and Ugaritic Psalms* (Jerusalem: Magnes, 1994), 111–205. See also Robertson, *The Books of Nahum, Habakkuk, and Zephaniah*, 212–48.

16–19: שמע/*šm'* (vv. 3, 16); רגז/*rgz* (vv. 3, 16), establishing a frame for Yahweh's actions in the middle part of the poem. The Hebrew here is awkward and difficult, but sensible. I have rendered my translation of v. 2 from the Hebrew above with little emendation. However, the text may plausibly be *slightly* emended with a clearer reading:

> "O Yahweh, I heard (of) your renown; I was awed, O Yahweh (at) your work.
> In these years, O Yahweh, In these years, you will be known
> Though angry, may you remember mercy."

This is Avishur's attempt to make sense of a difficult verse. "Your renown" is how one can read the Hebrew word שִׁמְעֲךָ/*šim'ăkā*. "In these years" is an idiomatic way to translate the more literal "In the midst of years." The third vocative "O Yahweh" is explainable as changing the verb "make it live" (חַיֵּיהוּ/*ḥayyêhû*) to the divine name (יהוה/*YHWH*). The verb that he emends to "you will be known" (תִּוָּדַע/*tiwwāda'*) is explainable as a slight change of the vowels from "make it known" (תּוֹדִיעַ/*tôdîa'*).[11] This is a possible reconstruction, but not essential, for an understanding of the meaning of the verse.

The verse indicates that the prophet now has an expanded understanding of God and his actions, and wants God to make his mercy present in the time of Habakkuk. The prophet has heard a "report" (my rendering of שִׁמְעֲךָ/*šim'ăkā*) about Yahweh and has "seen" (יָרֵאתִי/*yārē'tî*) his "wondrous work" (פָּעֳלְךָ/*po'ălĕkā*). As indicated in figure 3, above, the repetition of this language draws our attention back to God's wondrous work from Hab 1:5 in raising up the Babylonians.[12] That the prophet sees and hears this indicates that he understands that Yahweh is utterly committed to this trajectory. The latter half of the verse is interesting because it is as if the prophet is pleading that Yahweh would enact the judgment soon! Why would the prophet ask for this judgment on his own people? It is because Yahweh's judgment is followed by Yahweh's salvation.

As has been argued in Hab 2, Israel will experience Yahweh's salvation *in and through* judgment. They will not escape. In Yahweh's wrath, the prayer is that he would remember mercy (רְחֵם/*raḥēm*)—a covenant characteristic of Yahweh that makes possible Israel's restoration. Although Hab 3:2 uses an in-

---

11. Avishur, *Studies in Hebrew and Ugaritic Psalms*, 148.

12. By prioritizing these lexical connections between Hab 1 and 3, I diverge from Avishur, who thinks the report mentioned in Hab 3:2 is actually the old psalm of Yahweh's mighty deeds in vv. 3–15.

finitive absolute, the same root is used in the pivotal exilic affirmation of hope in Lam 3:21–23: "It is due to Yahweh's proofs of covenant faithfulness that we are not consumed. Indeed, his mercies [רַחֲמָיו/*raḥămāyw*] do not fail. They are new every morning. Great is your faithfulness." The mercy of Yahweh constitutes the hope of life *after* and *beyond* judgment. Habakkuk 3:2 and 3:16–19 frame Yahweh's actions that are described in Hab 3:3–15.

**3:3–7** From his affirmation of hope beyond judgment, even beyond exile, the prophet then turns to a memory of Yahweh's former act of salvation. This is a well-structured poetic section that is identifiable from a shift from second-person address (vv. 2, 8) to third-person address (vv. 3–7). In this middle section of historical memory, the poetry describes God's movement to save his people; this description is overlaid with symbolism that holds cosmic significance:

a) Yahweh rises like the sun to deliver his people with rays of light shooting from his hand (v. 4).
b) Yahweh marches forward with both plague and pestilence serving as his divine retinue, both before and behind (v. 5).
c) In his march, the earth and mountains shatter, and the celestial orbits are ruined ("the ancient paths" of v. 6).

This section is a unit of thought that rehearses the memory of God's march *down* to Egypt to deliver his people from their oppression. It is tempting to think that God's march in this section is a move northward *with* God's people *out of* Egypt toward the promised land, with miraculous deliverance from the sea (Exod 14), the provision in the desert (Exod 16–17), and the triumphal conquest (Josh 1–12) firmly in view. Yet, Andersen rightly notes that the poetry does not best fit "the conquest of Canaan. The March of Yahweh is, accordingly, a march from the desert into Egypt *via* Sinai to rescue his people (v 13)."[13] In short, God rises from the east (Teman) and heads westward (Paran) to deliver his people in vv. 3–7. The section closes in v. 7 with a reference to Cushan and Midian. Both terms likely indicate the southern part of the Transjordan region in the same general region as Teman and Paran. So vv. 3 and 7 parallel one another as geographical regions from which Yahweh makes his march. This interpretation, then, does not understand the term "Cushan" as another toponym for Cush, which is often identified as Ethiopia. This entire section fills in the gaps of exodus narrative from Exod 2:23–25. Yahweh saw, heard, and knew the suffering of his people (see the discussion

---

13. Andersen, *Habakkuk*, 292.

on Hab 1:2, above), and then went on the march to save them. The structure of the verses is as follows:[14]

(A) v. 3a: Place (Teman//Paran)
   (B) v. 3b: Celestial focus (sky) and terrestrial focus (earth)
      (C) v. 4: God compared to the sun
      (C¹) v. 5: God's retinue (plague and pestilence)
   (B¹) v. 6: Terrestrial focus (earth, nations, mountains, hills) and celestial focus (ancient paths)
(A¹) v. 7: Place (Cushan//Midian)

Yahweh "rises" like the sun from Teman and marches his way toward Egypt. His march is accompanied by praise and majesty in the earth and sky. This is mirrored in v. 6 with the worship and reverence of the heavenly circuits of the stars ("ancient paths") and the ancient hills. In short, in his march, God's creation reveres and worships him with praise and majesty. Yet Yahweh is not alone in his march, as two figures accompany him as both front guard and rear guard: pestilence and plague. These two terms (דֶּבֶר/*deber*, "pestilence," and רֶשֶׁף/*rešep*, "plague") are identified as pagan deities in cultures surrounding Israel. This idea may lie in the background, but in this text pestilence and plague are not gods who accompany Yahweh in his march.[15] Rather, these terms demarcate the pestilence that will afflict the Egyptians (cf. Exod 9:3, 15). In this way, despite the mythological background, both pestilence and plague are indicators of divine judgment against the wicked, which is important for Habakkuk, as was evident in the woe oracles in Hab 2.[16] In vv. 3–7 Yahweh is pictured as a warrior marching to judge the wicked and to liberate the innocent sufferers: Israel in Egyptian bondage.

If this represents an accurate understanding of the verses, then the backdrop of God's deliverance of Israel becomes an analogy that foreshadows Yahweh's deliverance of the prophet. In both the Egyptian oppression and now in Habakkuk's experience of suffering, Yahweh "heard," "saw," and "knew" the suffering and then marched to deliver. On this reading, allusion to the exodus experience stands at the opening (Hab 1:2–3) and closing (Hab 3:3–7) of the book of Habakkuk, indicating an intentional composition. This composition reveals that humanity's cries to God for help are matched by his divine response.

14. My chiasm differs slightly from that of Andersen, *Habakkuk*, 289.

15. For a different understanding, see Andersen, *Habakkuk*, 300–308.

16. In the Old Testament the term רֶשֶׁף/*rešep*, "plague," is used to describe a kind of judgment against the wicked, even God's people Israel (cf. Deut 32:24; Ps 78:48).

**3:8–15** These verses compose another unit that is related to vv. 3–7, although not identical to it. The structures of the two sections remain somewhat similar, as Avishur insightfully recognizes.[17] As vv. 3–7 display a chiasm, so do vv. 8–15. It is a kind of thematic or topical chiasm that has some lexical correspondence at various levels. I have identified the lexical repetitions in this section with the terms in italics. Note, however, the break in this structure in the transposition of $B^1$ and $C^1$, below:

(A) v. 8:   *Waters, sea,* and *horses*
  (B) v. 8:   *Anger* and rage; *salvation*
    (C) v. 9:   *Staff*
      (D) v. 9:   God makes the *earth* burst
        (E) v. 10: Terrestrial convulsion (mountains and deep)
        ($E^1$) v. 11: Celestial convulsion (sun and moon)
      ($D^1$) v. 12: God treads the *earth*
    ($B^1$) v. 12: *Anger* and fury; *salvation* (v. 13)
  ($C^1$) v. 14: *Staff*
(A$^1$) v. 15: *Sea, horses,* great *waters*

This section no doubt is archaic in its poetic style, and may indeed be part of an early poem. However, this section has been transfixed into the context of Hab 3. These verses present the notion that Yahweh's march down to Egypt carries with it cosmic significance; indeed the entire earth responds to Yahweh's movement in the world. Avishur notes the themes and language in this section that corresponds to Ugaritic literature, especially the Ba'lu myth.[18] There are similarities, to be sure. The very terms for "sea" (יָם/*yām*) and "rivers" (נְהָרִים/*nĕhārîm*) in vv. 8 and 15 seem to correspond to Ugaritic deities *Yammu* and *Naharu*.

However, if these concepts do lie in the background of the poetry, then they have been transposed into Habakkuk's poetic context to show how Israel's God (the true God!) demonstrates his power. In other words, the depiction of Yahweh's power in vv. 8–15 cannot be reduced to a mere recycling of Canaanite story. Rather, Israel's God is shown to be the one who marches to deliver his people, and the entire created order (not Ugaritic deities) responds to his deliverance.[19]

His traverse through the desert is at once a march of judgment against the wicked and move of deliverance for the righteous. This point stands out

17. Avishur, *Studies*, 118–21.
18. Avishur, *Studies*, 125–29. For the exact text, see *COS* 1:249.
19. In this way, I diverge from the explanations of Avishur, *Studies*, 125–29.

because the language of divine wrath, anger, and rage occurs in vv. 8 and 12; yet it is here that we also find the language of salvation: "your chariots of salvation [יְשׁוּעָה/*yĕšûʿâ*]" (v. 8) and "you have gone out to save [לְיֵשַׁע/*lĕyēšaʿ*] your people" (v. 13). In other words, Yahweh's judgment against the wicked is immediately a move of justice for the righteous. Thematically, this connects quite nicely to the turnabout prophesied in Hab 2:6–20. In both texts, Yahweh responds to the cries of his righteous. Habakkuk has cried out for salvation (Hab 1:2) and now God sends his chariots of salvation (Hab 3:8). God is on the move . . . let all the earth respond with terror and wonder!

Habakkuk 3:2–15 imaginatively retells the story of God's deliverance of his people in the exodus narrative. These verses promote the power of *memory*. Fascinatingly, however, this passage bucks the overwhelming trend of *how* that experience is remembered in the Bible. Michael Fishbane has argued, and his insight still holds true, that the exodus narrative is "the consummate expression" of Yahweh's power and national redemption in the Old Testament. It became for Israel the "archetypal expression of its own future hope."[20] Deuteronomy picks up the exodus narrative as a way of showing Yahweh's grace, which is matched by Israel's recalcitrance. The echoes of the exodus reverberate, for example, in the first chapters of the book of Joshua: Moses's mantle of leadership is picked up by Joshua (Josh 1:1–9, 16–18), while the crossing of the sea in Exodus is matched by the crossing of the river Jordan in the conquest (Josh 3:1–17). The Psalter, too, celebrates the exodus as a testimony of the faithfulness and power of Yahweh (Pss 78:12–16, 42–55; 106:7–11; 111:4; 114:1–6; 135:8–12; 136:10–16). While Fishbane is correct to note that the exodus narrative becomes the framework of future hope, Habakkuk, however, uniquely presents this hope.

---

### Excursus: The Power of Memory

Habakkuk focuses upon Yahweh's *initial* response to the cries of his people. He presents the backstory of Yahweh's march to save his anointed people (Hab 3:13) from Egypt. This recollection is not a mere regurgitation of past events, but rather a framing of hope in the present. As Yahweh delivered in the past, so shall he do now! This, at least, is his prayer. So the plea in Hab 3:2 stands out: "In the midst of years, declare it; In the midst of years, make it known. Though angry, may you remember compassion."

---

20. Michael Fishbane, *Biblical Text and Texture: A Literary Reading of Selected Texts* (New York: Schocken, 1979), 121; see also 121–40.

It is as if the prophet is looking at a vast painting of the exodus experience that hangs in the gallery of Israel's faith. The prophet surveys the landscape of this painting, sees its contours, and his eyes stop on one place . . . an underviewed space off in the corner of the painting, a little corner that in fact holds the tenor and hues of the rest of the painting. It is the spot where the painting portrays Yahweh's march down to Egypt. Other prophets and psalmists have been inspired by other parts of the canvas and then have painted their own masterpieces in response (Pss 78; 106; and 114 come to mind). But not Habakkuk. It is *here* that he is captured . . . this little spot. But then our prophet does something surprising. He *steps into* the painting, and walks alongside Yahweh as he marches through the desert to deliver. As he walks with the Lord, Habakkuk wonders at the majesty and power of God. He is overwhelmed by Yahweh's move to save his people, to save his anointed (v. 13). He is encouraged and inspired, and from this newfound joy, the prophet casts his gaze outward, back into the space outside the painting that he just occupied. From his new perspective, he can see his place in a whole new way, encouraged by the power and compassion of Yahweh at his side. With this new perspective, the prophet then makes his last traverse. He steps out of the painting and settles back into his place. What had been a memory, off in a little corner of a painting in Israel's experience, now has become part of *his own experience*. It is no longer a memory of what Yahweh has done for Israel back *then*; Yahweh's march down to save has become part of Habakkuk's reality in the present. The way Habakkuk remembers his God paves the way for an enlarged understanding of his present suffering.

Memory is indeed God's gift that remains formative for the life of faith. On the one hand, people rightly think of memory as a *technique* or *skill* that enables us to regurgitate right information. To be sure, the prevalent call for God's people to remember the Lord, or his law, or his grace, or his character pervades Scripture. Indeed, in the Minor Prophets, the call to remember the torah is a significant and abiding command (Mal 4:4 [H 3:22]). Further, the practice of memory is a constituent feature of two ordinances for the church: baptism and Eucharist. In both, the memory of God's saving work in the past (in the Hebrew Passover, or the deliverance from the sea, or the crossing of the Jordan River) climaxes with the reality of God's saving work in Jesus Christ (in his cross, death, resurrection, and ascension). Believers are called to *remember* as they celebrate. Forgetfulness of God and his works equates to a loss of love for our Creator. No, memory is vital for Christian life.

But as a gift, memory is more than a technique to master in the life of faith. Rather, rightly understood, memory is formative for believers. Indeed, Habakkuk's own experience, and his reaction to it, are shaped and molded by his knowledge of his maker. His memory of Yahweh provides the frame by which Habakkuk sees his own context and responds to his situations. His memory of Yahweh becomes the tracks on which his response to the Lord may run. We have seen this often in the book up to this point. Habakkuk is *empowered* to respond to Yahweh on the basis of what he *already* knows of his maker, which then shapes his complaint (see Hab 1:14). Jesus's memory of Israel's wisdom texts shaped *how* he taught: parables, wisdom instruction, proverbs, and so forth. Memory is formative in the life of faith. But more than this, memory provides the opportunity for the believer to *actively emplace* one's present situation *in light of* God's work in the past.

This is an act of reconfiguration and application. In the ancient practice of *lectio divina*, this is what is known as *contemplatio*. Mariano Magrassi says that *contemplatio* is an experience that "is rooted in love. It continues God's historical plan of salvation in each of us. When genuine, it is directly inspired by the Spirit and exists in radical dependence on the written Word of God."[21] In this way, active remembrance of God and his work that is recorded in Scripture becomes the horizon by which we see our world; and in fact, the vast horizon of Scripture breaks *onto* our world so that the word of God "lives again in every vital Christian experience."[22] So it was for Habakkuk. The word he knew so well—God's word of salvation in the exodus experience—became the ground of his hope. Its light illumined the landscape of his day.

---

**3:16–19** Habakkuk offers his final response to Yahweh in these verses, and his words become a pattern for all those who suffer. He has just rehearsed Yahweh's march in the desert, and that has now set the stage for what comes in these verses. Israel's God *can* save and *will* save. Yet the repetition of the Hebrew roots שׁמע/*šmʿ* (vv. 3, 16) and רגז/*rgz* (vv. 3, 16) draws the reader's attention back to the present time. What God has done in salvation and deliverance in the *past* is set for the *future,* but the *present* is set for Israel's judgment at the hands of the Babylonians: he has heard and now his bones quake. As the prophet again focuses upon the present situation, he recognizes that judgment awaits. But this time, the impending judgment leaves the prophet responding in various (and surprising!) ways.[23] He quakes before the justice of God in v. 16, accepts the coming devastation in v. 17, and delights in Yahweh in v. 18.

21. Magrassi, *Praying the Bible,* 30.
22. Magrassi, *Praying the Bible,* 30.
23. So I diverge from the interpretation of Andersen, *Habakkuk,* 344, who thinks that the prophet's response in v. 16 is a result of the report in vv. 3–15. To my mind, this is unlikely.

It is tempting to see discord between the grand picture of salvation in vv. 3–15 and the prophet's responses in (especially) vv. 16–18. Yet Andersen rightly states that only "a bloodless rationalistic analysis" would find contradiction here.[24] In fact, when humans are confronted with the holiness of God, we find ourselves at a loss of what is sufficient: should we fall on our face (Gen 17:3; Lev 9:24; Num 20:6), delight in his word (Ps 37:4), confess sin (Isa 6:5), tremble before God (Ezra 9:4; Pss 96:9; 99:1; 114:7), or something else altogether? Habakkuk quakes in holy fear (v. 16), accepts coming destruction at Yahweh's hand (v. 17), rejoices in Yahweh's salvation (v. 18), and then discovers joy in his future with Yahweh beyond destruction (v. 19). Andersen believes that the poems closest to Habakkuk present varied responses to Yahweh's revelation as well (see Exod 15; Judg 5; Pss 18 and 68).[25] He also argues that vv. 16–19 fit a chiastic structure that depicts the prophet's responses to God. The chiasm of vv. 16–19 complements the other chiastic structures in vv. 3–7 and vv. 8–15:

Terror (v. 16)
    Deprivation (v. 17)
    Satisfaction (v. 18)
Confidence (v. 19)[26]

Habakkuk's terror is a result of his clear acknowledgment that a nation is "coming to attack us" (v. 16). Interestingly, as he acknowledges this, his lips quiver and he is left speechless. In effect, Habakkuk has moved from complaint in the first poem to silence in the third poem! God's persistent presence in and through the prophet's prayers have ushered this change. The holy awe of Yahweh's coming destruction ironically leads to acceptance.

The complaints of Hab 1:12–17 now undergo a reversal. Whereas he formerly questioned the use of the Babylonians for various (very good!) reasons, he now has an enlarged perspective on Yahweh's ways. He will now "wait quietly for the day of distress, for a nation to come to attack us" (v. 16b). The language here is somewhat unusual, as what is translated "I will wait quietly" derives from the Hebrew root נוח/*nwḥ*, which ordinarily means "to rest." Hebrew does have a root that means "to wait," namely קוה/*qwh*. Only here does the Hebrew root נוח/*nwḥ* connote the idea of "resting quietly" or "waiting quietly" for distress. Still, the idea that Habakkuk can rest in the day of distress represents an illogicality and a paradox, if not for Yahweh's clear pronouncement that salvation for

---

24. Andersen, *Habakkuk*, 345.
25. Andersen, *Habakkuk*, 345.
26. Andersen, *Habakkuk*, 342.

his people comes *through* judgment (Hab 1:5-11), and that Babylon in the end will get its just deserts (Hab 2:5-20). The prophet then comes to a place where, in the midst of terror, still he can rest in God. Verses 17-18 carry this notion forward to the point of seeming absurdity! Here the prophet pronounces that even if the world turns upside down and there is no fecundity whatever in God's land (v. 17), *still* he will exult in Yahweh and rejoice in the God of his salvation (v. 18). When we look back to his complaint in Hab 1:14, God's creation order is the ground on which Habakkuk builds his case. But in Hab 3:17, the prophet acquiesces to even creation turning upside down if that is what Yahweh deems appropriate! All the failures mentioned in v. 17 are natural devastations and not the result of an invading army. Even if the world that God has created for fecundity turns against itself and produces only aridity, the prophet will not be moved; rejoicing is his only song now. This is a powerful turnabout of perspective. Andersen captures the essence of Habakkuk's transformation: "Even if the devastation is total, even if there is no retribution or restoration, Yahweh, my God, my Lord, my Strength, my Salvation, has become the sole and sufficient object of Habakkuk's ecstatic hope and joy."[27]

The prophet has come to a place of joy because his God has come to him. As he wrestled with God in complaint and prayer, God has opened him up to the wonder of the Lord's ways. God has opened up Habakkuk not *to* faith, as the prophet *already* believed his God, but *to a fuller, richer* faith. Habakkuk trusted in Yahweh only to discover a deeper trust in and through suffering and prayer. He discovered what it is to walk by faith and not by sight. The touch of God upon his life has brought him unspeakable joy (vv. 18-19):

> Yet I shall triumph in Yahweh,
> I shall rejoice in the God of my salvation.
> My Lord Yahweh is my strength
> He makes my feet like the deer's (feet),
>     And upon the heights he causes me to tread.

These verses use all of the typical language associated with praise to God. Psalm 18:33 [H 34] is almost identical to Hab 3:19b: "He made my feet like the deer's (feet), and upon the heights he causes me to stand." Interestingly, the praise in Ps 18:33 rejoices in God's already experienced deliverance. In Hab 3:19b, however, the prophet anticipates Yahweh's deliverance. Whatever may come, Yahweh is the prophet's hope and joy. Yahweh is the prophet's ultimate security.

27. Andersen, *Habakkuk*, 345.

The biblical text says over and again that Israel's God does answer the cries of his people. If it were not so, Habakkuk could *not* have prayed as he did. God likes to give his people bread, not stones. He relishes in answering the cries of justice uttered by the vulnerable (as Jesus teaches in Luke 18:1–6). However, the prophet draws out a deadly serious question of faith, as Gowan poignantly reminds us. What shall believers do when God does *not* answer our prayers? Shall we lose heart, or faith?[28] Habakkuk leaves no room for compromise. Even if the violence of the day seems to have won sway over Yahweh's world, the prophet affirms that Yahweh nonetheless remains his hope, joy, and salvation. If death comes, Yahweh is the hope beyond death: "upon the heights he causes me to tread."

28. Gowan, *Triumph of Faith*, 86.

# PART II

# THEOLOGICAL HORIZONS

# Major Themes in the Minor Prophet:
Habakkuk and Biblical Theology

## Introduction

This section expounds upon Habakkuk's contribution to biblical theology. Of course, it is evident that the vitality of faith is central to Habakkuk's message and reception in the Bible, but as we have already seen, faith in God's salvation cannot be easily divorced from the primary notion of God's faithfulness; and Habakkuk keeps God's faithfulness fully in view, of which human faith is a subset. This perspective is received by Paul in both Romans and Galatians, and is essential to the teaching on faith in Hebrews.

## Habakkuk in the Old Testament

The communicative strategy of Habakkuk extends in a series of horizons outward from its originating context. The book communicates to real Judahite readers facing the upcoming Babylonian threat in the latter years of the seventh century BCE. As such, it speaks to that context with particular acuity on faith and faithfulness to this God over all nations, including the terror of Babylon. And yet, extending from the theological insights to these readers, there are secondary and tertiary horizons for readers of the book. As discussed above, when Habakkuk is coupled with Nahum, the emphasis upon God's justice and his authority over nations extends not only to the present situation of the Neo-Babylonian threat, but also to the larger question of God's justice over nations and for Israel, a question that spans centuries. With theodicy lying central in this reading, the question of the Neo-Babylonian threat and God's dealings with an idolatrous nation is extended theologically to a larger scale—*when* will God deal with idolatrous nations (Babylon in Habakkuk, Assyria in Nahum) in a final sense, as he has promised to do?

### Destructive Power of Sin

Habakkuk teaches, with the other prophets, an uncompromising message on the destructiveness of sin. In this, the prophet is an enforcer of God's covenant with Israel. Amos's proclamation of judgment against Israel and Judah horrifically presents a society governed by lies, corruption, cruelty, neglect, and sexual perversion that leave the vulnerable abused and suffering (Amos 2:4–8). Jeremiah, too, lambasts his people for their various sins, including treachery, unjust riches, crimes, lack of proper judgment, and lack of care for the vulnerable in society (Jer 5:27–28; cf. 6:28–30). Sin is destructive and generates divine punishment. This is the case of God raising up the Babylonians, a point Jeremiah saw as well as did Habakkuk.

But in another sense, sin does not just engender divine punitive measures; sin is fundamentally *self*-destructive. The Old Testament prophets reveal that sin creates a society where suffering and oppression become the norm. The sins of Israel's leaders are a source of pain for the populace of God's people, as shown in Mic 3:1–3 (cf. Amos 8:4–8). The prophet suggests that the leaders' sins "tear the skin off" of God's people, leaving them mutilated. In Isaiah, sin is an unacknowledged and untreated sickness (Isa 1:5–6) that is real and destructive, even if it is not recognized. When one interprets the enemies of Hab 1:1–4 as God's wicked people, their violence and devastation bring the prophet to cry out to God in pain: "How long have I cried for help, but you do not listen?" (Hab 1:2).

The problem of sin remains a persistent problem in the Minor Prophets. Hosea opens the corpus by reminding Israel that God has loved her with an everlasting love, as a husband loves his bride. But Israel is a faithless bride that sins against her husband with multiple lovers. Amos circumnavigates the Levant in Amos 1–2 to depict God's judgment against the nations, only to identify sin in the heart of Israel and Judah. As God will judge the nations, God will judge his people as well. Micah depicts God's lawsuit against his own people when he executes judgment against them for rebellion and sin (Mic 1:5). Perhaps nothing is so terrifying as Zephaniah's oracle, where God says that he will utterly sweep away everything from the face of the earth (Zeph 1:2). The sin identified there is the sin of idolatry (Zeph 1:4–6). The sin of both Israel and Babylon is bound for divine judgment. God will not allow sin to persist.

### Waiting on the Lord

Habakkuk teaches the value of waiting on God, which is a theme running through the Minor Prophets as well. This corpus reminds its readers that God is justified as righteous. God enacts restoration of a broken Israel and Judah (see Hos 1:1–2:1), and eventually this restoration will encompass all of creation (cf. Mic 4) because God is the Lord of creation itself. For Israel, divine judgment is shown to be only a step along the way to restoration. This is a message that coheres with the teaching of Habakkuk concerning the end. The recurrence of the language of Exod 34:6–7 reinforces that while God's judgment is in force it still remains an extension of the "steadfast love of Yahweh" so that his mercy and compassion might be demonstrated.[1] In God's wrath, Habakkuk prays, may he remember his covenant love of mercy (Hab 3:2). Indeed, it is his divine faithfulness, another covenant characteristic from Exod 34:6–7, that ensures the vision will come to fruition. God in his mercy will restore his people and land—even creation itself—because of his justice and righteousness (Mic 4:1–7). And yet, the restoration, the end, that so many texts envision still stands far off. Notwithstanding real historical returns to the land (as Haggai and Zechariah confirm), in the canonical presentation of the Twelve, God's day of vindication is pressed forward eschatologically, creating space between the now of suffering and the not-yet of justice and restoration as exemplified in Habakkuk's expectant waiting in Hab 3:16–19 (cf. Mal 3:16–4:6 [3:16–24]). The challenge of waiting and watching for God's future redemption still remains. This now/not-yet dimension of both Habakkuk and the other Minor Prophets reveals the spiritual virtue of waiting on God. The wait is not a futile one, though, because the end will not tarry and it will not delay. In the meantime, however, there remains room for prayer and honest questioning as God's people persevere in faith.

The call to faithfulness is a serious one that connects Habakkuk to the Major Prophets. Watson correctly observes that faithful waiting upon the Lord's saving activity becomes a vital message to be heard. The reader who waits on Yahweh (Hab 2:3) becomes the person who exercises fidelity to God's coming salvation (Hab 2:4). The certainty of God's coming salvation enables strength and vitality to live in the present, or "to run," as Hab 2:2 suggests. Watson relates the verse to Isa 40:31, "Those who wait on Yahweh shall renew their strength; they shall mount up on wings of eagles; they shall run and not grow weary." Waiting on God's impending salvation is the fundament for hope and the paradigm for faith. For Watson, "It is the entire Book of the Twelve that is written 'so that one who reads it may run.' The assurance that 'the righteous shall live by his faithfulness' lies at the heart of this book."[2]

---

1. Hos 2:21–25; Joel 2:13–14, 18; Amos 9:9–15; Jonah 3:7–10; 4:2; Mic 7:18–20; Nah 1:3; Hab 3:2; Zeph 3:16–20; Zech 1:15–17; 8:8, 13; 10:6.

2. Watson, *Paul and the Hermeneutics of Faith*, 125–57, quotation on p. 157.

### Righteous Suffering

Suffering remains a complex feature in the prophets. It is borne by individuals and community, Israel and the nations, creation, and even God himself. There are a number of sources and responses to suffering as well, none of which can be discounted. But the future of suffering is certain: it will be swallowed up by the decisive act of God in the future. It is the end appointed in Hab 2:2–3. Yet the Old Testament in general and Habakkuk in particular open up the biblical theme of righteous suffering. This is already present in Ps 22 and is well known in Isa 53 with the work of the servant, but it is true of Habakkuk as well.

Martin Buber's analysis of Jeremiah initiates us to the theology of righteous suffering. He suggests that in the prophetic faith, the transcendent God of the universe wants to demonstrate his immanence to the creation, and in particular, his covenant people. He does this through the lowly and contrite of heart. He does this through his prophets. Buber says that the presentation of Jeremiah opens a theology where

> He Who is infinitely above the domains of the mighty and secure descends to those who lie in the dust of the earth and shares their afflictions. His growing incomprehensibility is mitigated and even compensated by His becoming the God of the sufferers and by suffering becoming a door of approach to Him. . . . Between God and suffering a mysterious connection is opened.[3]

This extraordinary insight applies clearly to the experience of Habakkuk. The prophet is an exemplar of righteous suffering; he is one who experiences the presence of God in both protest and pain. Habakkuk's fate is exile and death, and yet through this suffering he is trained to wait expectantly for the day of distress, knowing that God's presence is enough. Indeed, God mysteriously sets the prophet's feet on high places (Hab 3:19) and is his salvation.

This theme is not incidental or accidental in the biblical material. The prophets bear the burdens of both the people and the Lord, even at points speaking for the suffering of God in divine laments (Jer 9:9; 12:7–12; 15:5–9; 48:29–33; Ezek 27:3–11, 26–36). God suffers *with* those who are suffering in the prophets (Isa 15:5; 16:9–11; Jer 9:10, 17–18; 12:7; 31:20; 48:30–36). In these texts, God mourns with the mourning, hurts with the hurting, and thereby identifies with suffering from the inside.

3. Buber, *Prophetic Faith*, 183.

### God, Israel, and the Nations

Habakkuk clearly indicates the judgment of God against Babylon . . . and his own people. How can God use and judge both his own people and the nations? What gives him the prerogative? In the Old Testament, the God that Habakkuk enjoins in debate is none other than the God of Israel, the nations, and creation itself. We have seen in Hab 3 that God goes down to judge Egypt and deliver his people. In the broader vision of the Old Testament, the ultimate vision of Israel and the nations is for *all* peoples to be purified of sin and to join in worship of the Lord.

God's justice revealed in the temple in Hab 2:20 connects to the broader theme of Zion in the prophetic corpus. As a theological symbol, Zion reveals God's plan for Israel and the nations. Zion as a physical entity encapsulates both God's people and his holy dwelling (whether the sanctuary or holy city). In the Minor Prophets, Joel associates Zion with the day of Yahweh (Joel 2–3). Like the day of Yahweh, the symbol of Zion appears in the context of God's judgment against his people and city (Joel 2:1–17) as well as God's salvation (Joel 2:23–32). Zion regularly appears as a people/city judged (Amos 1:2; 6:1; Mic 3:12) or saved (Obad 17; Mic 4:1–10) by God's work. Zion is the place of future hope where God's kingship will be manifest on the earth (Mic 4:7; cf. Pss 95–100).

In Zion, the destiny of Israel intertwines with that of the nations. As those who have been judged and remain, the nations *and* Israel will find refuge in Zion under the protection of God, the instruction of God, and his appointed king (Mic 4:1–2; Zeph 3:9; Zech 2:10–11; 8:1–23). God's final judgment and salvation, which we only see in part in Habakkuk, are for Israel *and* the nations. After purification of sin, Israel *and* the nations are incorporated into a new humanity in Zion. Zion, then, is an important theological theme because it presses the future hope well beyond any former localization in the Old Testament's presentation of history. As an eschatological symbol, Zion provides the implied reader of the Twelve a vision in which future life is portrayed. In Zion, ideal Israel is restored before God, and war, death, and sin are no more. Zion represents a renewed creation united under God's reign. In the eschatological future, Zion is the locale where God's kingship will be exercised in creation (Mic 4:7; cf. Pss 95–100). In this way, Zion cannot be limited to Israel alone. Zion as a symbol intertwines the destiny of Israel with the nations. As those who have been judged and remain, the nations and Israel will find refuge in Zion under the protection of God, the instruction of God, and his appointed king (Mic 4:1–2; Zeph 3:9; Zech 2:10–11; 8:1–23).

## The New Testament

### *Future Hope*

As indicated in the exegesis on Hab 2:4a, there is some indication the LXX translation of Hab 2:4b employs translation techniques that betray a messianic expectation. The one who has faith in God's fidelity is none other than "The Righteous One," the messiah. As indicated, Hays suggests that in the New Testament Paul employed an apocalyptic understanding of the messianic Righteous One from Hab 2:4b to identify Jesus. On this line of interpretation, what is envisioned in the reception of Hab 2:4b in Rom 1:17 and Gal 3:11 (and Heb 10:38) is a prophecy concerning the Righteous One, Jesus Christ, who was coming.[4]

Hays's suggestion, however, is not entirely persuasive. First, Jesus is the eschatological fulfillment of God's work, to be sure, but that is not sufficient reason—even with his supporting evidence in the exegesis of the Pauline texts—to conclude that the term ὁ δίκαιος/*ho dikaios* in Rom 1:17 and Gal 3:11 serves as a messianic title. Paul's citation of Hab 2:4 diverges from the LXX in both Romans and Galatians (his citation exhibits neither the third-person pronoun "his/its" from the Hebrew nor the first-person pronoun "my" from the Greek). In Gal 3, Paul depicts the type of person that embraces God's faithfulness. This is distinguished from the kind of person that is essentially self-sufficient, trusting in the works of law in Gal 3:10–12. Instead, the faithful person simply trusts and believes in God's faithfulness, which is manifest in the gospel of Jesus Christ. As Bae Gil Lee says of Gal 3:11, "Paul emphasizes that both Jews and Gentiles must respond to God's eschatological provision for their deliverance from the curse, by having faith in Christ crucified."[5] In other words, the text is not using Hab 2:4b to predict the coming messiah, but rather the one to whom we should look in faith to see the incarnation of God's faithfulness in this present age.

Romans 1:17 strikes a very similar note, but with a different nuance that emphasizes God's righteousness. According to Peter Stuhlmacher, Rom 1:17 is part of Paul's larger argument to demonstrate God's righteousness (or faithful activity of God) which believers (i.e., the righteous) embrace by faith in Jesus. More than this, by placing their faith in Jesus, these righteous are

---

4. Hays, *Conversion of the Imagination*, 119–42.

5. Bae Gil Lee, "A Developing Messianic Understanding of Habakkuk 2:3–5 in the New Testament in the Context of Early Jewish Writings" (PhD diss., Southwestern Baptist Theological Seminary, 1997), 141.

enfolded within the righteousness of God; they become living testimonies of God's faithfulness/righteousness.[6] So again, in Rom 1:17, Paul is not using a messianic title for the righteous but is describing the kind of person who will live faithfully as a result of God's faithfulness. That person becomes part of the righteousness of God that has been revealed. In both cases, Paul is not talking about the coming of the messiah. At any rate, Jesus has already come, so it would be out of place to speak about the coming messiah in these texts, unless it has something to do with the return of Christ in his *second* coming (as one sees in 1 Cor 15). Stuhlmacher says of the righteousness of God and faith that

> Paul made the expression "the righteousness of God" the center of the gospel in that, together with the Christians before and beside him, he spoke of God's salvific activity for the sinful world in and through Christ and related God's righteousness strictly to faith. Through faith in Jesus Christ as redeemer and Lord, every individual Jew and Gentile obtains a positive share in the work of the one, just God who brings forth through Jesus Christ peace, salvation, and deliverance for Israel, the Gentile nations, and the (nonhuman) creation.[7]

Hebrews 10:38 uses Hab 2:4b as an encouragement for believers to express fidelity to God. It is true that Heb 10:37 uses the Greek rendering of Hab 2:2–4a to depict the coming messiah (particularly the second coming of Jesus), but this is simply a word of encouragement for the saints to persevere in their faith: Jesus is coming, so do not shrink back. The writer of Hebrews admonishes believers to look to God in faith.

The identity of the righteous in Habakkuk is the one who maintains allegiance to God in light of the vision he has given. This emphasis upon faithfulness is also the note that is rung out in Gal 3:11, Rom 1:17, and Heb 10:38. God is worthy of faith precisely because of his extraordinary divine faithfulness, both in guaranteeing the vision (vv. 2–3) and in guaranteeing Christ the Lord (per the New Testament evidence). Placing faith in God's faithfulness exhibits the fitting behavior of the follower of God.

---

6. See Peter Stuhlmacher, *Paul's Letter to the Romans: A Commentary* (Louisville: Westminster John Knox, 1994), 25–32.

7. Stuhlmacher, *Paul's Letter to the Romans*, 31.

### Faith in the Faithfulness of God

Habakkuk speaks to the people of God in expanding horizons that comport with the message of the book in its originating context. As Christian Scripture and a word from God, Habakkuk is understood as a present word for the church. Paul especially saw a central tenet of God's faithfulness and the faith of Israel as deriving from Habakkuk. Although space here prevents a full discussion of this major theological theme, Rikki Watts demonstrates that Paul employs both thematic and lexical ties to the book of Habakkuk in Rom 1 that culminate in the (altered) citation of Hab 2:4: "The righteous will live by faith."[8] The purpose of the citation is to advance a line of thought in Romans that parallels the situation of Habakkuk. Paul relates the stance of the faithful follower of God in Habakkuk's day to the stance of the faithful follower of God in light of what he has done in and through Christ. In both historical situations, God is vindicated as just and righteous in his activity of salvation. Through the connections, Paul centralizes and proves God's work in Christ as the decisive act of salvation. Watts concludes, "The gospel, then, is the revelation of Yahweh's faithful exercise of his power in effecting salvation (Hab 3:18–19; Rom 1:16), but it is a salvation on the basis of faith in the revealed gospel (Rom 1:17b; cf. the vision of Hab 2:1–4)."[9]

I step beyond Watts in this discussion. The presentation in Habakkuk is one of God's extraordinary faithfulness to vindicate the righteous and judge the wicked. This will be enacted in the eschatological future, or the end (Hab 2:2–3). The point of the vision is to validate for his people his commitment to justice and to his covenant with his people. The surety that God's vision will come at the end is the very definition of God's faithfulness. His followers will respond to their covenant Lord by trusting in his faithfulness, thereby validating their designation as righteous. If this is the case, then Paul draws in both aspects of Hab 2:4: God's faithfulness/righteousness (as defined as his commitment to justice and the covenant) and believers' faithfulness/righteousness (as defined as trusting, or faith, in God's righteousness). So Paul can say that the righteousness of God is revealed through the gospel "from faith to faith" (Rom 1:17), or from the time of the Jews in Habakkuk's

---

8. Rikki E. Watts, "For I Am Not Ashamed of the Gospel: Romans 1:16–17 and Habakkuk 2:4," in *Romans and the People of God*, ed. Sven K. Soderlund and N. T. Wright (Grand Rapids: Eerdmans, 1999), 3–25. As is well known, Paul's citation does not directly quote the Hebrew or Greek and instead omits the pronoun—whether a 3ms suff. in the Hebrew, "his faith," or a first-person pronoun in the Greek, "my faith"—that otherwise accompanies the noun "faith" in Hab 2:4.

9. Watts, "I Am Not Ashamed," 23.

day to the time of the Greeks, to whom Paul now ministers.[10] Paul illumines God's faithfulness attested in Habakkuk with God's faithfulness triumphantly on display in the victory of Christ. Those who demonstrate faith (e.g., Rom 1:8) do so by virtue of belief and obedience to Christ the Lord: allegiance to the God and Father of the Lord Jesus Christ. Christ Jesus is the ultimate demonstration of the righteousness of God, wherein he climaxes his mighty work of redemption and reconciliation of all things to himself—the promised end of Habakkuk.[11]

The faith on display in Habakkuk is reiterated in Paul but with a crucial difference. Expected divine salvation in Habakkuk (i.e., the overthrow of a wicked nation and the restoration of God's people in righteousness) demands God's followers to place their faith and trust in his goodness and trust that he would do what he said he would do to enact salvation. Paul, however, uses this former logic from Habakkuk as a springboard to launch his view of faith in light of Jesus. Faith for Paul is allegiance to God and a belief in his goodness and salvation in Christ that comes as the culmination of God's redemptive work. Those who give their lives trusting in God's salvation place their faith in Christ and rightly live under the Son. God's salvation for Israel is fulfilled ultimately in Jesus. As such, God's ways are vindicated. One need only trust in God's salvation: Jesus.

But this faith in the Son demands perseverance at present. God's salvation has been vindicated through God's word and Christ's death and resurrection (e.g., Rom 1:1–6), but for both Habakkuk and Paul, present suffering remains potent. The issue is how to live in light of the suffering. As with Habakkuk, who in light of God's word of salvation nonetheless waited for it to be enacted in his days (Hab 3:2), Paul calls for Christ's followers to endure (cf. Rom 4:18–25; 5:1–5; 8:18–27). God called Habakkuk to faith and endurance, as Paul does his readers. For Paul, perseverance produces something inwardly in the believer (it is soul-building), but it is certainly more than this. It is an anticipation that suffers in the present as it eagerly awaits the certainty of new creation and the consummation of God's reign over creation, in Christ (e.g., Rom 8). Ultimately, perseverance is not merely introspective to see what might be gained in suffering but rather it is fundamentally prospective, anticipating the work of God in Christ.

Paul, then, develops an analogical readership between the audience of

---

10. Quarles rightly argues that "from faith to faith" (Rom 1:17) indicates a span of time. See Charles L. Quarles, "From Faith to Faith: A Fresh Examination of the Prepositional Series in Romans 1:17," *NovT* 45 (2003): 1–21.

11. See Stuhlmacher, *Paul's Letter to the Romans*, 25–32.

Habakkuk's day and the Christian audience of the first century CE. Although the primary audience has changed (the church may theologically be related to ancient Israelite/Judahite communities but should not be collapsed into them), nonetheless the communicative strategy of Habakkuk does not change in the Christian reception. In Paul's rhetoric, the base message of Habakkuk is extended theologically in the light of God's salvific work in Christ. Through the analogy between Israel and the church, a Christian reception of this book can be productively maintained. Human faith is placing complete trust in God's faithfulness and living faithfully before him. Another way of conceiving of the idea is that believers come to recognize and hold onto the fact that they are *already* caught up in the faithfulness of God, and in the light of his faithfulness, they rest in God. In this, God's divine faithfulness through Christ is affirmed without neglecting the need for proper human response in light of it: faith in Christ and fidelity to him.

Faith in God's faithfulness is exactly what is needed for God's people. Luke presents Paul as using Hab 1:5 as a warning to believe in God's work of faithfulness, to believe in Jesus. Luke records the situation of Paul's message to the synagogue in Antioch of Pisidia (Acts 13:13–43). Paul's message centered upon God's mighty choice of Israel and of God's faithfulness through the messiah that was prophesied in the Old Testament. As the climactic final warning to the synagogue, Paul calls his brothers to believe in the Messiah Jesus for the forgiveness of sins (Acts 13:38–39). He closes with a warning: "Beware lest what is said in the prophets should come about: 'Look, you scoffers, be astounded and perish; for I am doing a work in your days, a work that you will not believe, even if one tells it to you.'" This citation of Hab 1:5 clearly diverges from the Hebrew version of the same. In fact, it follows the Greek translation (LXX) more closely, but not fully. Essentially, Paul places his audience in the place of the audience of Habakkuk, who would not believe in the message of God's judgment and salvation. For Habakkuk's audience, the believer is the one who sees God's salvation but will not shrink back and believes. Paul calls his audience to do the same: to believe in God's work in Christ. In the full light of his sermon, this insertion of Hab 1:5 calls the Pisidian Antiochene Jews to a choice: Will they trust in Jesus for the forgiveness of sins, or will they be like the scoffers who reject God's work in Christ? "If they do not believe, they will perish in the coming judgment of God."[12]

---

12. David G. Peterson, *The Acts of the Apostles*, PNTCS (Grand Rapids: Eerdmans, 2009), 395.

### Righteous Suffering

The New Testament affirms that suffering remains a reality for the church. L. Ann Jervis argues that suffering lies at the very center of the gospel itself: those who follow Christ will experience pain in their life.[13] Despite the fact that pain and death are defeated through Christ, both remain with us. Jervis suggests that suffering serves in a variety of ways in the New Testament: it is a battle in Christian growth; it is a marker of a broken world; and it is part of what it means to be "in Christ." Still, suffering may be borne in the manner of Christ: "By virtue of our being caught between the time of Christ's resurrection and the time of our own we recognize that we will suffer as we hope for glory."[14] This insight draws attention to the fact that for the New Testament, suffering can be borne because Christ is victorious and raised (Matt 28; Luke 24; John 20–21; Acts 2; Phil 1:19–30), and new creation is assured (cf. Rom 8; Col 3:1–4; Rev 21). Paul's use of suffering should not be sought after; it is a marker that the world is out of joint, waiting to be fully clothed in a new creation in which suffering will no longer be operative. Instead, Christians ought to hope in Christ and bear suffering when it comes, knowing that future glory is assured.

### The Promised End

The New Testament finds that future resolution to suffering arrives in Christ Jesus. As the evangelists and apostles interpreted the life and death of Christ, they found in the Old Testament and in Jesus's teaching the resource to understand the meaning of both Christ's suffering and their own suffering. The vindication of the promised end that is expected in Hab 2:2–3 is brought to fruition in him. It is first at his death and resurrection. Christ's suffering deals the deathblow to sin and sets the world to rights in an ultimate vindication of God's actions with his creation. The evangelists affirm that as he suffered and died in the manner described in Isa 43 and 53, the man Jesus took the sin of Israel and the world upon himself. The victory of God in Christ puts an end to suffering. Ultimately, this victory is met in the new creation. The end where the righteous will be vindicated and the wicked will be punished comes to a cosmic finale in Rev 20, which gives way to Rev 21. Jesus is on the throne, death and hell are defeated, creation is remade, and Jesus says, "Behold! I make all things new."

---

13. L. Ann Jervis, *At the Heart of the Gospel: Suffering in the Earliest Christian Message* (Grand Rapids: Eerdmans, 2007).

14. Jervis, *At the Heart*, 109.

## Conclusion

With its emphasis upon the faithfulness of God in his work at the end, Habakkuk presses toward an eschatological hope. This hope, then, gives a shape to faithfulness and expectancy in the present. These themes are taken up in the New Testament. The end has come in the work of Jesus. Faith in him as the messiah is an affirmation of the very faithfulness of God. Considering God's now/not-yet work in Jesus, however, there remains the existential challenge of waiting expectantly in the present. Each of these themes merges together a rich theological tapestry that helps us see the beauty of God's work and live well before him because of it.

# Centering Shalom: Habakkuk and Prayer

## Introduction

This chapter is devoted to theological reflection on prayer from the foundation of Habakkuk and builds from the excursus on lament in Hab 1, above. There is a gap between biblical studies and theology, but when it comes to biblical studies and (what is commonly called) practical theology, the gap is considerably wider. Lament, as prayer, sits quite comfortably within practical theology. This is because prayer is a practice of communion with God. Theological discussion on the practice of lament is scarce except here and there, but where there has been such conversation, increasingly we gain more insight. Exceptional theological work arises in the edited volume *Evoking Lament*, which itself emerges from work in German circles specifically on lament in the *Jahrbuch für biblische Theologie*.[1] These discussions are a gift that complements the reflections on lament offered here.

Scripture is fundamental for theological reflection. If one speaks of another God other than the God of Abraham, Isaac, and Jacob, the God of Israel, the God and Father of our Lord Jesus Christ, then one does not speak of the Christian God. But this *scriptural* emphasis needs to be balanced by an emphasis upon *prayer*. *Lex orandi est lex credendi et agendi* ("the rule of prayer is the rule of belief and action").[2] These words, usually attributed to Pope Celestine I

---

1. Harasta and Brock, *Evoking Lament*; Martin Ebner et al., eds., *Klage*, JBTh 16 (Neukirchen-Vluyn: Neukirchener Verlag, 2001). See also Sally A. Brown and Patrick D. Miller, eds., *Lament: Reclaiming Practices in Pulpit, Pew, and Public Square* (Louisville: Westminster John Knox, 2005); Miriam Bier and Tim Bulkeley, eds., *Spiritual Complaint: Theology and Practice of Lament* (Eugene, OR: Pickwick, 2013).

2. Daniel B. Clendenin, ed., *Eastern Orthodox Theology: A Contemporary Reader* (Grand Rapids: Baker, 1995), 7.

(422–432 CE), rightly expose the union of theology and prayer. Without prayer, Scripture may become lifeless doctrines about a distant God far removed from either lost humanity or the saved community of faith. Barth's comments are evocative:

> God is the Father of Jesus Christ, and that very man Jesus Christ has prayed, and he is praying still. Such is the foundation of our prayer in Jesus Christ. It is as if God himself has pledged to answer our request because all our prayers are summed up in Jesus Christ; God cannot fail to answer, since it is Jesus Christ who prays.[3]

Jesus is disclosed in Scripture, and thereby scriptural prayer and prayer in Christ go hand in hand. Scripture *and* prayer ground sound theological reasoning.

Without prayer, theology becomes an ordering of the mind that puffs up the ego by facts about God. Dan Stiver, following the correct insight of Luther, powerfully suggests that "Theology first and last lives by prayer, or its reflection cannot avail."[4] This is because prayer is the explicit recognition of the need for God and the frailty of human finitude before the infinite Godhead. Indeed, prayer is essential to the discipline of theology.

As we have seen, prayer is foundational for the book of Habakkuk. And the prophet's prayers are poignant due to their relevance. Habakkuk laments. It is important to remember that the way I define lament throughout this work is as a specific kind of *prayer*, particularly a petitionary prayer that asks God to enact change. Lament can be reduced to emotional expression or catharsis (as mentioned in the excursus of Hab 1), but here I envision lament to be a prayer offered to God about a distress that the petitioner wants changed. In this way, Habakkuk's laments to God are the same that are perennial for followers of the Lord: Will God answer my prayers, or not? Is my prayer effective? Why is God so silent and distant from me? I feel like I am speaking to nothing, to no one. Where is the God of justice? How can God countenance such evil in the world? How long will God allow this to go on? What will he do about it? Who among us has approached holy God and not asked similar things? Habakkuk's prayers are typically human, and they remain perennial questions for those who wrestle in faith.

In many ways, prayer is a difficult practice to understand. I say "practice" rather than "topic" precisely because prayer is not to be discussed in an ab-

---

3. Karl Barth, *Karl Barth on Prayer*, TTCSST 26 (New York: T&T Clark, 2015), 14.

4. Dan R. Stiver, *Life Together in the Way of Jesus Christ: An Introduction to Christian Theology* (Waco, TX: Baylor University Press, 2009), 107.

stract sense, but enacted through regular discipline of communion with God. Prayer is that *practice*, perhaps above all others, that is open to all Christians, and yet neglected by most. This may be the case because we fear the terrifying intimacy of communion with God in prayer. We are intimidated by Martin Buber's famous "Thou" that demands an exacting encounter.[5] Or it may be that the church prefers the reduction of God to a list of doctrines or a mechanistic principle instead of encountering the numinous and personal God who encounters *us* in prayer just as we encounter *him*. Perhaps in these days it is easier to commodify God into a principle or a totem for consumption rather than treat him as the personal God that he is, who deserves (and demands) the reverence and awe that are due him in prayer.

Prayer is the practice of relationship with God. When we look to Jesus, we see humanity at prayer. Prayer is the first and best reflex of the church. When one thinks of the troubles of the world, one immediately is tempted to *act*, to *do*, to *perform*. Of course action is necessary; the gospel of Jesus Christ must be *proclaimed* and *obeyed*. We are to *speak* the truth, and we are to *live* the truth. These are actions all, and none indispensable to the Christian life. Yet Jesus was grounded in prayer. He *went* and *did*, but only after prayer. His ministry began with forty days of prayer. It concluded with a prayer on a cross. Prayer bookends our Savior's living ministry. We are to imitate our Savior's praying life because it models communion with the Father.

Prayer is a primary action. It is first, not least, because prayer leads the Christian to invest oneself in God, to rest in him and commune with him. Prayer encourages humans to embrace our creatureliness, the fact that we are God's handiwork under *his* care and utterly dependent upon him. Prayer reminds us that he is King of Creation, and we are not. Yet, we are under his extraordinary and loving care. At its best, prayer crucifies the ego because it provides the space and means to decenter the self and to recognize God on his rightful throne.

Prayer enables the worshiper to move along the grain of the universe. Discovering one's creaturely place in the world is liberating. The biblical portrait of God is neither one of extreme distance nor one of unmediated immanence. The God of the Old and New Testaments alike is the transcendent creator of the universe who also, almost paradoxically, walks with Adam and Eve in the garden of Eden. He majestically cares about the needs of his children. He speaks to Abraham, Isaac, and Jacob. He comforts poor Hagar in the wilderness. He judges his wayward people in their sin, yet redeems them in his love. In Jesus's teaching, God is the loving parent who gives his children bread and fishes, not

---

5. Martin Buber, *I and Thou*, trans. R. G. Smith, 2nd ed., (New York: Scribners, 1958).

stones or snakes (Luke 11:11–12). He hears their cries and judges their needs appropriately as the just and caring judge that he is (Luke 18:1–8). He has given the world his Son, who according to biblical testimony "lives to intercede" on our behalf (Heb 7:25). The God of Scripture is the God of immeasurable power and infinite care for all that he has made. For this reason, it is no surprise that one finds in the Scriptures God's people regularly calling out to *him*, in prayer. Prayer draws people into communion with God.

Despite the prevalence of prayer in the Scriptures, Bonhoeffer is surely right when he suggests that, naturally, humanity does not know how to pray. We need help and direction. Bonhoeffer says that true prayer is directed *to God who is disclosed in the Scriptures. Prayer goes to the one who has made all things, who has made even you and me.* Scripture discloses the true God who hears our address. It is to *this* God that his worshipers look for his response, his engagement, his interaction with his creatures.[6]

Truly, God's people expect him to respond to prayer. God's response may not be an answer but it will certainly be some sort of acknowledgment, a real presence with the petitioner. God's *response* rather than his *answer* should be in view. Answers to prayer are really only useful if we think that knowing *why* something is happening in tragedy, or being able to explain it, is going to some-how help the situation. But in fact, it may do little. On a rather personal note, knowing the answer to, say, why my wife miscarried does not necessarily dimin-ish the pain of the loss. Nor does *only* looking for answers in prayer. Answers to prayer may come. They did with the prophet Habakkuk (in surprising ways!). But it is the anticipated *encounter* that is truly necessary, his living response to the petitioner. True prayer leaves the answers to God. True prayer presses toward the person of God in communion with him.

When we consider the book of Habakkuk in light of the insights on prayer offered above, it becomes clear its poetry exposes not the *idea* but the *practice* of prayer. Habakkuk presses into God with his questions, looking to God for response. He acknowledges himself as a creature in God's creation, and God the creator and provider of all. He embraces his place in the world and looks to God for help. Now the prophet gets to engage in an audible *dialogue* with the Lord. We may not receive such a rich reward! However, the goal in our prayer is the same. We strain to hear the whispers or the shouts of God in the travails of life—and rest assured, God does speak.

---

6. Dietrich Bonhoeffer, *Life Together/Prayerbook of the Bible*, DBWE 5 (Minneapolis: For-tress, 2005), 155–56.

## Relating Shalom and Prayer

But it is vital to remind ourselves that prayer, as Bonhoeffer recognized, is grounded in biblical foundations, especially when we cry out over wrongs. One can recognize what is *wrong* only if one has an intimate sense of what is *right*. In this, lament prayer plays a vital role. Such is the case of our prophet. He is able to name evil in his world because he knows the good that God has set forth. This good at root might be identified as "shalom."

But what is shalom? Perhaps it could be defined as all of creation thriving before the face of God, under the reign of God, in perfect harmony. In the Bible, shalom is presented not with cold definitions, but in vibrant pictures. Psalm 85:10 [H 11] presents a beautiful picture of creation restored in a mighty act of God: "Faithful love and truth will join together, and justice and peace will kiss." The psalmist anticipates the time when God's glory will be demonstrable in the whole of his creation, when his divine attributes will meet creation with the intimacy of a lover. The psalmist employs in Ps 85:10–12 much of the language evidenced in Exod 34:4–6, a foundational text that discloses both the character and acts of God. God is known by his "covenant faithfulness" (חֶסֶד/*ḥesed*), "truth" (אֱמֶת/*ĕmet*), "justice" (צֶדֶק/*ṣedeq*), and "peace" (שָׁלוֹם/*šālôm*). Indeed, the entire created order will be at one, thriving before the face of God. This is a vision of God's world experiencing, even participating in, divine goodness fully, perfectly. This is but one picture of shalom. The psalmist's vision is a *glimpse* of the way the world *ought* to be and will be in the future, but is not at the present time.

The Old Testament, indeed the Bible, often touches on this picture of the future with the image of Zion in the prophets. It shows up in Isaiah and the Minor Prophets.[7] In Isa 2:1–4 and Mic 4:1–4, all nations will go up to Zion (Jerusalem) to be taught in the ways of the Lord. No more fighting or war will occur; swords will be fashioned into plowshares and spears into pruning hooks. Everyone will rest comfortably in peace. In Isa 11:6–8, the "lion will lie down with the lamb" and fear of death will not be a reality for God's people. In Isa 65:8–25, Zion is a renewed heaven and earth in which God's people live before him and are protected from harm. This expanding vision of shalom represents an ideal future reality that will appear in the last days (e.g., Isa 2:1; Mic 4:1).

Irenaeus described this time of shalom as the fulfillment of the kingdom of God, in which Jesus the king will drink with his followers the cup of the new covenant once again (cf. Luke 22:15–17). In this era, Irenaeus says, God will reign in Christ perfectly, and humanity will be restored to perfect union and

---

7. See Heath A. Thomas, "Zion," in *Dictionary of the Old Testament: Prophets*, ed. J. Gordon McConville and Mark J. Boda (Downers Grove, IL: InterVarsity Press, 2012), 907–14, esp. 910–13.

responsibility in God's creation. It is a time when "the creature, being renewed and delivered, shall bring forth plenty of all kind of nourishment, of the dew of Heaven, and of the fatness of the earth."[8] Irenaeus goes on to say that in this time:

> vineyards shall grow, having each 10,000 main shoots: and in one main shoot 10,000 branches and in one main shoot again 10,000 sprigs, and upon every sprig 10,000 clusters, and in every cluster 10,000 grapes, and every grape when pressed shall yield twenty-five measures of wine. And when any one of those saints shall lay hold of a cluster, another cluster shall exclaim, "I am a better cluster, take me, by me bless the Lord!"[9]

In other words, the created world will not produce thorns and thistles for humanity (cf. Gen 3:17–18), but it will produce life and fecundity. Irenaeus summarizes his exposition by saying that in the kingdom of God, all plants and animals "should come to be at peace and agreement with one another, submitting themselves to men with entire submission."[10]

Cornelius Plantinga, too, draws together biblical and theological testimony on shalom. He draws from the prophets, Irenaeus, and the insights of Nicholas Wolterstorff.[11] He summarizes shalom as follows:

> The webbing together of God, humans, and all creation in justice, fulfillment, and delight is what the Hebrew prophets call *shalom*. We call it peace, but it means far more than mere peace of mind or a cease-fire between enemies. In the Bible, shalom means *universal flourishing, wholeness, and delight*—a rich state of affairs in which natural needs are satisfied and natural gifts fruitfully employed, a state of affairs that inspires joyful wonder as its Creator and Savior opens doors and welcomes the creatures in whom he delights. Shalom, in other words, is the way things ought to be.[12]

Plantinga outlines a state of affairs in the world that is fitting to the grace and delight of the divine: the whole creation flourishing under the rule of God.

---

8. Irenaeus, *Five Books of Saint Irenaeus against Heresies*, §5.33.1, 3; pp. 526–27.

9. Irenaeus, *Five Books of Saint Irenaeus against Heresies*, §5.33.3; p. 528.

10. Irenaeus, *Five Books of Saint Irenaeus against Heresies*, §5.33.3; p. 528. Irenaeus goes on in §5.33.4 to quote Isa 11:6–9 to describe the time when this will happen, thus confirming the prophetic linkage of future shalom.

11. Nicholas Wolterstorff, *Until Justice and Peace Embrace* (Grand Rapids: Eerdmans, 1983), 69–72.

12. Cornelius Plantinga Jr., *Not the Way It's Supposed to Be: A Breviary of Sin* (Grand Rapids: Eerdmans, 1995), 10.

Plantinga (following Wolterstorff) rightly draws from the Old Testament prophetic tradition to inform this vision of shalom.

Yet this vision is not only an eschatological future reserved for the time described in Isa 11 or 65, or for that matter, Rev 21. *Shalom is an anticipated state of affairs in the prophets due to the fact that shalom is a remembered state of affairs disclosed from earlier biblical testimony.* Plantinga and Wolterstorff's helpful outline of shalom derives, I suggest, not first from the prophets but from the creation account in Genesis.


## God's Shalom World and Prayer

Shalom is given its primary shape in the creation account of Gen 1:1–2:3. This is the great entryway that marks the story set out in the Bible. Its presence is neither accidental nor incidental. For most of the twentieth century, scholars and theologians treated the creation account as the prologue to the real story of the Bible: God's revelation in history. However, Hiebert reminds us that such thinking is not true to the biblical agenda.[13] Creation is not a prologue or backstory for the real stuff of Scripture. History itself is the story of created beings working out of (or against) the order God has established in creation. "Yahweh founded the earth by wisdom, by understanding he established the heavens; by his knowledge the deeps split open, and the clouds drop down dew" (Prov 3:19–20). Redemption and creation remain correlates of one another. Oswald Chambers says: "The redemption is not only for humankind, it is for the universe, for the material earth; everything that sin and the devil have touched and marred has been completely redeemed by Jesus Christ."[14] Adrio König reminds us that

> The same God who redeems is the Creator. This God has an identity, and he remains eternally true to himself; he is the God of love. So we are warranted in expecting that *all* his acts will evince a structural correspondence, and this includes creation and redemption. . . . Consequently we may expect redemption to be expressed in creation terms and creation in those of redemption.[15]

---

13. Theodore Hiebert, *The Yahwist's Landscape: Nature and Religion in Early Israel* (Oxford: Oxford University Press, 1996), 3–22.

14. Oswald Chambers, *Conformed to His Image and the Servant as His Lord: Lessons on Living Like Jesus* (Grand Rapids: Discovery House Publishers, 1996), 13.

15. Adrio König, *New and Greater Things: Re-Evaluating the Biblical Message on Creation*, StOri 1 (Pretoria: University of South Africa, 1988), 145.

If one does not understand *more* of God's creation, then one will understand *less* of God's redemption. If one attempts to tease these two ties apart or to marginalize one to the neglect of the other, then Christian doctrine on both is under threat of unraveling. The creation account sets the agenda for the whole of reality, and the redemption of that reality, under the lordship of Jesus Christ (Col 1:15–20).

Another temptation for Christians lies waiting in the wings with this text, that is, to read this text with a *simple* lens, viewing it as *mere* description of God's creative fashioning of the world. Of course, this point is undeniable: the account *does* give the true story of the creation of the world. However, it is much more than this, and it is by no means *simple*. It not only gives the "what" of God's activity in creation, it also gives the "how" of God's activity in creation, and both the what and how help to elucidate how creation is linked with shalom. This discussion also clarifies why the prophet Habakkuk appeals to the God of creation when he sees his world fundamentally gone wrong, and appeals to him to act in a redemptive manner (so Hab 1:4, 14; see commentary above).

But here we must be very careful. The how of God's creative activity in this account is neither simple, nor is it simply described. In the modern world, the creation account has been compartmentalized into camps of "creationism" versus "evolution" or "intelligent design" versus a purely material biological process of development ("Darwinian evolution"). Of course, these discussions are fruitful *and* necessary. However, what can be overlooked in these debates is, in fact, the biblical text. I am interested particularly in the literary structure and theological outlook of the text rather than a precise scientific harmonization of the text with natural phenomena, though no doubt such investigations are important. But what I would like to suggest is that the literary and theological data from the creation account are the clue that provides greater insight into scientific investigation.[16] It is the beacon that illumines the way for scientific investigation rather than obscuring or darkening it. So, it is important to draw out (rather briefly) the literary structure of the creation account in Gen 1:1–2:3. In so doing, the close relationship between God's act of creation and the reality of shalom will emerge.

Note the structure of the account. The text begins with God's speech-act of creation: a word that ordains the world (Gen 1:1). God pronounces the world into existence, but does so in six days. There is a time when the earth is a "no-world," being "formless" and "void," shapeless and empty, and darkness covers the face of the deep (v. 2). This is, for all practical purposes, day 0, because it is a period of formless emptiness. But this no-time no-world is not without God,

---

16. I use the language of "clue" from the popular but helpful work by Timothy Keller, *The Reason for God: Belief in an Age of Skepticism* (New York: Dutton, 2008).

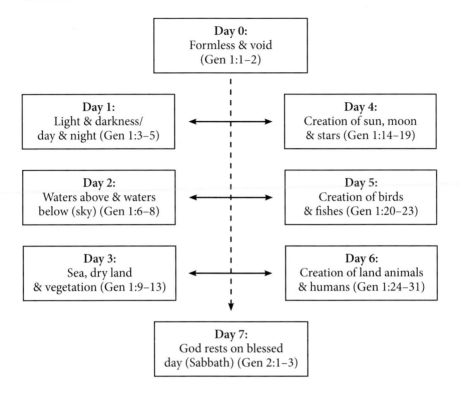

for the "spirit of God was hovering upon the face of the waters." God's spirit is present even in the midst of nothingness, moving, hovering and waiting to instill his creative purpose. God's six days of creative activity (called the "hexameron" in Christian tradition) display a distinctive order that reveals both the domains of creation (days 1–3) and the filling of those domains (days 4–6).

Several significant theological insights derive from the literary structure of the account. The first has to do with *the orderliness of God's world*. There is a close correspondence between days: day 1//day 4; day 2//day 5; day 3//day 6. This pattern exposes symmetry and order in the creative act of God. The world that God has created displays regularity, symmetry, and a discernible structure. God could have made other worlds, but this is the actual one that is comprehensible to his creatures. As William Brown says of God's creation:

> All hints of conflict and opposition are effectively banished from this account. The elements of creation are poised to fulfill God's bidding at the drop of a word. Creation is gently yet decisively led to its fulfillment in a process of formfullness, an execution of separation and fulfillment. Nothing

lies outside of God's creative direction and approbation, not even "chaos."
... First and foremost, God is creator of an order par excellence.[17]

*The goodness of God's world* constitutes the second insight. On all the days of
creation, the pronouncement is made that the world is "good." Indeed, the term
"good" (טוב/*ṭôb*) occurs seven times in the creation account, identifying the complete goodness of the created world, its completion.[18] The goodness of the created
world is found in God's declaration, in his ordaining it for order and purpose, that
his ways might be actualized for all of its inhabitants. It is the goodness of God's
creation that sets the stage for Habakkuk's complaints to God *about* the world
when it turns upside down. Present experiences of tragedy and horror are terrible
in part because there is an innate sense that this is not the way the world ought to
work: God did not make it that way. It is also in place to note that the goodness
of the creation is not an accident that is denied after the turn toward sin. Rather,
the goodness of creation is affirmed even after sin, by the confirmation of God's
covenant after the deluge in Gen 6–9. The flood was a purifying judgment from
sin rather than an annihilating judgment that denies creation. The created order
is good, but purified by God's activity, first by water, then by fire (2 Pet 3:6–13).

The third insight has to do with *the hierarchical pattern of God's world*.
Each of the days in the creation account is ordained of God, but each of the
days cannot be counted as equal. Day 1 establishes light and darkness, but day
4 ordains how those domains will be ordered: the great lights will govern day
and night, times and seasons. Birds and fishes fill the sky and seas in day 5, while
animals are created to inhabit the land in day 6. Humans and animals alone are
blessed by God in days 5 and 6, and are given the commands to "be fruitful"
and "multiply" (Gen. 1:22, 28). Further, the Jewish scholar Leon Kass beautifully
exposes the hierarchical and ordered world according to Gen 1:

- Humanity as the peak of creation as stewards of it (day 6).
- Humanity has the rational capacity to discern and govern, higher than
  the remainder of the created order (day 6).
- Humanity alone images God in the world (day 6), as opposed to the other
  animal worlds (land animals, day 6; fish and fowl, day 5).
- Animals (fish, fowl, and land animals) are higher than heavenly bodies
  (day 4) by virtue of the fact that they have greater freedom (day 5).

---

17. William P. Brown, *The Ethos of the Cosmos: The Genesis of Moral Imagination in the
Bible* (Grand Rapids: Eerdmans, 1999), 46, 47.

18. Several elements in the narrative are associated with the number seven. For discussion,
see James McKeown, *Genesis*, THOTC (Grand Rapids: Eerdmans, 2008), 308–9.

- All animals are blessed and commanded to multiply (days 5 and 6).
- All animals produce according to their kind (days 5 and 6), and unlike the heavenly bodies (day 4), animals display the powers of awareness (such as the gift of hearing).[19]

He goes on to say about this hierarchy, "Living things are higher than nonliving things; and among living things, some are more alive than others—that is, their powers of awareness, action and desire are more fully developed. Who could disagree? The special powers of human beings make the case most boldly."[20]

The fourth insight is that Gen 1 reveals *the unique place of humanity in creation*. To be sure, humans are creatures. They stand neither above nor apart from creation. So, humans are inevitably creaturely. Humans are blessed to be fruitful and multiply like the other animals. Still, *only* humanity is stamped with the image of God (vv. 26–27). Although they are formed from the dust of the ground, Brown suggests "human beings are, however, not 'landlings'; they are rather 'landlords,'" so that humanity has the "tasks and trappings of royalty and cult, the offices of divine representation and habitation." The author of Gen 1 has "imbued humanity with royal blessing and task in the world."[21] Humanity is blessed by God, indeed, but to be a blessing to the rest of the created order, to rule and subdue it (Gen 1:28). Humans are given the great privilege and responsibility of being God's vice-regents in the world that he has made.

How does the image of God (or *imago Dei*) relate to humanity, theologically speaking? Initially, the creation account treats the *imago Dei* in terms of what humanity is called to *do*. So God says, "Let us make humanity in our image, according to our likeness. They will rule over the fish of the sea, and over the bird of the sky, and over the beast, and over all of the earth, and over every creeping thing that creeps upon the earth" (Gen 1:26). Verse 28 reiterates this command and forms an *inclusio* around the poetic center of v. 27:

> And God created humanity in his image.
> In the image of God he created him.
> Male and female he created them.

19. Leon R. Kass, *The Beginning of Wisdom: Reading Genesis* (Chicago: University of Chicago Press, 2006), 35–36.

20. Kass, *Beginning*, 36. Kass goes on to say that evolutionary theorists would disagree with him! However, he provides a compatibilist view between the biblical vision of Gen. 1 and evolutionary theory, which he supports.

21. Brown, *Ethos*, 44.

Considering the dual commands surrounding and highlighting v. 27, the literary structure of Gen 1:26–28 indicates that image-bearers of God exercise dominion over creation; this humanly prerogative, granted by God, *imitates* divine governance. As God has bestowed his world with order and purpose, God gives his landlords/stewards the command to order the creation under his authority.

This humanly task is both a great privilege and an enormous responsibility. The unique terminology of governance given by God for humanity is the language of royal power ("to rule," from the Hebrew root רדה/*rdh*) that is coupled with the terminology used to describe how humans can fashion the created world into a state of productivity ("to subdue," from the Hebrew root כבשׁ/*kbš*).[22] On the meaning of "to subdue," Brown perceptively comments: "Human beings must work *in* creation in order for creation to *work* for human beings by providing sustenance and the means of their livelihood. Nevertheless, such a commission does not require exploiting the earth's resources, as the specific language of subduing might suggest."[23] Bearing God's image connotes the kind of rule and dominion that promotes the flourishing of the whole of creation. As Bartholomew states,

> The creation comes into existence progressively as a coherent whole, and part of humankind's stewardship will be to continue to ensure that the earth brings forth vegetation in a way that is "good," so that birds, fish, and animals are able to flourish in the environments designated for *them*.[24]

Acknowledging this point alerts us to the fact that *proper exercise of dominion for the good of the world* is a significant aspect of what it means to image God well.

Yet, it is also vital to state that being God's image-bearers is what humanity *is* as much as what humanity *does*. Humans *are* image-bearers *by virtue of* being human rather than being another member of God's created world: the privilege of bearing God's image is not relegated to the other species within creation (fish, fowl, land animals, vegetation, luminaries, sky, or sea). Humanity is also known as human by *who it is*. Gordon Spykman rightly avoids any reductionistic account of the image of God in humanity, emphasizing one facet of what it means to be human rather than another, for instance, human action versus human ontology.[25]

22. So Brown, *Ethos*.

23. Brown, *Ethos*, 44–45.

24. Craig G. Bartholomew, *Where Mortals Dwell: A Christian View of Place for Today* (Grand Rapids: Baker Academic, 2011), 16 (emphasis original).

25. Of course, some Christian theology argues that the "soul" is the center of the image

Human action is a *part* of imaging God, but not the only, or perhaps even primary, part. For instance, an infant does little but coo, cry, or smile. An infant cannot rule or reproduce as described in the language of Gen 1:26, 28. Yet an infant images God all the same. A sleeping person loses nothing of God's imprint upon them because of sleep. A body at rest images God beautifully. This is to draw out a simple but profound theological point: although it is appropriate to suggest that bearing God's image is *closely* tied up to the language of governance in the creation language from Gen 1 (rule and subdue, vv. 26, 28), it is not *exclusively* tied to this functional terminology. The *whole* human, in all the countless vicissitudes of what it means to be human (physical, psychological, spiritual, emotional, social, placial),[26] wholly images the Triune God. Imaging God is not a property of humanity, as if one could take it off like a coat. "Imaging [God] is not a choice but a given. We *are* imagers of God. Imaging God represents our very makeup, our constitution, our glory, and at the same time our high and holy calling in God's world."[27]

It remains highly suggestive that Habakkuk has difficulty understanding how or why God would use the Babylonians for his purposes. This foreign nation would not image God *well* but rather would obscure the glory of God. The Babylonians would devote to an idol what properly belongs to God: his creative power, his glory, his fame. Habakkuk cannot imagine that this fits the way the world is supposed to work. Humans are to honor and praise God in all things. Their lives are to be a glowing beacon that draws attention to the true light, God himself.

Finally, the literary structure of the creation account establishes another key theological insight. Namely, *the seventh day marks the goal (aim) of creation.* It is true that the sixth day is the longest day in terms of the amount of words describing the day. And it is further true that the sixth day is climactic in terms of God establishing his image in humanity to govern the created world. It is further apparent that it is after he completed the sixth day that God pronounced the world "very good" (v. 31). Yet creation is not complete without the Sabbath,

---

of God, due to the fact that the soul goes to heaven after death. However, I would immediately rebut that the biblical vision is not an escape from the world, but rather a return to it through the redemption of Christ. A disembodied soul is not fully human until it is reunited with the body in the new creation, as Paul perceptively notes in Rom 8:22–25.

26. By "placial" I mean being set within the structure of God's world, established in particular "places" over the globe. Humans are to live in different places all over God's world, they are "emplaced" in the created order. This is a significant feature of being human. My placial terminology is informed by Bartholomew, *Where Mortals Dwell*.

27. Gordon Spykman, *Reformational Theology: A New Paradigm for Doing Dogmatics* (Grand Rapids: Eerdmans, 1992), 224 (emphasis original).

because the Sabbath is the culmination of creation itself: all of creation enjoying God and God enjoying all his creation.

While the hexameron reveals a world that is habitable for God's vice-regents/imagers, the creation account identifies that the aim of creation is Sabbath rest. God takes "formless and void" (day 0) and ordains a world: "the heavens and earth and all their array" (Gen 2:1). The seventh day is unique for both literary and theological reasons:

LITERARY

1. The merism of "heaven and earth" (Gen. 1:1) appears again (Gen. 2:1), bracketing day 0 and day 7 as the diagram on p. 177 shows.
2. The formulaic conclusion "it was evening and it was morning" that appears with days 1–6 is notably absent in day 7, leaving the time frame of the day open-ended. It is a day not bounded by the evening/morning constraints of the other days. For this reason, it is doing something other than providing a rationale for the later Sabbath law. The Sabbath in the creation account is not bounded in time, even if demarcated by the term "day."

THEOLOGICAL

1. God blesses (only) the seventh day.
2. God declares (only) the seventh day holy.
3. God rests from his creative activity described in the hexameron.
4. The "formless" and "void" (Gen 1:2) is now fully established and identifiable as the "heavens and earth and all its array" (Gen 2:1). This alerts the careful reader to the progression of creation: from empty to filled, from a formless mass to an ordered world.

One may be tempted in a theological interpretation of the seventh day to collapse it onto the laws regarding the Sabbath in both Exod 20:8–11 and Deut 5:12–14. This is a fundamental error, in my judgment. The seventh day in Gen 2:1–3 does not appear in the narrative to explain the (later) laws: it is *not* an aetiology for the Sabbath law.[28] If we interpret it as such, we underread its theological freight. The later laws are, in fact, theological reflections *on the reality of the Sabbath*. They elucidate the characteristics of God as creator (Exod

---

28. Calvin leans toward this interpretation: John Calvin, *Commentaries on the First Book of Moses Called Genesis*, trans. John King (repr., Grand Rapids: Baker, 2009), 1:102–8. See, too, otherwise the beautiful analysis of Dennis T. Olson, "Sacred Time: The Sabbath and Christian Worship," in *Touching the Altar: The Old Testament for Christian Worship*, ed. Carol M. Bechtel (Grand Rapids: Eerdmans, 2008), 2–34.

20:8–11) and God as redeemer (Deut 5:12–14) for Israel considering God's role as the Sabbath lord.[29] The laws provide space and time in the normal week to reflect upon the grandeur of God as well as to provide rest from painful toil in the land of thorns and thistles (Gen 3:18).

Yet in the creation account, the Sabbath day stands as a timeless time, with no evening and no morning, one in which thorns and thistles are not present. It is the *culmination* of creation, where God enjoys his creation and all his creation works in proper order before him. It is the time in which God takes up his reign over his finished, created world. As the divine King ascends to his throne, he rules over the good world, all in order, all thriving before him. Later texts in the Old Testament depict God granting the king of Israel rest from enemies so that the king can rule the kingdom in peace under God (2 Sam 7:1–6; 1 Kgs 5:4–5; 8:56; 1 Chr 22:9–10, 18–19; 23:25–26).[30] The Israelite king now enjoys his rule in the land under God, resting in his reign. This point echoes the rest of God in creation.

God's rest on the seventh day indicates his divine reign over the ordered world that he has made. In this, there is enjoyment and worship before the creator. This reveals that the function of the Sabbath day in Gen 2:1–3 is different from the others. God made the world in the first six days of creation, but he sustains the created world in the seventh day, reigning over the good order and rhythm that he established in days 1–6.[31] He ceases from the creative work of days 1–6 because the world he has established stands as complete, good, ordered, thriving. Day 7 is reserved for all creation thriving and enjoying God.

So, it is apparent that the rest of God has little to do with God's cessation of work. As Augustine knew so well, the idea of a cosmic-creator God needing a twenty-four-hour period of leisure for recuperation was nonsense! Indeed, it was a Manichean heresy that he combated.[32] Augustine codifies a Christian interpretation that presents the rest of God as a metonymy: the rest

---

29. So helpfully disclosed by Olson, "Sacred Time," 12–14.

30. Note the discussion of G. K. Beale, *The Temple and the Church's Mission: A Biblical Theology of the Dwelling Place of God*, NSBT 17 (Downers Grove, IL: InterVarsity Press, 2004), 62–63.

31. "God's rest both at the conclusion of creation in Gen 1–2 and later in Israel's temple indicates not mere inactivity but that he had demonstrated his sovereignty over the forces of chaos (e.g., the enemies of Israel) and now has assumed a position of kingly rest further revealing his sovereign power" (Beale, *Temple and the Church's Mission*, 62).

32. See the discussion of Augustine on Gen 2:1–3 and his refutation of the Manicheans; Saint Augustine, *Saint Augustine on Genesis: Two Books on Genesis against the Manicheans and on the Literal Interpretation of Genesis*, trans. Roland J. Teske, FC 84 (Washington, DC: Catholic University of America Press, 1991), §1.22.33–34, pp. 81–83.

of God is the reign of God in which all creation rests before him. God *causes* the Christian rest and thriving before him on the seventh day. He appeals to three other scriptural instances for support of this view (Rom 8:26; Deut 13:3; Matt 24:36).

Further, the seventh day is, for Augustine, the indicator of the seventh age of the world. It is the age that is hoped for, the heavenly and eschatological beatific vision:

> After this evening [the sixth age of the world, where Christ returns to judge the living and the dead] there will come the morning, when the Lord himself will come in glory. Then they to whom he said, "Be perfect as your Father, who is in heaven, is perfect," will rest with Christ from all their works. For such men perform works that are very good. After such works should one hope for rest on the seventh day, which has no evening. Words in no sense express how God made and created heaven and earth and every creature that he created, but this exposition according to the order of days recounts it as a history of works he did so that it has special regard for the prediction of what is to come.[33]

Augustine demarcates the seventh day as prophetic, depicting the age of the kingdom of God. His interpretation that links the seven days of creation with the seven ages of the world is, to my mind, highly evocative (but not essential). His great insight is his connection between the seventh day and the goal of creation: the divine King reigning over creation. The real world that is revealed in the seventh day discloses what will come about finally, fully, after the great defeat of sin. For those who place their faith in the King of Creation (Jesus Christ), they will experience the Sabbath rest that awaits the whole of creation, nothing less than a new heavens and new earth under the reign of Christ (Heb 4:1–11). The writer of Hebrews views the rest of God as being the restoration of all things, the hope of the suffering Christian.

All told, the vision that Gen 1 affords is God's creation of the world for shalom: ordered, everything in its place and performing according to its function, and thriving under God in his kingdom of peace. Shalom is a picture founded in creation.

> Shalom is the human being dwelling at peace in all his or her relationships: with God, with self, with fellows, with nature. . . . In shalom, each person enjoys justice, enjoys his or her rights. . . . Shalom at its highest is *enjoyment*

---

33. Augustine, *Saint Augustine on Genesis*, §1.23.41, p. 88.

in one's relationships . . . to *enjoy* living before God, to *enjoy* living in one's physical surroundings, to *enjoy* living with one's fellows, to *enjoy* life with oneself. . . . Shalom is the *responsible* community in which God's laws for the multifaceted existence of his creatures are obeyed.[34]

What could be clearer? The seventh day depicts shalom at its ultimate: the created world, in perfect order and complete harmony, thriving before the King, God himself. In this sense, the created world of Gen 1, especially in the seventh day, depicts a world of justice and righteousness at every level: God's rule over creation, humanity's relationship to God, one another, and over the rest of the created world.

True prayer knows what is *right* in the world so as to flag up what has gone *wrong*. True prayer, then, understands the tenets and goal of God's creation. True prayer knows that creation was built for thriving and fecundity before God. Literally, prayer that understands the fullness of God's world as described in his word has the foundation and power to pray with all seriousness that God's kingdom *would* manifest itself on earth as it is in heaven. To pray against wrong in the world, one needs to know what is right. The biblical teaching on creation is foundational for biblical prayer. Prayer that understands God's creation design prays along the grain of the universe.

## Shalom Shattered

Despite its compelling portrait of peace, the vision of the seventh day is only a memory, an echo to the song that was once the glory of creation under the peace of God. We live in the land of thorns and thistles, east of Eden, which is the focus of most of the Old Testament. Human rebellion broke trust between the image-bearer and image-giver and as a result, sinful humanity broke loose upon the world.

For Habakkuk, and for all those who live through injustice, it is evident that sin shatters shalom. This point theologically illumines for us Habakkuk's pleas. His prayers in Hab 1:1–4, 12–17 affirm that the shalom world remains only a specter of what once was in the beginning of all things. In Hab 1:1–4, the prophet cries out because of Judah's pervasive violence, a misdirection of dominion. Particularly, it is a misdirection of their covenantal responsibilities

---

34. Wolterstorff, *Until Justice and Peace Embrace*, 69–72 (emphasis original). Wolterstorff, however, founds his understanding of shalom in the prophets. But his view, as has been shown above, fits with what is revealed in the creation account.

before God. If justice is a kind of wholeness, goodness in the order of things, recognition and enactment of the way the world ought to work under God's rule, then it is apparent that Habakkuk lives apart from justice. He partici- pates in a world where only "crooked justice goes forth" (מִשְׁפָּט מְעֻקָּל/*mišpāṭ mĕʿuqqāl*; Hab 1:4). This is a world marked by sin that chokes out life before it can even spring forth from the ground. For Hab 1:12–17, Habakkuk cries out because of Babylon's idolatrous ways. Idolatry is for so many reasons a perver- sion because it takes the glory of God away from him properly and attributes it to an idol. That Babylon does or would do this is the exact opposite of imaging God well in his world. In this case, the prophet uses the language of dominion from Gen 1 to press God to response: Is it true that humanity is reduced to the status of a creeping thing rather than the true image-bearer of God? Idolaters like the Babylonians will not image God well; they will only give glory to an idol. Humans have rejected their creational calling: to image God in his world. Habakkuk cries out precisely because, in contrast to the vision of the psalmist above (Ps 85:10 [H 11]), justice and peace *do not kiss* and he knows that only God can set things right.

When we pray for justice in the world, we do so with a firm eye to the problem of sin. Sin that springs forth from the heart of humanity is the ulti- mate enemy of God's shalom for creation. When we pray, we pray that God would defeat sin and swallow up suffering—our suffering. And indeed he does so. We should remember that Jesus, too, suffered at the hands of angry men. "He was despised and rejected by men, a man of sorrows who was acquainted with grief" (Isa 53:3). Yet, what seems to be defeat in Christ's death ultimately is victory over suffering. We are reminded that God's ultimate vindication of sin and suffering is in the person and work of his Son, Jesus Christ. "He became sin who knew no sin so that in him we might become the righteousness of God" (2 Cor 5:21). God reconciled all things, whether in heaven or in earth, to himself through Jesus Christ (Col 1:20). God takes both sin and suffering into himself in Christ and bears it on the cross, so that God's world might be reconciled and renewed. But still we pray with the expectant appeal that God's kingdom, which comes with Christ, may be done "on earth as it is in heaven," and it may be done *today*.

As we live in the in-between-time between the kingdom-come and the kingdom-not-yet, naming sin remains a powerful practice. Only after sin is named and identified can it be rightly lifted in prayer. In his powerful book *Peo- ple of the Lie*, M. Scott Peck labors to identify and categorize evil. As a psychol- ogist, he wants to see how evil permeates human experience, how it manifests itself, how to identify it, and then how to respond to it. He sees evil as a kind of facade of truth but bereft of truth's power. As a result, whenever there is evil, a lie is not far behind. Whether one agrees with Peck's analysis or conclusions, one of the great insights of his work is the attempt to *name* evil. Naming is a human responsibility. In the garden, Adam was given the charge to name animals. Naming, classifying, and categorizing is a human capacity given to us by God.[35] Sin can, and should, be named. But sometimes it is a struggle to name sin. Sin can stretch our abilities to name and classify it. Yet, we must make the attempt.

Habakkuk does just that. In Hab 1 alone, he identifies idolatry, rebellion, and strife among God's people, wicked people surrounding the righteous, violence, and iniquity. When one names sin, one admits to oneself the starkness of reality. Instead of papering over the brokenness of this world or pretending that it does not exist, naming sin keeps the corruptions of this world in view. In this, we are called to be truth-tellers: the world is broken in countless ways and we are sinful in countless ways. We must learn to count them.

In his meditation on John's Apocalypse, Eugene Peterson draws attention to Rev 6. It is here, he says, that evil is named.

> Christians do not shut their eyes to the world's cruelty in themselves or others. St. John has trained us to be especially attentive to it, to name it with honesty—no euphemisms, no evasions—and deal with it courageously. . . . Christians, for the most part, are the very persons in our society who can be counted on to have no illusions about the depth of depravity in themselves or the world at large. No other community of people has insisted so consistently through the centuries on calling evil by its right name.[36]

Once sin is named, it must be offered to God in prayer. Emmanuel Katongole and Chris Rice speak of the challenges the church faces in places like Rwanda, where the butchery of the genocide is a specter that looms over the nation—but more pointedly, the church. In their work, they attempt to *name* sin. They note that prior to the slaughter (over eight hundred thousand were killed), it was known that Rwanda was one of the most evangelized countries in Africa![37] How was the church complicit in this violence? What can be said of this? What went wrong? Where does the church move forward from here? To wrestle with these questions adequately the church must learn to name her sins. Only then will we begin to face up to our *full brokenness* and *deep need* of

---

35. M. Scott Peck, *People of the Lie: The Hope for Healing Human Evil* (New York: Simon and Schuster, 1983).

36. Eugene H. Peterson, *Reversed Thunder: The Revelation of John and the Praying Imagination* (San Francisco: Harper San Francisco, 1991).

37. Emmanuel Katongole and Chris Rice, *Reconciling All Things: A Christian Vision for Justice, Peace, and Healing* (Downers Grove, IL: InterVarsity Press, 2008), 75.

God's grace. After naming, the church can move forward in prayer. Katongole and Rice write:

> The first language of the church in a deeply broken world is not strategy, but prayer. The journey of reconciliation is grounded in a call to see and encounter the rupture of this world so truthfully that we are literally slowed down. We are called to a space where any explanation or action is too easy, too fast, too shallow—a space where the right response can only be a desperate cry to God. We are called to learn the anguished cry of lament.[38]

These are the same prayers of Habakkuk: desperate cries to a wholly holy God. The book presents no normal prophetic action, no normal prophetic word. The actions and strategies for prophetic rebuke are left to the other biblical prophets, to Jeremiah, who calls his people to repentance and warns them of (inevitable) judgment. The words of rebuke are left to Isaiah, Jeremiah, and Ezekiel to perform sign-acts that present God's message to the people: Jeremiah's dirty undergarments, Ezekiel's exile-food cooked over excrement, Isaiah's strangely named children. Habakkuk, by contrast, cannot *act*. He cannot *move*. He can only cry out to God with his "anguished cry of lament."

Habakkuk's prayers do not shake an angry fist at God in the fashion of a petulant teenager moaning about the injustice of having to carry out the rubbish to the bin at the parent's request. As Christian Polke rightly says, "To lament is not to whine."[39] Nor can lament be called the words of a rebellious human railing against a holy God, an act of willful indolence at God's goodness. The lamenter does not impudently walk away in disgust at the Lord's silence. No. The lamenter's prayers are neither petty nor petulant. Katongole and Rice's words capture the prayers of Habakkuk when he sees injustice and wrong in God's world. His prayers are like "those who see the truth of the world's deep wounds. . . . It is the prayer of those who are deeply disturbed by the way things are. . . . If we are to participate in God's plan to reconcile all things in Jesus Christ, we must begin to listen to this cry."[40]

---

38. Katongole and Rice, *Reconciling All Things*, 77.

39. Christian Polke, "God, Lament, Contingency: An Essay in Fundamental Theology," in Harasta and Brock, *Evoking Lament*, 44.

40. Katongole and Rice, *Reconciling All Things*, 78.

## Shalom in the New Creation

The bookends of the Bible give a Christian vision of the world, moving from creation (Gen 1–2) to new creation (Rev 21). The new creation ushered in by God comprises the ultimate hope of the Christian life, because it is in this place where we see Christ on his throne and all of God's created order worshiping him in harmony (Rev 21:1–5). In short, new creation is God's shalom world that has come to its consummation. The biblical prophets give portrait to this vision with the eschatological concept of Zion, which is picked up in the New Testament. It is in Zion where Yahweh reigns over Israel and the nations, and the nations make their pilgrimage to worship Israel's God (Isa 2:2–3; 27:13; 60:3–16; Mic 4:1–8; Zeph 3:9–10). It is in Zion where God issues judgment, vindicating the faithful but punishing the wicked (Joel 3:12–16). It is in Zion where God administers peace and all the world experiences fecundity and life. The Psalter celebrates this shalom vision as the time when God reigns among his people in his kingdom, which crystallizes in Zion: "Yahweh is great and is highly praised in the city of our God, his holy mountain. (It is) beautiful in elevation, the joy of the whole earth. Mount Zion, in the far north, is the city of the great king" (Ps 48:1; cf. Ps 99:1–5). J. Clinton McCann says that, "for believers, Jerusalem [or Zion] becomes a spatial, temporal symbol for the reality of God's rule in all times and places."41 Isaiah identifies future, purified Zion as nothing short of the new heaven and new earth (Isa 65:17). When one sees the image of Zion in the Old Testament, one sees the promise of God's shalom world.

When one sees the image of new creation in the New Testament, particularly Rev 21:1–22:5, one sees the reality of God's shalom world. God sets the world to rights and reigns in and through his Son, Jesus Christ. The kingdom of God has finally come on earth, as it is in heaven. God's kingdom was assumed to be real in the Scriptures: *that God would really reign on the earth justly, righteously, and eternally*; and it is in Christ that the real and present suffering of the world is embodied as well as (finally) overcome by God's real and present reign. But Christ's victory at the cross, and in the resurrection, remains a *prolepsis*.[42] Christ's victory reveals (and anticipates) the reality of its future completion. As Paul describes it: first Christ, then the church, then the world will have its resurrection day (1 Cor 15:12–58). Only those who have expressed faith in the gospel of Jesus Christ inherit the kingdom of God (1 Cor 15:50). Christ's victory

---

41. J. Clinton McCann Jr., *A Theological Introduction to the Book of Psalms* (Nashville: Abingdon, 1993), 151.

42. For discussion on the kingdom of God in the Old and New Testament, see Wright, *New Testament and the People of God*, 299–338; Wright, *Jesus and the Victory of God*, COQG 2 (London: SPCK, 1996), 443–74, 612–53.

ensures that he makes all things new (Rev 21:5). However, all Christians still face sin or the outcomes of sin, and they die in their physical body (Rom 8). Death is defeated by Christ, but the Christian fully experiences this reality at the *culmination* of the kingdom. God's kingdom is established *now* because of Christ's victory, but God's kingdom will be consummated by Christ at the *end* of all things. Looking back to Saint Augustine's thought that the Sabbath day was prophetic, perhaps he *was* right to read the end at the beginning: "Words in no sense express how God made and created heaven and earth and every creature that he created, but this exposition according to the order of days recounts it as a history of works he did so that it has special regard for the prediction of what is to come."[43] The Sabbath day at creation will be the Sabbath world at the end of all things.

The church prays in anticipation of this certainty. Praying lament faithfully is nothing less than a cry for the kingdom of God to be made manifest in the world. "Every truly Christian prayer of petition is, implicitly at least, a request that the Kingdom may come."[44] If this is true for lament as well, then there is an analogical relationship between the hope present in the prayers of lament and the hope set on display in the kingdom of God. Ultimately, in the grand movement of the biblical story, death is defeated and suffering will also be swallowed up in the end because of the work of Christ and the movement of his kingdom. What is interesting is the kingdom of God that Christ has inaugurated *now* through his life, death, burial, resurrection, and ascension is not fully consummated . . . until *then*, in the future.

What about meantime? What of the period between then—vindication—and now—present suffering? This is where the cries of lament break in. We cry out that God's kingdom would be made present now amid the world and all its brokenness. The church is mindful that we cannot usher in God's kingdom; it comes with the return of Christ, and he comes whenever the Father deems it appropriate. This mystery of faith enables us to press into God, pray to him, and await his response. But we know that if we wait for his promised end (Hab 2:2–3), then surely it will come. Even if it tarries, we should wait for it. We should hold faith and not turn back. As we pray "Your Kingdom come, your will be done, on earth as it is in heaven," we pray in faith and obey the Christ who gave us the words.

---

43. Augustine, *Saint Augustine on Genesis*, §1.23.41, p. 88.

44. Gabriel Daly, *Asking the Father: A Study of the Prayer of Petition* (Wilmington, DE: Glazier, 1982), 80.

# Dead Ends to Doorways:
## Habakkuk and Spiritual Formation

## Introduction

The previous chapter discussed the power of prayer that is opened to us in and through the book of Habakkuk. This chapter explores how this prophet opens us to spiritual formation. As I understand it, spiritual formation intends the shaping of the whole person (not just the mind) into the image of Christ. This shaping process, however, is not narcissistic and self-actualizing for the sake of self alone. In short, spiritual formation is the process by which we discover the glorious blessings in Christ so that we might be a blessing to the world.

Ruth Haley Barton draws upon two Pauline metaphors to describe this process. The first comes from Gal 4:19, where Paul indicates that he is in "the anguish of childbirth until Christ is formed" in the Galatian church. The idea here is powerful, but it is a mixed metaphor. The notion of "anguished childbirth" is when a child is delivered. This is the pain that he undergoes, until they reach maturity in Christ and live according to their Savior. And yet "until Christ is formed" is the idea of Christ growing to full maturity inside a person. This is not a childbirth image but rather an image of growth in the mother's womb. Paul is pained to see God's people grow into maturity, but that maturity comes by Jesus maturing in the believers. This is the process of spiritual formation: Christ growing to full maturity in his body, the church. The other Pauline image comes in Rom 12:2, where Paul appeals to the Roman church not to be conformed to the image and pattern of the sinful world, but rather to be transformed by the renewal of the mind. The transformation is nothing less than a "metamorphosis" (hence the Greek word μεταμορφόω/*metamorphoō*).[1]

---

1. Ruth Haley Barton, *Sacred Rhythms: Arranging Our Lives for Spiritual Transformation*, Formatio (Downers Grove, IL: InterVarsity Press, 2006), 11–13.

Believers are renewed by Christ and his word, and thereby they morph into something different, namely, new creations in Christ (see Rom 8).

These images that depict change have some things in common. First, these images are all processes that develop over time. They are not automatic nor are they microwave-quick. Childbirth, maturation, and metamorphosis each take time, and so it is evident that the progress of time remains essential for spiritual formation. God does not expose our deepest wounds, desires, or sins in a moment. This is because, in part, our woundedness and sinfulness reach to the very core of our being, and our understanding of ourselves stands in a far-off country that only God can go to and bring back for us. Psalm 139 reminds us that only God knows us. He has searched us and known us from the foundation of time. It is *our* process to allow God to go into that distant land of self, bring it back to us, so that we can become aware of what God already knows. This takes time. It was the time that Habakkuk spent with God that provided the space for change. The process of formation *over time* will give us space to change as well.

Second, those in Christ who undergo such change do not do it themselves! We are transformed by the renewing of our minds, but we do not transform ourselves by the renewing of our minds. No, Christ is formed *in us*. The point is clear. Spiritual formation is a process to which we commit that takes time and that God instigates and achieves in us. It is God's work, not ours. In his reflection on his own spiritual transformation, Henri Nouwen says it this way: "*You* cannot make yourself different. *Jesus* came to give you a new heart, a new spirit, a new mind, and a new body. Let him transform you by his love and so enable you to receive his affection in your whole being."[2]

Spiritual formation, while deeply effective in the life of the believer in his or her transformation into a new creation in Christ, is not solely for oneself. If God is doing the deep work in us, it is for others as well. The great danger of talk about spiritual formation is that it centers the self on self. This kind of egoism can divorce us from the world. In his classic work on intellectual life, Antonin-Dalmace Sertillanges argues that true Christian spirituality is deeply connected to the world:

> A true Christian will have ever before his eyes the image of the globe, on which the Cross is planted, on which needy men wander and suffer, all over which the redeeming Blood, in numberless streams, flow to meet him.

2. Henri J. M. Nouwen, *The Inner Voice of Love: A Journey through Anguish to Freedom* (New York: Doubleday, 1996), 41 (emphasis original).

The light that he has confers on him a priesthood; the light that he seeks to acquire supposes an implicit promise that he will share it.[3]

True Christian spirituality does go deeply inward, but the journey inward is instrumental for the journey outward, in service with the Lord for the sake of others. For example, one reason that we will not proclaim the good news of the gospel of Jesus Christ is that we, as Christians, are simply selfish. Spiritual formation is the process where we die to self, and Christ is formed in us. The selfishness is transformed into love and compassion. Love and compassion, given by Christ, then compel us to proclaim Christ to a world that needs him. Spiritual formation, in this vein, is a process that is for the sake of Christ and his gospel for all people.

This chapter argues that Habakkuk opens us up to the process of spiritual formation. Pain and suffering, so often a clear dead end for cultivating faith in God, become a doorway into the full reality of life. Christian faith is transformative of the human person, even in the face of horrendous pain. God must enable and walk us through this process of transformation, just has he has done with the prophet Habakkuk.

## Dead Ends

But if spiritual formation is a process, some experiential dead ends prevent its movement in us. Two stand out. The first is the experience of *violence*. I define violence as an act or deportment that causes pain (physical, social, emotional, psychological, or even spiritual) to an Other.[4] And although the above definition does not demand it, it is not unusual to associate violence with inherent negativity: something immoral, unjust, or harmful. Some herald the death of God, in part, by claiming the overwhelming violence of the world and the overwhelming violence of religion.[5] Because God is violent, he is neither worthy of worship nor of existence. Some observe pervasive violence and misfortune in

---

3. Antonin-Dalmace Sertillanges, *The Intellectual Life: Its Spirit, Conditions, Methods*, trans. Mary Perkins Ryan (Washington, DC: Catholic University of America Press, 1998), 13.

4. Heath A. Thomas, "Divine Violence, Pain, and Prayer in Lamentations," in *Wrestling with the Violence of God: Soundings in the Old Testament*, ed. M. Daniel Carroll R. and J. Blair Wilgus, BBRS 10 (Winona Lake, IN: Eisenbrauns, 2015), 94.

5. Sam Harris, *The End of Faith: Religion, Terror, and the Future of Reason* (New York: Norton, 2004); Daniel Dennett, *Breaking the Spell: Religion as a Natural Phenomenon* (New York: Penguin, 2006).

the world and simply leave the faith.[6] Because of negative human experience of violence, devout people abandon their religious tradition. In these scenarios, violence equates to a negative experience, particularly an injurious experience of harm.

Another dead end is *silence*. By silence I intend the perceived nonresponsiveness of God to cries for help, comfort, or relief. Silence remains a powerful barrier to faith, and it leads people to walk *away* from faith. In Phil Zuckerman's empirical research on why people leave religious tradition, he reveals that one of the reasons is because of "the failure of prayer." Zuckerman says that these formerly devout folk "had faith, they prayed to God, their prayers weren't answered, and apostasy is the result."[7] Divine silence can be a dead end to spiritual formation. If God does not speak, then how can the devout hear and respond in faith?

Christian faith is transformative of the human person, even in the face of horrendous pain. In the exploration that follows, we will see how the experience of speech overcoming silence marks the shape of spiritual formation. God must enable and walk us through transformation, just as he has done with the prophet Habakkuk.

### Violence

The persistence of violence remains a dead end of faith for many. Indeed, violence in its varied forms leads many to question the comprehensibility of life, the viability of Christian faith, and even the possibility of God. At least three manifestations of violence in Scripture are problematic:

1. The problem of a violent God portrayed in Scripture
2. The problem of violent people of God portrayed in Scripture
3. The problem of a divine text (Scripture) that authorizes violence[8]

The book of Habakkuk presents all three manifestations. God is violent in Habakkuk: he judges the Babylonians *and* the Israelites, causing pain. People are violent in Habakkuk: God raises up the Babylonians to do his bidding—namely, to reprove his people, causing pain. One can argue that Scripture authorizes

---

6. Phil Zuckerman, *Faith No More: Why People Reject Religion* (Oxford: Oxford University Press, 2012).

7. Zuckerman, *Faith No More*, 46.

8. These are identified by Jerome F. D. Creach, *Violence in Scripture*, IBC (Louisville: Westminster John Knox, 2013), 2.

the violence in Habakkuk in at least two ways: the vision of Hab 2:2–3 inscribes divine judgment (and salvation) for Israel and Babylon; the canonical text of Habakkuk preserves and enshrines violence on its pages.

As one might suppose from the above paragraph, this essay does not avoid the association of God and violence in the Scripture. At the level of biblical material, one cannot bypass the notion that God is violent, if the above definition of violence is cogent at all. Apart from definitional gymnastics, scholars have attempted to shift God away from, or disassociate God from, violence in various ways, whether through Christus Victor theological models against penal-substitutionary models (a relatively modern theological move), or disassociating the God of the Old Testament from Jesus (the more ancient Marcionite instinct). Still, the persistence of violence in the Bible cannot be dismissed, however one attempts to sidestep its presence in Scripture, or in its relation to God.

Violence, as we have seen, draws the prophet Habakkuk to wonder about God's ways. "I cry out to you 'Violence!' but you do not save" (Hab 1:2b). But by the end of Hab 3, the prophet embraces impending death with the glad welcome of a friend, inviting him to hasten speedily home. What a strange transformation!

For those outside of Habakkuk's faith, this might be construed as a dark form of masochism: a love for God that is demonstrated by embracing pain, death, and humiliation. Psychologists in the Freudian tradition have identified the willingness, even giddiness by some Christians, to suffer and die for the faith as a kind of neurosis.[9] Further, it is not uncommon to discover that a willingness to suffer and die for God is indicative not only of neurosis but also of an irrational belief in an abusive God. Regina Schwartz suggests that violence is inherent to the Bible and this sets a violent legacy for the church.[10] This violent legacy, then, becomes the seedbed that cultivates martyrdom and further violence.

In this line of thought, embracing hurt or abuse remains (horrifically) rational for the Christian faith. After all, the New Testament seems to revel in the glorification of death. Jesus called his followers to embrace death as a marker for fidelity to him, to take up their cross and follow the way of Christ (Luke 9:23). The apostle Paul reminded the Philippian church that for him "to live is Christ and *to die is gain*" (Phil 1:21). And the writer of Hebrews instructs his audience

9. Sigmund Freud, "A Child Is Being Beaten: A Contribution to the Study of the Origin of Sexual Perversions (1919)," in *The Standard Edition of the Complete Psychological Works of Sigmund Freud*, ed. J. Strachey (London: Hogarth, 1957), 17:179–204, cited in Jaco Hamman, "The Rod of Discipline: Masochism, Sadism, and the Judeo-Christian Religion," *JRHe* 39 (2000): 322–24.

10. See, e.g., Regina Schwartz, *The Curse of Cain: The Violent Legacy of Monotheism* (Chicago: University of Chicago Press, 1998).

to embrace pain from God, because it is soul-building (Heb 12:5–11). With these (and other) texts in view, Jaco Hamman argues that Christianity enables violence against both self and others: Christianity is a violent and neurotic religion.[11]

One could object to the kinds of constructions of God and violence identified above. It is possible to quibble with this line of analysis as a facile presentation of Christianity that does not comprehend its distinctive presentation of the defeat of violence. Still, its pertinence should give us pause as a serious threat or dead end to the faith.

### Silence

Alongside violence, the shuddering silence of God in the life of faith is a dead end to faith for many. When it comes to prayer, C. S. Lewis states, "We can bear to be refused but not to be ignored. In other words, our faith can survive many refusals if they really are refusals and not mere disregards. The apparent stone will be bread to us if we believe that a Father's hand put it into ours, in mercy or in justice or even rebuke."[12] True prayer, Lewis understands, is the practice of setting one's request before God with the expectation for divine response. But silence? What to do with silence?

The Old Testament again and again throughout its corpus addresses the perennial problem of divine silence. It does so in Habakkuk, as well. A myriad of texts speak to God's silence, hiddenness, and unresponsiveness (Job 13:24; 30:20; 31:35; Pss 13:1, 3; 27:4, 7; 44:24; 55:2; 69:16–17; 86:1; 88:14; 102:2; 119:45; 143:7; Mic 3:4; Lam 3:8). Lamentations depicts God as hiding himself in a cloud so that no prayer can go through (Lam 3:44). That picture adequately summarizes the life of faith at certain times. God hidden, concealed, and silent. A rosy spirituality may suggest otherwise, but for those who walk in the valley of the shadow, they know better. It leads us to ask "Why?" and "How long?" with no answer whatever. Note these are the leading questions of the prophecy of Habakkuk (1:2–4).

Nouwen, in a time of deep spiritual depression, suggested time and again that it is wrong to deny the experience of pain, because pain is a reality that we all must embrace for growth.[13] A spirituality that leads to a kind of denial of pain is no spirituality at all. The pain that is being addressed here is the abject silence of God. Afraid to admit this silence of God, a sunny spirituality denies

---

11. So Hamman, "Rod of Discipline," 319–27.
12. C. S. Lewis, *Letters to Malcolm: Chiefly on Prayer* (London: Bles, 1964), 75.
13. Nouwen, *Inner Voice of Love*, 3, 26–27, 47–48, 61–62, 88, 103.

its very existence. Yet such denial is delusion. The biblical evidence says something fundamentally different. Sometimes God *is* silent. No voice, no sound. God-not-here-and-not-speaking. We must learn to reckon with divine silence to come to its full awareness. Nouwen says that denial of pain prevents growth. Another danger comes from denying God's silence. It prevents us from pressing through to God—hence, a true dead end. When one comes to the impasse, all one can do is simply turn around and walk back the road from which one came. Therein lies the real danger of divine silence. It leads to no more speech, no more pressing, no more anything. Defeated by silence, the praying person effectively loses faith and walks away from God.

Fear of walking away from the faith often is the reason why people ignore divine silence. The sunny side of spirituality is much more palatable. It is easier to speak about divine silence (if it exists) as essentially God's way of teaching us that we were prideful to ask for God's presence or speech in the first place. God has not removed ourselves from *us*, but we have removed ourselves from *him*. Thus, only penitence is the appropriate response. God will respond when we repent; only then will his silence become speech. There is something to this, to be sure.

Yet, it is not appropriate for our text in Habakkuk. Neither is it appropriate for Ps 88, or Ps 44, or the book of Job. In each of these texts, the wicked surround the righteous, and God is far off. Habakkuk's pain and complaints are met with divine silence. Yet these very texts that address divine silence are not content to walk away from the God they address—and neither should we. But the point of pressing through silence in prayer brings us to a doorway that will be addressed below.

## Doorways

The dead ends of violence and silence should not be underestimated. They are real and persistent experiences of pain that complicate faith. Yet, what seem to be dead ends do not have to be so. How can dead ends become doorways to spiritual formation?

Negative experiences of violence and silence can become pathways to new life and a deeper communion with God. Martin Laird powerfully captures the way that violence is overcome in the victory of Christ: "God in Christ has taken into Himself the brokenness of the human condition. Hence, human woundedness, brokenness, and death itself are transformed from dead ends to doorways into Life."[14] So, too, are the violence and silence that seem to divide

---

14. Laird, *Into the Silent Land*, 119.

the vital communion between God and his people. Still, God, who suffers in Christ, provides a gateway that helps us see suffering not as an end in and of itself but as a way toward spiritual formation.

### Violence, Hospitality, and Christ

In the Christian tradition, two scholars have unveiled the ways that God and violence relate and open the possibility of spiritual formation. Hans Boersma and René Girard enable us to see how violence, despite its horrors, can be a doorway to deeper faith.

Boersma relates violence to hospitality. He says that the Christian God, in his essence, is love and pure hospitality. This is his nature. Boersma envisions God as providing, through creation and especially new creation, pure love and hospitality—in which a perfect love for God, self, one another, and the world is not an ideal but a reality lived and borne before the presence of God. However, in a broken world, violence, even divine violence, is necessary for the revelation of God's love. For divine hospitality to take hold in the future, divine violence is instrumentally necessary at present:

> God's hospitality requires violence, just as his love necessitates wrath. This is not to say, of course, that God's violence and wrath are his essential attributes. God *is* love, not wrath; he *is* a God of hospitality, not a God of violence. There is an absolute primacy, therefore, of hospitality over violence. Hospitality bespeaks of the very essence of God, while violence is merely one of the ways to safeguard or ensure the future of his hospitality when dealing with the humps and bumps of our lives. Divine violence, in other words, is a way in which God strives toward an eschatological situation of pure hospitality.[15]

Boersma sees violence, especially divine judgment, as necessary as one moves toward the new creation, or "an eschatological situation of pure hospitality." In the present age, where sin and evil still hold sway, divine violence safeguards love. "Love, it seems, requires passionate anger toward anything that would endanger the relationship of love."[16]

If one applies Boersma's thought to Habakkuk, his insights immediately become apparent. Habakkuk's complaint about violence (Judah, Babylon, and

---

15. Hans Boersma, *Violence, Hospitality, and the Cross: Reappropriating the Atonement Tradition* (Grand Rapids: Baker Academic, 2004), 49.

16. Boersma, *Violence, Hospitality, and the Cross*, 48-49.

even God) is correct. But God lifts the prophet's vision to see the instrumentality of that violence. God's work with the Babylonians against Judah is a step along the way toward the knowledge of the glory of Yahweh being revealed over the entire earth, as waters cover the sea (Hab 2:14). God reveals the knowledge of glory of Yahweh through his violent use of, and retribution against, the Babylonians. His action, seemingly problematic, is necessary so that the knowledge of the glory of Yahweh will be manifest among all peoples.

In this configuration, violence in Habakkuk becomes a doorway toward a deeper understanding of, and relationship with, Yahweh. Notice that in Hab 2:14, above, what is central in the justice that God brings against the Babylonians, which includes the vindication of the righteous, is the revelation of the "*knowledge* of the glory of Yahweh." This is not abstract knowledge about God's glory. Rather, what is envisioned here is experiential and relational knowledge of God and his glory. As Steven Tuell perceptively comments: "As a noun, the Hebrew *da'at* ('knowledge') occurs ninety times in the Hebrew Bible, forty times in Proverbs. Here, however, *da'at* appears in a verbal form that intensifies the experiential, relational sense of the word: Habakkuk speaks not of the intellectual grasp of static data about God but of *knowing* God."[17]

Such knowledge of God is impossible, at least in Habakkuk, without the experience of, and wrestling with, violence. So the necessity of divine violence in Habakkuk becomes a doorway to renewed life in God. Without walking down the confused path of violence, Habakkuk would not come to the knowledge of the glory of Yahweh. Neither shall readers today. The faithful must come to grips with the fact that God becoming knowable to us does not come without Habakkuk's journey of confusion and pain.

Boersma's exploration of the relationship between God and violence is theological while René Girard's is sociological. Both, however, penetrate the relationship between God and violence by way of Scripture. Girard's life work has been to explore, philosophically and theologically, the problem of violence, and his great insight is that humanity enacts violence in the form of "mimetic desire."[18] That is, humans mimic what we love. It can be a child mimicking the parent, or a student mimicking her professor. This is a good thing at first, because we are formed by this modeling process, and we learn how to be in the world through it. However, it is always possible that the model becomes a *rival*, and when this happens, a "scandal" breaks loose. For Girard, a scandal is when we try to overcome or kill our rival. The desire to kill the rival represents desire

17. Steven Tuell, *Reading Nahum–Malachi: A Literary and Theological Commentary* (Macon, GA: Smyth & Helwys, 2016), 91 (emphasis original).

18. René Girard, *I See Satan Fall Like Lightning* (Maryknoll, NY: Orbis, 2001).

run amok: those whom we love and imitate we now have the desire to topple and kill. The very ones we love become a scapegoat for our destructive desire, and we must murder the scapegoat to achieve self-actualization. Justifying our violence, we kill those that we love so that we might become liberated selves. Girard calls this process the cycle of mimetic desire. This is always a potential reality for humanity, but potentiality becomes actualized again and again in a destructive recurrent cycle of violence. For this reason, Girard calls mimetic desire *the identifying characteristic* of humanity.

What can free us from the violence of mimetic desire? Girard says that the pagan myths offer no real help, because again and again these myths identify with the one who kills rather than the victim who has become the scapegoat. In his view, the myths of the world side with the victors of violence rather than the victims.

But the movement that alters and finally breaks the cycle of mimetic violence comes in the Jewish and Christian tradition. In the Old Testament, God sides *with* victims of violence rather than against them. In this way, to use Abraham Heschel's language, God suffers suffering from the "inside."[19] Girard suggests that God suffers with the victim—even himself becoming the victim—of violence. In the Old Testament prophets especially, God and his prophets are rejected and abused by nations and even by God's own people. So it is evident that the mimetic cycle of violence is present among God's people. Rather than capitulating to it, however, the Bible presents God as siding with the suffering victim rather than siding with the mob. This is crystallized in triumphant notes in the suffering of his very own son, Jesus Christ, who suffers violence at the hands of the mob (which wished to make him king) who, though loving him, now crucify him. The very voices that cried, "Hosanna! Hosanna!" in a mimetic twist of desire, now shout, "Crucify him! Crucify him!" The reason? Jesus did not become the king they fashioned him to be. He was, in effect, the paradigmatic scapegoat that was killed. Yet in stark contrast between the real death of Christ and the myths of the pagan world, Jesus is not divinized in a false way; he is resurrected to be Christ and Lord, who defeated death, sin, hell, and mimetic violence. Girard says:

> The Gospel revelation is the definitive formulation of a truth already partially disclosed in the Old Testament. But in order to come to completion, it requires the good news that God himself accepts the role of the victim of the crowd so that he can save us all. This God who becomes a victim is not another mythic god but the one God, infinitely good, of the Old Testament.[20]

19. Heschel, *Prophets*, 109–19, 151–52.
20. Girard, *I See Satan Fall*, 130.

Girard argues that the triumph of the cross is utterly unique because of its absolute victory over violence. God does not perpetuate violence of mimetic desire, but rather defeats it through the cross of Christ. The triumph of the cross bears out because of the resurrection, in which God says the divine "No!" to victimization and violence. The resurrection of Jesus becomes the pattern for all of those who embrace the way of God in Christ. It is Satan that is the ultimate example of mimetic desire, because it was Satan who aped God and killed him, literally in Jesus, as the rival. Yet it is precisely in Jesus that the satanic engine of mimetic violence that fuels the world is defeated and sin overcome. It is Jesus who, through his own work, saw "Satan fall like lightning from heaven" (Luke 10:18). And it is here that Girard sees the picture of Jesus's defeat of Satan, which becomes a picture of Jesus's defeat of violence at the cross.

Violence emerging from mimetic desire is the thing that exposes us as typically human, and yet God defeats violence through becoming the victim at the cross. This victimization is not a defeat, however, but a victory over violence through nonviolence.

> Christ does not achieve this victory through violence. He obtains it through a renunciation of violence so complete that violence can rage to its heart's content without realizing that by so doing, it reveals what it must conceal, without suspecting that its fury will turn back against it this time because it will be recorded and represented with exactness in the Passion narratives.[21]

"Until we come to the place of exile we are not minded to undergo the disciplined quietness and passionate waiting that bring us to the point of hearing, seeing, and receiving God's fullness."[22] For Girard, violence against Jesus on the cross becomes a disclosure of how Jesus defeats the violent cycle of mimetic desire. His work on the cross is the dead end that becomes a doorway to hope, to the defeat of violence. This is true for those who are in Christ. His death and resurrection become the site of our resurrection (both literally and symbolically). His body becomes our home. In his wounds at the hands of violence, we are healed, experiencing peace. Girard's emphasis upon Christ as the solution to violence at the very least draws our gaze back to Jesus.

Jesus stands as the center of Scripture, and fundamentally at the center of creation itself, and so any response or resolution to the problem of violence should be found in relation to him. Karl Barth describes the centrality of Jesus in this way:

---

21. Girard, *I See Satan Fall*, 139.
22. Peterson, *Reversed Thunder*, 90.

This man is the secret of heaven and earth, of the cosmos created by God. To know Him is to know heaven and earth in their diversity, unity and createdness, and to know God as their Creator. The Old Testament insight into this matter can thus be understood as meaningful and practicable only if it is understood as the promise, or prototype, of the knowledge of the Messiah.[23]

Barth exposes two fundaments to our exploration on God and violence. If violence is present as a problem in creation—which it is, and Habakkuk exposes it—then any response to violence must find articulation through Jesus as the center. Second, if violence recorded in Habakkuk is a problem, then Habakkuk's response to the problem of violence cannot be fully answered without reference to Jesus in the full Christian canonical witness of Old and New Testaments. Habakkuk's vision of justice and setting the world to rights (seen, e.g., in Hab 2:2–5, 14, 20; or in Hab 3) is a promise of God's work ultimately fulfilled in Jesus. New Testament evidence, as witnessed in Rom 1:17 and Heb 10:36–39, confirms this. As I summarize elsewhere, in the light of the New Testament evidence,

> Those who embrace him [Jesus] are declared "righteous" in the sight of God and find new life, both now and through eternity. They live faithfully before their Maker in and through the whole of life. Those who embrace Christ in faith, then, are righteous and will live. The birth, death, resurrection and second coming of Jesus comprise the substance of God's faithfulness.[24]

God's faithfulness in Jesus becomes an ultimate response to, and defeat of, the problem of violence. Christ's victory is sure. The future reign of God in Christ, that is, a kingdom of perfect peace, is certain. But we await that kingdom as a future hope. Our embrace of Christ's victory over violence through the cross and resurrection in our own experiences comes through suffering, through our negative experiences of violence. Instead of turning away from faith in our experience of pain and suffering, God calls for a deeper faithfulness to him in the midst of it, in the fashion of our Savior: "For we have become participants in Christ if we hold firmly until the end the reality that we had from the start" (Heb 10:14 CSB). As the Lord Christ bore suffering and violence, his people can bear suffering in the fashion of our Savior so that we become "participants in Christ."

23. Barth, *CD* III.1:21–22.
24. Thomas, *Faith amid the Ruins*, 81–82.

### Divine Silence and Prayer

Being deeply formed in the victory of Christ through suffering requires the thunder of prayer. Eugene Peterson finds in the book of Revelation the ultimate end to prayer, even lament prayer. He explores the vision of Rev 8:1–6 and its depiction of prayer. There, at the opening of the seventh seal, the angel of God mixes the prayers of the saints with incense. Then, in a powerful reversal, the prayers that have gone up to God are thrown back down to earth, in what Peterson calls a "reversed thunder."[25] The prayers strike the world, creating lightning and thunder on earth. This is a visual presentation of God's answer to prayer: literally heaven coming back to earth.

What are we to make of this vision? In short, the prayers of God's people are not lost on a silent and aloof deity. He has heard, he has seen, and he *will* respond. It is a presentation of the end, where God vindicates the prayers of the righteous and enacts justice and judgment on the earth. The cry in Rev 6:10, "How long, O Lord, holy and true, until you judge and avenge our blood from those who live on the earth?" has now come to a resounding divine response. We should remember the prayer, "how long," because it has a familiar ring to it! It is the cry of our prophet, and it is the lament prayer of all of us who want to see God's kingdom come and justice done on this earth—and God offers his sure response. Peterson says that when we see that our lives and our suffering are not lost on God, that our prayers and our cries are not rebuffed by his indifference, then we can begin to see that his "delay is not procrastination, that our waiting is not because of someone's indifference, that we have not been forgotten, then the waiting is not intolerable."[26] Peterson says the response of God in Revelation to the prayers of his people reveals that prayer "orients us to God's design."[27] Prayer sets us within the purposes of God and, simultaneously, opens us up to God's response. "Prayer pulls the actions of heaven and earth into correspondence."[28] Only in the prayers of "how long" do we open ourselves to God's response, where he sets our feet on high places (Hab 3:19).

When we think along these lines, it becomes apparent that prayer develops within us spiritual virtue that leads to a deeper understanding of ourselves and a deeper communion with God. It is possible to see that there are practical benefits for lament in the Christian life. Lament facilitates certain habits in the church that are integral for her transformation.

---

25. Peterson, *Reversed Thunder*, 88.
26. Peterson, *Reversed Thunder*, 94.
27. Peterson, *Reversed Thunder*, 95.
28. Peterson, *Reversed Thunder*, 97.

1. *Lament slows the church down*. Lament prayer is uttered from the perspective of the *victim*, the one who often goes through the horrors of violence and oppression again and again, if not physically, then certainly emotionally and psychologically.[29] The lamenter lives and relives trauma. Lament shifts attention away from the process of resolution from pain and draws the focus back again and again *to* the pain of the sufferer. It allows space and time for suffering to be known, experienced, and voiced. This inevitable slowing down process enables the church, at either an individual or communal level, to recognize and *own* their wounds. We must slowly learn to trace the scars in our own lives even as we look to the scars of the risen Christ for comfort.

Slowing down is vital. Alan Lewis suggests that the church learns this from the gospel of Jesus Christ. The church needs to rehearse its fundamental and world-shaping gospel account again and again: the death, burial, and resurrection of Jesus. Moving too quickly to the *resurrection* neglects fundamental insight of the *whole* gospel. The Apostles' Creed affirms that Jesus "suffered under Pontius Pilate, was crucified, dead, and buried. He descended into hell. The third day he rose again from the dead." He ascended and now sits at the right hand of the Father, to be sure, but still he suffered, was crucified, dead, and buried. By slowing down, by meditating upon the *death* of Jesus can we understand God's power being made manifest through folly and weakness, which is the crucifixion. The *burial* of Jesus (the day between days) marks the great silence, the question mark of uncertainty, in history. Jesus's claims were met with an awkward silence on the Sabbath day he rested in the grave. But Jesus's *resurrection* marks the triumph of God in history. Jesus's resurrection is the guarantee that sinful humanity can be made new; the whole of creation will be refitted with its Easter garments of joy. Lewis contends,

> What theme could be more impeccably biblical, and more central to the life and mission of the Christian church, than that Christ, by his cross and resurrection, has defeated sin and destroyed the powers of death and hell? Yet precisely because it is not *without*, but *through*, the cross, that newness of life and death's defeat are accomplished—that God uses what is *weak* to overcome what is powerful (1 Cor 1:27)—the good news of resurrection is itself under threat when the suffering and the folly, the humiliation and

29. Suffering is not a one-stop process, where pain is experienced and then done away with. Rather, pain of the order that Habakkuk attends to is often serial trauma, which recurs in the memory and emotion of the sufferer. So chronic pain, for instance, cannot be solved by a simple cure. See the discussion of Swenson, *Living through Pain*, 30–68.

the impotence, the godlessness and the finality of the cross of Christ are minimized.[30]

Precisely. Only by slowing down, allowing itself to embrace the pain of suffering and resisting the impulse to move too quickly to resurrection, can the hope of new heavens and new earth—shalom made certain in and through the work of Christ—be fully appreciated as the Christian hope. Lament is that space to meditate, to slow down, to name the brokenness of the world and bring it before the Lord.

2. *Lament fights powerfully against blissful naiveté and sterile ambivalence.* There is a temptation to see the world as fundamentally "on the way." Every year things will get better. Hope, however, comes with the next new thing: with a new election, a new leader, or new technology, we suppose our world will improve. This perspective betrays an old edifice that casts its shadow on us still. It is the shadow of an Enlightenment view that thought the goal of humanity was to create "cosmopolis," or a society ordered by perfectly exact rational categories.[31] Once these categories were set in place, a perfect society would ensue. But the present world knows better. At the dawn of the twenty-first century, the old specter of pain, irrational abuse, genocide, and injustice still haunts us and shows little sign of flight. Bob Goudzwaard, Mark Vander Vennen and David Van Heemst suggest that there is a crisis in the current world: we look for solutions to the problems in the world but cannot find them. These problems— global violence, environmental devastation, and global poverty—leave us on the precipice of disaster. Newer ideologies in our world that arise to address these problems (material progress and prosperity, guaranteed security and freedom) remain in large degree as vacuous as older ideologies of the twentieth century (such as the ideologies of revolution).[32] This view is hopelessly naive. Christianity powerfully reveals the brokenness of humanity and culture due to prevalent sin. God has created both good, but they are misdirected in so many ways. Leaning upon the "new" thing to bring hope—whether leaders, rationality, or technology—equates to leaning upon a tower doomed to fall, and great is the fall. Lament drives through the emptiness of naiveté and looks the brokenness of the world square in the face with all seriousness. Lament prayer knows that only *God* in Christ sets things aright, and so it is to *him* that we appeal.

30. Alan E. Lewis, *Between Cross and Resurrection: A Theology of Holy Saturday* (Grand Rapids: Eerdmans, 2001), 40.

31. Stephen Toulmin, *Cosmopolis: The Hidden Agenda of Modernity* (Chicago: University of Chicago Press, 1992).

32. Bob Goudzwaard, Mark Vander Vennen, and David Van Heemst, *Hope in Troubled Times: A New Vision for Confronting Global Crises* (Grand Rapids: Baker Academic, 2007), 47–126.

But apart from the temptation to naively envision the world as "on the way to progress," the harshness of the world can also tempt us to respond to it with an attitude of ambivalence. In the latter half of the twentieth century, Jacques Ellul characterized the world as being in an age of abandonment, where there is little hope for the future, only ambivalence. Ellul suggested that hopes set in technology, ideology, material prosperity, and revolution proved to be empty. Because of the broken promise, a sense of disillusionment and ambivalence set in. Ambivalence leads to paralysis of action and, eventually, our withdrawal from the world. Instead of crying for life, the world that Ellul saw was offering a different word: an attitude of scorn, habits of derision, and a disavowal of life that leads to suicide.[33]

Lament, however, offers a different word. It cannot abandon hope and withdraw. This special kind of prayer sets us in the fray, engaged in God's world for the sake of shalom. What is out of joint *must* be set right, but only God can do this. The hope in lament prayer lies not in withdrawal, but in *God* who hears and answers prayer. Lament drives the church to see the way the world actually is: good and created by God, but terribly broken and awaiting redemption that can only come from God.

3. *Lament offers the church a cruciform shape to suffering.* The church is caught up in the suffering of the world, not excluded from it. I have been challenged to consider how often the modern, Protestant (and Evangelical) church embraces suffering in its worship. On a personal note, I have no expertise in the modern praise and worship movement. Indeed, that with which I am acquainted, I very much appreciate. However, I have yet to find a modern worship song that even approaches lament in the fashion of Pss 22, 44, 69, 88, or, for that matter, Rev 6:10.

When suffering, God's people lament, and Jesus is the prime exemplar of the practice. Stephen Ahearne-Kroll has suggested that Mark presents Jesus as *the* Davidic lamenter par excellence.[34] So as the kingly sufferer without peer, Jesus exclaims his experience of dereliction in Mark 15:34 (which quotes Ps 22:1). His exclamation is, at root, a cry for help and a proclamation of deep pain. God does not remove his Son from suffering, but sustains him through it; and prayer enables the Christ to cry to God in the time of suffering. If Jesus is the exemplar of the one who utters such lament prayer, then we see that such prayer is valuable. We are reminded that rightly uttered lament remains a fully Christian prayer that imitates the model of the master.

---

33. Jacques Ellul, *Hope in a Time of Abandonment*, trans. C. Edward Hopkin (New York: Seabury, 1973), 16–17, 38–70.

34. Stephen P. Ahearne-Kroll, *The Psalms of Lament in Mark's Passion: Jesus' Davidic Suffering*, SNTSMS 142 (Cambridge: Cambridge University Press, 2007).

It is fascinating that lament prayer is offered during Holy Week in the Christian calendar, where the church celebrates the suffering king. But in the Free Church tradition (and the Baptist tradition of which I am a part), the neglect of both liturgy and the historical understanding of the church's worship practices remains pervasive. This forgetfulness tends to obscure the vital significance that the suffering of Christ displays in the liturgy of Holy Week.[35] These traditions tend to focus upon the victory that Jesus achieves on Easter morning. But the liturgies in the Catholic, Greek Orthodox, Anglican, and Lutheran traditions, for example, draw our gaze to Christ's *suffering* and his *prayers of lament* from Maundy Thursday to Good Friday. As Lewis's remarks above indicate, the desire to run to the victory of Easter prevents us from experiencing the suffering of our Lord. The liturgies of Holy Week, however, enable us to see our suffering in the light of Christ's suffering. Lament is one of the ways the church can learn the cruciform shape to suffering. Christ embraces his suffering before he achieves his victorious resurrection. We too may pray in our suffering, knowing that as we experience pain Christ has won the victory that will one day be ours. One day, too, we will be clothed with our Easter garments of joy. Until that day, we pray.

4. *Lament opens us to divine response.* Habakkuk is a book that reveals that God does respond to our cries. God engaged the prophet's prayers, both the prayers about the injustice of his own people and the prayers about the injustice of the Babylonians. Yet, God takes the prophet's prayers and through them moves the prophet toward a deeper realization of God and his ultimate ways. The vision for the end and appointed time issues forth nothing short of the verdict of ultimate cosmic justice: "Yahweh is in his holy temple, let all the earth be silent before him!" (Hab 2:20). Habakkuk's laments, ironically, were the doorway deeper into the mystery of God.

If we take Jesus's teaching on prayer in Luke 18:1–6 seriously, then we are left with this conclusion: God responds to prayer. Notice in these verses that Jesus is talking about a desperate issue of injustice that the widow faces . . . this is not a petty thing! In short, the question that the widow asks again and again is the question of lament: "How long?" Jesus's teaching here is that God *will* respond because God is a good and just and loving God. But the key point about this parable is that Jesus teaches about prayer and faith. When he comes in glory, will Jesus find a persistent-widow kind of faith among God's people? This is a radical faith that presses into God.

---

35. See, for instance, the illuminating discussions of Eugenia S. Constantinou, "Lamentations for the Lord: Great and Holy Friday in the Greek Orthodox Church," in *Great Is Thy Faithfulness? Toward Reading Lamentations as Sacred Scripture*, ed. Robin Parry and Heath A. Thomas (Eugene, OR: Pickwick, 2011), 131–38; A. Cameron-Mowat, SJ, "Lamentations and Christian Worship," in Parry and Thomas, *Great Is Thy Faithfulness?*, 139–41.

The challenge of, and solution to, suffering are present whenever a prayer is offered: God himself. But it is also important to note that on the full biblical revelation, our prayers for justice are not *our prayers* alone. The Scriptures indicate that Jesus intercedes on our behalf (John 17) and "ever lives to make intercession for us" (Heb 7:25). They record that the Spirit intercedes as well, *groaning* on our behalf in our suffering (Rom 8:26–27). This shows us that even within the Godhead, the Spirit and the Son make intercession to the Father about the affairs of humanity, praying about sin and the mediating salvation of Christ (Heb 7:23–25), praying for support and fidelity to God (John 17), and groaning and interceding over suffering (Rom 8:26–27). In this, we are not alone in prayer, even in prayers of lament. God has gone before and behind us in the Son and the Spirit, drawing our prayers into his. As Peterson reminds us, the prayers of God's people are answered in the end in his final verdict. Wickedness, divine silence, and violence are all given a final shape in the new creation, where God throws death away and all suffering is set to rights. Pain and tears will no longer haunt the human experience. Although we, like him, will still have scars, our marks will draw us to a deeper understanding and love for the One who was wounded for our transgressions, and bruised for our iniquities.

### Learning to Suffer for the Sake of Others

It is not true that Christian life is carefree. Habakkuk reveals clearly that pressing into the space called discipleship brings great care, and pain. The prophet likely would go into exile with his compatriots. He would suffer a similar fate to that of Jeremiah, Ezekiel, Daniel, Hananiah, Azariah, and Mishael. Either he would be exiled into a foreign land or die in the siege of Jerusalem. But the prophet is not defeated by God's word. Rather, it is God's very word that leads him to high places by Hab 3:19. Habakkuk was deeply formed by his communion with God, which led him to a deeper account of his own self and his faith in God. But the call made by God is total, a complete surrender, even to the point of death.

Dietrich Bonhoeffer understood total surrender to God. His famous statement from *The Cost of Discipleship* is that when "Christ calls a man, he bids him come and die."[36] Myriads of Christians, no doubt, eager to respond to the call, have wrongly understood Bonhoeffer's point here with a kind of warped masochism. If so, the Christian faith *is* what people have accused it to be: a kind of masochistic perversion. It is a kind of neurotic belief that has no real warrant

---

36. Dietrich Bonhoeffer, *The Cost of Discipleship* (New York: Macmillan, 1963), 99.

and is destructive to life. If God's desire is to see myriads of martyrs die in his name, then perhaps he is a god of death after all, unworthy of worship or praise.

No, this is not the kind of faith of which Bonhoeffer speaks, nor is it the God that he describes. In fact, he argues that our death to self is the path to life. Not just in the life to come, but life *now*. What is hard, however, is that the denial of self and abandonment to God mark a real death of *our* wants, *our* needs, and *our* desires. This unholy trinity must be crucified so that, with Jesus, we can begin to pray, "Not *my* will, but yours be done." Suffering is a process that *can* root out these counterfeits and replace them with the authentic desires of the Holy Trinity for life. So Bonhoeffer says, "The call to discipleship, the baptism in the name of Jesus Christ means both death and life."[37] Truly, life is borne out of death. Saint Paul uses the metaphor: "I have been crucified with Christ and therefore it is no longer I who live, but Christ who lives in me. And the life I now live in the flesh I live by faith in the Son of God, who loved me and gave himself for me" (Gal 2:20).

The God of Scripture is the God who ordained, created, sustains, and guarantees life. To suggest otherwise is to deny God's vitality. For God life, not death, is the ultimate aim and goal of all his creation. It is life that comes through death and suffering that marks Christian spirituality. Moreover, death is not *sought out* but borne. Foolish people seek suffering. Jesus himself asked that the cup of suffering be taken from him in the garden of Gethsemane. Suffering is never sought, but when it comes, it can be borne in faith. Habakkuk learned this. In this way, his life becomes an early picture of Christ and a paradigm for Christian suffering as well. We bear suffering because, as the God of life, we know that God grants resurrection. The martyrs under the throne in Rev 6:9–10 got their answer. Habakkuk did as well. So did Jesus. So will we. Suffering is a process that can be borne in faith because we know it is not, in the movement of God's story, the end. Rather, the end is the vindication of the righteous by the God of life.

But when we bear suffering, we discover that our painful process is not for us alone. This is a powerful mystery: suffering builds a community of comfort. When bearing the weight of suffering, a general feeling is abject loneliness. We learn from Jesus that this human experience is not ours alone. The master came to his followers after agony in prayer: "Can you not watch and pray with me one hour?" His loneliness was complete. Abandoned by his people, abandoned by his friends, and ultimately on the cross Jesus prayed, "My God! My God! Why have you forsaken me?" (Mark 15:34). Yet he who was abandoned has not abandoned us. Rather, as we remarked above, Jesus now prays for us. And he

---

37. Bonhoeffer, *Cost of Discipleship*, 99.

creates a community for support and comfort. The apostle Paul encourages through his letter to the Corinthian church:

> Blessed be the God and Father of our Lord Jesus Christ, the Father of mercies and God of all comfort, who comforts us in all our affliction, so that we may be able to comfort those who are in any affliction, with the comfort with which we ourselves are comforted by God. (2 Cor 1:3–4)

This comfort might be the comfort from the sting of sin. But suffering is not always related to sin. Sometimes suffering is simply suffering for what seems to be no good reason. Or if there is a reason, as in the experience of Job, it is hidden from us. We may never know why we suffer. Still, God's comfort is available in suffering; and when we experience this comfort, we can begin to share it with others who suffer. We should certainly rejoice with those who rejoice, but profoundly Christians can and should be a community that weeps with those who weep (Rom 12:15). Overly sunny spirituality might miss this rich opportunity for comfort. In this way, we suffer, but for the sake of others. We are a community connected to the Crucified One, who suffered on our behalf, so that we might be able to suffer with others. Suffering, then, is a doorway to spiritual formation.

Even at the doorway, however, we must learn from the prophet Habakkuk. His suffering, although so much like Jeremiah's or Job's, was utterly unique. As indicated in the exegesis in the first half of this commentary, Habakkuk's experience of call and response from God has no real equal in the Bible. His experience of suffering was distinctive, as was his interaction with God. Habakkuk opens a door to see his house of pain. But his house does not have our address. Rather, we must own our own suffering and allow God to speak to us in our particularity.

This fact serves as a warning of further damaging those who hurt with the best of intentions. Nouwen describes how human suffering is deeply related to specific situations and circumstances that bear the marks of individuality and nonrepeatability. When we suffer, we do not suffer, as he says, "in the abstract." Real people and real events give specific shapes to individual suffering. Because of this, he says, "all suffering is unique."[38]

As we move to comfort others, we must never lose sight of the fact that those we might console have their own house of pain that does not carry our address. Our role as comforters is not to make our experience of comfort *their* experience of comfort. To do so would be to move their pain into our house.

---

38. Nouwen, *Inner Voice of Love*, 103.

Such an action, even with the best of intentions, is a move of deflection. It deflects the pain of the sufferer into the world of one who has already met with God. Another process is necessary. Rather than bringing their pain into our house, we draw them to God, and sit with them until he arrives at their house. We must usher them to God, and God will meet them in their place of pain. Because all comfort is from God, our role as comforters is to release those who suffer to the God of life, so that he might heal their hurts as he sees fit. We wait with them. We weep with them. We pray with them. We hurt with them. But we cannot force our way upon them. This is the folly of Job's would-be comforters. They forced their way upon Job, to disastrous results (Job 16:2) and God's rebuke (Job 42:7–8). Rather, as comforters we draw them toward the wounded and risen Christ, who is the master healer, who has wounds himself. In his wounds, they are healed. This cautionary note on comfort is important, because it shifts our role from that of fixer to friend. We cannot comfort those who hurt by fixing them, but we can open ourselves to God, so that he might work through us and serve them well. As did our prophet, Habakkuk. As he opened himself to God, he discovered spiritual transformation in which the Lord moved him from the depths of pain and confusion to set his feet upon high places (Hab 3:19).

# Select Bibliography

Achtemeier, Elizabeth. *Nahum–Malachi*. IBC. Atlanta: John Knox, 1986.

Ahearne-Kroll, Stephen P. *The Psalms of Lament in Mark's Passion: Jesus' Davidic Suffering*. SNTSMS 142. Cambridge: Cambridge University Press, 2007.

Albertz, Ranier, James D. Nogalski, and Jakob Wohrle, eds. *Perspectives on the Formation of the Book of the Twelve: Methodological Foundations, Redactional Processes, Historical Insights*. BZAW 433. Berlin: de Gruyter, 2012.

Andersen, Francis I. *Habakkuk*. AB 25. New York: Doubleday, 2001.

Andrew of St. Victor. *Expositio super duodecim prophetas*. Edited by Franciscus A. van Liere and Mark A. Zier. CCCM 53G. Turnhout: Brepols, 2007.

Angel, Hayyim. "Biblical Prayers and Rabbinic Responses: Balancing Truthfulness and Respect before God." *JBQ* 38 (2010): 3–9.

Aquinas, Thomas. *Questiones Disputatae de Veritate*. Translated by R. W. Schmidt. Chicago: Regnery, 1954.

Augustine. *City of God*. NPNF 1/2.

———. *On Christian Teaching*. Translated by R. P. H. Green. Oxford: Oxford University Press, 1999.

———. *Saint Augustine on Genesis: Two Books on Genesis against the Manicheans and on the Literal Interpretation of Genesis*. Translated by Roland J. Teske. FC 84. Washington, DC: Catholic University of America Press, 1991.

Avishur, Yitzhak. *Studies in Hebrew and Ugaritic Psalms*. Jerusalem: Magnes, 1994.

Balentine, Samuel E. "Afterword." Pages 193–204 in *Seeking the Favor of God: Volume 1, The Origins of Penitential Prayer in Second Temple Judaism*. Edited by Mark J. Boda, Daniel F. Falk, and Rodney A. Werline. EJL. Atlanta: Society of Biblical Literature, 2006.

———. *Prayer in the Hebrew Bible: The Drama of Divine-Human Dialogue*. OBT. Minneapolis: Fortress, 1993.

Barr, James. *The Concept of Biblical Theology: An Old Testament Perspective*. London: SCM, 1999.

Bartholomew, Craig G. *Introducing Biblical Hermeneutics: A Comprehensive Framework for Hearing God in Scripture*. Grand Rapids: Baker Academic, 2015.

———. *Where Mortals Dwell: A Christian View of Place for Today*. Grand Rapids: Baker Academic, 2011.

Bartholomew, Craig G., and Heath A. Thomas, eds. *A Manifesto for Theological Interpretation*. Grand Rapids: Baker Academic, 2016.

Bartholomew, Craig G., and Ryan P. O'Dowd. *Old Testament Wisdom Literature: A Theological Introduction*. Downers Grove, IL: InterVarsity Press, 2011.

Barton, John. *The Nature of Biblical Criticism*. Louisville: Westminster John Knox, 2007.

———. *Reading the Old Testament: Method in Biblical Study*. London: Darton, Longman, & Todd, 1984.

Barton, Ruth Haley. *Sacred Rhythms: Arranging Our Lives for Spiritual Transformation*. Formatio. Downers Grove, IL: InterVarsity Press, 2006.

Bates, Matthew W. *The Birth of the Trinity: Jesus, God, and Spirit in New Testament and Early Christian Interpretations of Old Testament*. Oxford: Oxford University Press, 2015.

———. *Salvation by Allegiance Alone: Rethinking Faith, Works, and the Gospel of Jesus the King*. Grand Rapids: Baker Academic, 2017.

Bavinck, Hermann. *Our Reasonable Faith: A Survey of Christian Doctrine*. Translated by Henry Zylstra. Grand Rapids: Eerdmans, 1956.

Beale, G. K. *The Temple and the Church's Mission: A Biblical Theology of the Dwelling Place of God*. NSBT 17. Downers Grove, IL: InterVarsity Press, 2004.

Beck, Martin. *Der "Tag YHWHs" im Dodekapropheton: Studien im Spannungsfeld von Traditions- und Redaktionsgeschichte*. BZAW 356. Berlin: de Gruyter, 2005.

Bede, Venerable, *The Complete Works of Venerable Bede, In the Original Latin, Volume 9: Commentaries on the Scriptures*. Translated by John A. Giles. London: Whittaker and Company, 1846.

———. *On Tobit and the Canticle of Habakkuk*. Translated by Seán Connolly. Portland, OR: Four Courts Press, 1997.

Begrich, Joachim. "Das priesterliche Heilsorakel." *ZAW* 52 (1934): 81–92.

Beker, J. Christiaan. "Echoes and Intertextuality." Pages 64–69 in *Paul and the Scriptures of Israel*. Edited by Craig A. Evans and James A. Sanders. JSNTSup 83. Sheffield: JSOT Press, 1993.

Ben Zvi, Ehud. "Twelve Prophetic Books or 'The Twelve': A Few Preliminary Considerations." Pages 125–57 in *Forming Prophetic Literature: Essays on Isaiah and the Twelve in Honor of John D. W. Watts*. Edited by James W. Watts and Paul R. House. JSOTSup 235. Sheffield: JSOT Press, 1996.

Ben Zvi, Ehud, and James D. Nogalski. *Two Sides of a Coin: Juxtaposing Views on Interpreting the Book of the Twelve/the Twelve Prophetic Books*. Introduction by Thomas Römer. Analecta Gorgiana 201. Piscataway, NJ: Gorgias Press, 2009.

Berrigan, Daniel. *Minor Prophets, Major Themes*. Eugene, OR: Wipf & Stock, 2009.

Bier, Miriam J., and Tim Bulkeley, eds. *Spiritual Complaint: Theology and Practice of Lament*. Eugene, OR: Pickwick, 2013.

Billings, J. Todd. *The Word of God for the People of God: An Entryway to the Theological Interpretation of Scripture*. Grand Rapids: Eerdmans, 2010.

Bliese, Loren F. "The Poetics of Habakkuk." *JOTT* 12 (1999): 47–75.

Block, Daniel I. *The Book of Ezekiel: Chapters 1–24*. NICOT. Grand Rapids: Eerdmans, 1997.

———. "Preaching Old Testament Law to New Testament Christians." *STR* 3 (2012): 195–221.

Boda, Mark J., Daniel F. Falk, and Rodney A. Werline, eds. *Seeking the Favor of God: Volume 1, The Origins of Penitential Prayer in Second Temple Judaism*. EJL. Atlanta: Society of Biblical Literature, 2006.

Boersma, Hans. *Violence, Hospitality, and the Cross: Reappropriating the Atonement Tradition.* Grand Rapids: Baker Academic, 2004.

Bonhoeffer, Dietrich. *The Cost of Discipleship.* New York: Macmillan, 1963.

———. *Life Together/Prayerbook of the Bible.* DBWE 5. Minneapolis: Fortress, 2005.

Borght, Eduardus van der, ed. *The Unity of the Church: A Theological State of the Art and Beyond.* SRTh 18. Leiden: Brill, 2010.

Brown, Sally A., and Patrick D. Miller, eds. *Lament: Reclaiming Practices in Pulpit, Pew, and Public Square.* Louisville: Westminster John Knox, 2005.

Brown, William P. *The Ethos of the Cosmos: The Genesis of Moral Imagination in the Bible.* Grand Rapids: Eerdmans, 1999.

Browne, George Forrest. *The Venerable Bede: His Life and Works.* London: SPCK, 1919.

Broyles, Craig C. *The Conflict of Faith and Experience in the Psalms: A Form-Critical and Theological Study.* JSOTSup 52. Sheffield: JSOT Press, 1989.

Bruce, F. F. "Habakkuk." Pages 2:831–96 in *The Minor Prophets: An Exegetical and Expository Commentary.* Edited by Thomas E. McComisky. 3 vols. Grand Rapids: Baker, 1993.

Bruckner, James. *Jonah, Nahum, Habakkuk, Zephaniah.* NIVAC. Grand Rapids: Zondervan, 2004.

Brueggemann, Walter. *The Message of the Psalms: A Theological Commentary.* Minneapolis: Augsburg, 1984.

———. "Psalms and the Life of Faith: A Suggested Typology of Function." *JSOT* 17 (1980): 3–32.

Buber, Martin. *I and Thou.* Translated by R. G. Smith. 2nd ed. New York: Scribners, 1958.

———. *The Prophetic Faith.* New York: Macmillan, 1949.

Budde, K. "Die Bucher Habakuk und Zephanja." *TSK* 66 (1893): 383–93.

Calvin, John. *Commentaries on the First Book of Moses Called Genesis.* Vol. 1. Translated by John King. Repr., Grand Rapids: Baker, 2009.

———. *Commentaries on the Twelve Minor Prophets: Habakkuk, Zephaniah, Haggai.* Vol. 4. Translated by John Owen. Repr. Grand Rapids: Baker, 2009.

———. *The Institutes of the Christian Religion.* Trans. Henry Beveridge. Repr., Peabody, MA: Hendrickson, 2008.

Cameron-Mowat, Andrew. "Lamentations and Christian Worship." Pages 139–46 in *Great Is Thy Faithfulness? Reading Lamentations as Sacred Scripture.* Edited by Robin A. Parry and Heath A. Thomas. Eugene, OR: Pickwick, 2011.

Carroll, Robert P. "Eschatological Delay in the Prophetic Tradition?" *ZAW* 94 (1982): 47–58.

———. "Habakkuk." Pages 268–69 in *A Dictionary of Biblical Interpretation.* Edited by R. J. Coggins and J. L. Houlden. London: SCM, 1990.

Chambers, Oswald. *Conformed to His Image and the Servant as His Lord: Lessons on Living Like Jesus.* Grand Rapids: Discovery House, 1996.

Cherry, Conrad, ed. *God's New Israel: Religious Interpretations of American Destiny.* Englewood Cliffs, NJ: Prentice Hall, 1971.

Childs, Brevard S. *Introduction to the Old Testament as Scripture.* Philadelphia: Fortress, 1979.

Cleaver-Bartholomew, David. "An Alternative Approach to Hab 1,2–2,20." *SJOT* 17 (2003): 206–25.

Clendenin, Daniel B., ed. *Eastern Orthodox Theology: A Contemporary Reader.* Grand Rapids: Baker, 1995.

Coggins, Richard, and Jin H. Han. *Six Minor Prophets through the Centuries: Nahum, Habak-*

*kuk, Zephaniah, Haggai, Zechariah, and Malachi*. BBC. Chichester: Wiley-Blackwell, 2011.

Collett, Donald C. "Prophetic Intentionality and the Book of the Twelve: A Study in the Hermeneutics of Prophecy." PhD diss., University of St. Andrews, 2007.

Collins, John C. "The Zeal of Phinehas: The Bible and the Legitimation of Violence." *JBL* 122 (2003): 3–21.

Constantinou, Eugenia S. "Lamentations for the Lord: Great and Holy Friday in the Greek Orthodox Church." Pages 131–38 in *Great Is Thy Faithfulness? Reading Lamentations as Sacred Scripture*. Edited by Robin A. Parry and Heath A. Thomas. Eugene, OR: Pickwick, 2011.

Copeland Klepper, Deana. *The Insight of Unbelievers: Nicholas of Lyra and Christian Reading of Jewish Text in the Later Middle Ages*. JCC. Philadelphia: University of Pennsylvania Press, 2007.

Creach, Jerome F. D. *Violence in Scripture*. IBC. Louisville: Westminster John Knox, 2013.

Cyril of Alexandria. *Commentary on the Twelve Prophets*. Translated by Robert C. Hill. FC 116. Washington, DC: Catholic University of America Press, 2008.

Daly, Gabriel. *Asking the Father: A Study of the Prayer of Petition*. Wilmington, DE: Glazier, 1982.

Dangl, Oskar. "Habakkuk in Recent Research." *CurBS* 9 (2001): 131–68.

Day, John. *Psalms*. OTG. Sheffield: JSOT Press, 1992.

———. *Yahweh and the Gods and Goddesses of Canaan*. JSOTSup 265. Sheffield: Sheffield Academic, 2002.

Dennett, Daniel. *Breaking the Spell: Religion as a Natural Phenomenon*. New York: Penguin, 2006.

Dietrich, Walter. "Three Minor Prophets and the Major Empires: Synchronic and Diachronic Perspectives on Nahum, Habakkuk, and Zephaniah." Pages 147–57 in *Perspectives on the Formation of the Book of the Twelve: Methodological Foundations—Redactional Processes—Historical Insights*. Edited by Ranier Albertz, James D. Nogalski, and Jakob Wöhrle. BZAW 433. Berlin: de Gruyter, 2012.

Dorman, Ted M. "The Joint Declaration on the Doctrine of Justification: Retrospect and Prospects." *JETS* 44 (2001): 421–34.

Driver, G. R. "Hebrew Notes." *VT* 1 (1951): 241–50.

Duhm, Bernhard. *Das Buch Habakuk*. Tübingen: Mohr, 1906.

Eaton, John H. *Obadiah, Nahum, Habakkuk, and Zephaniah*. TBC. London: SCM, 1961.

———. "The Origin and Meaning of Habakkuk 3." *ZAW* 76 (1964): 144–71.

Ebner, Martin, Paul D. Hanson, Ottmar Fuchs, and Bernd Janowski, eds. *Klage*. JBTh 16. Neukirchen-Vluyn: Neukirchener Verlag, 2001.

Eichrodt, Walther. "Hat die alttestamentliche Theologie noch selbständige Bedeutung innerhalb der alttestamentlichen Wissenschaft?" *ZAW* 47 (1929): 83–91.

Eissfeldt, Otto. *The Old Testament: An Introduction*. Translated by Peter Ackroyd. San Francisco: Harper & Row, 1965.

Ellul, Jacques. *Hope in a Time of Abandonment*. Translated by C. Edward Hopkin. New York: Seabury, 1973.

———. *The Technological Society*. Translated by John Wilkinson. New York: Knopf, 1964.

Emerton, J. A. "The Textual and Linguistic Problems of Habakkuk II.4–5." *JTS* 28 (1977): 1–18.

Eszenyei Szeles, Mária. *Wrath and Mercy: A Commentary on the Books of Zephaniah and Habakkuk*. ITC. Grand Rapids: Eerdmans, 1987.

Evans, Jeremy. *The Problem of Evil: The Challenge to Essential Christian Beliefs*. BHSCA. Nashville: B&H Academic, 2013.

Eynde, Ceslas van den, ed. *Commentaire d'Išoʿdad de Merv sur l'Ancien Testament, IV. Isaïe et les Douze*. CSCO.S 128. Louvain: Secrétariat du CorpusSCO, 1969.

Feinberg, Charles L. *The Minor Prophets*. Chicago: Moody Press, 1990.

Ferreiro, Alberto. *The Twelve Prophets*. ACCS 14. Downers Grove, IL: InterVarsity Press, 2003.

Fiddes, Paul S. *The Creative Suffering of God*. Oxford: Clarendon, 1988.

———. *Participating in God: A Pastoral Doctrine of the Trinity*. Louisville: Westminster John Knox, 2000.

Filipović, Zlata. *Zlata's Diary: A Child's Life in Sarajevo*. New York: Penguin, 1995.

Fishbane, Michael A. *Biblical Text and Texture: A Literary Reading of Selected Texts*. New York: Schocken, 1979.

Fitzmyer, Joseph A. *The Biblical Commission's Document "The Interpretation of the Bible in the Church": Text and Commentary*. SubBi 18. Rome: Pontifical Biblical Institute, 1995.

Floyd, Michael H. *Minor Prophets: Part 2*. FOTL 22. Grand Rapids: Eerdmans, 2000.

———. "Prophecy and Writing in Habakkuk 2,1–5." *ZAW* 105 (1993): 470–90.

———. "Prophetic Complaints about the Fulfilment of Oracles in Habakkuk 1:2–17 and Jeremiah 15:10–18." *JBL* 110 (1991): 397–418.

Foot, Sarah. "Women, Prayer and Preaching in the Early English Church." Pages 59–76 in *Prayer and Thought in the Monastic Tradition: Essays in Honour of Benedicta Ward, SLG*. Edited by Santha Bhattacharji. London: Bloomsbury, 2014.

Fowl, Stephen. *Engaging Scripture: A Model for Theological Interpretation*. CCTh. Oxford: Blackwell, 1998.

———. *Theological Interpretation of Scripture*. Cascade Companions. Eugene, OR: Cascade, 2009.

Fox, Michael V. *Proverbs 10–31: A New Translation with Introduction and Commentary*. AB 18B. New Haven: Yale University Press, 2009.

Freud, Sigmund. "A Child Is Being Beaten: A Contribution to the Study of the Origin of Sexual Perversions (1919)." Pages 17:179–204 in *The Standard Edition of the Complete Psychological Works of Sigmund Freud*. Edited by James Strachey. London: Hogart, 1957.

Gadamer, Hans-Georg. *Truth and Method*. Translated by Joel Weinsheimer and Donald G. Marshall. 2nd ed. New York: Continuum, 2002.

Garrett, James Leo, Jr. *Systematic Theology: Biblical, Historical, and Evangelical*. Vol. 2. Grand Rapids: Eerdmans, 1995.

Girard, René. *I See Satan Fall Like Lightning*. Maryknoll, NY: Orbis, 2001.

Goheen, Michael, and Michael Williams. "Doctrine of Scripture and Theological Interpretation." Pages 48–71 in *A Manifesto for Theological Interpretation*. Edited by Craig G. Bartholomew and Heath A. Thomas. Grand Rapids: Baker Academic, 2016.

Goudzwaard, Bob, Mark Vander Vennen, and David Van Heemst. *Hope in Troubled Times: A New Vision for Confronting Global Crises*. Grand Rapids: Baker Academic, 2007.

Gowan, Donald E. *The Triumph of Faith in Habakkuk*. Atlanta: John Knox, 1976.

Gross, Walter, and Karl-Josef Kuschel. *'Ich schaffe Finsternis und Unheil!' Ist Gott verantwortlich für das Übel?* 2nd ed. Mainz: Grunewald, 1995.

Guillaume, Philippe. "A Reconsideration of Manuscripts Classified as Scrolls of the Twelve

Minor Prophets (XII)." *JHS* 7 (2007): 2–10. http://www.jhsonline.org/Articles/article_77.pdf

Gunkel, Hermann, and Joachim Begrich. *An Introduction to the Psalms: The Genres of the Religious Lyric of Israel.* Translated by James D. Nogalski. MLBS. Macon, GA: Mercer University Press, 1998.

Haak, Robert D. *Habakkuk.* VTSup 44. Leiden: Brill, 1992.

Haimo of Halberstadt. *Enarratio in duodecim prophetas minores.* PL 117.

Hamman, Jaco. "The Rod of Discipline: Masochism, Sadism, and the Judeo-Christian Religion." *JRHe* 39 (2000): 319–27.

Harasta, Eva, and Brian Brock, eds. *Evoking Lament: A Theological Discussion.* London: T&T Clark, 2009.

Harris, Sam. *The End of Faith: Religion, Terror, and the Future of Reason.* New York: Norton, 2004.

Haupt, Paul. "The Poems of Habakkuk." *Johns Hopkins University Circular* 39/325 (1920): 680–84.

Hauser, Alan J. "Judges 5: Parataxis in Hebrew Poetry." *JBL* 99 (1980): 23–41.

Hays, Richard B. *The Conversion of the Imagination: Paul as Interpreter of Israel's Scripture.* Grand Rapids: Eerdmans, 2005.

Henry, Matthew. *The Comprehensive Commentary on the Holy Bible: Vol. 3; Psalm LXIV–Malachi.* Edited by William Jenks. Philadelphia: Lippincott, 1849.

Heschel, Abraham J. *The Prophets: An Introduction.* Vol. 1. New York: Harper, 1962.

Hick, John. *Evil and the God of Love.* 2nd ed. San Francisco: Harper-Collins, 1977.

Hiebert, Theodore. *God of My Victory: The Ancient Hymn in Habakkuk 3.* HSM 38. Atlanta: Scholars Press, 1986.

———. *The Yahwist's Landscape: Nature and Religion in Early Israel.* Oxford: Oxford University Press, 1996.

House, Paul R. *The Unity of the Twelve.* JSOTSup 97. Sheffield: Almond Press, 1990.

Houtman, Cornelius. *Exodus.* 4 vols. HCOT. Leuven: Peeters, 1993–2002.

Howard, George E. "The Twelve Prophets." Pages 807–10 in *A New English Translation of the Septuagint.* Edited by Albert Pietersma and Benjamin E. Wright. Oxford: Oxford University Press, 2007.

Huff Byrne, Patricia. "'Give Sorrow Words': Lament—Contemporary Need for Job's Old Time Religion." *Journal for Pastoral Care & Counseling* 56 (2002): 255–64.

Hughes, Henry Trevor. *Prophetic Prayer: A History of the Christian Doctrine of Prayer to the Reformation.* London: Epworth, 1947.

Irenaeus. *The Demonstration of the Apostolic Preaching.* Translated by J. Armitage Robinson. London: SPCK, 1920.

———. *Five Books of Saint Irenaeus against Heresies.* Translated by John Keble. Oxford: Parker, 1872.

Janowski, Bernd. *Konfliktgespräche mit Gott: Eine Anthropologie der Psalmen.* Neukirchen-Vluyn: Neukirchener Verlag, 2003.

Jepsen, A. "חָזָה." *TDOT* 4:280–90

Jerome. *Commentaries on the Twelve Prophets: Volume 1.* Edited by Thomas P. Scheck. Ancient Christian Texts. Downers Grove, IL: InterVarsity Press, 2016.

———. *Commentarii in Prophetas Minores.* CCSL 76, 76a. Turnholt: Brepols, 1969–1970.

Jervis, L. Ann. *At the Heart of the Gospel: Suffering in the Earliest Christian Message*. Grand Rapids: Eerdmans, 2007.

Jöcken, Peter. *Das Buch Habakuk: Darstellung der Geschichte seiner kritischen Erforschung mit einer eigenen Beurteilung*. BBB 48. Bonn: Hanstein, 1977.

Johnson, Marshall D. "The Paralysis of Torah in Habakkuk I 4." *VT* 35 (1985): 257–66.

Kass, Leon R. *The Beginning of Wisdom: Reading Genesis*. Chicago: University of Chicago Press, 2006.

Katongole, Emmanuel, and Chris Rice. *Reconciling All Things: A Christian Vision for Justice, Peace, and Healing*. Downers Grove, IL: InterVarsity Press, 2008.

Kaufmann, Yehezkel. *The Religion of Israel: From Its Beginnings to the Babylonian Exile*. Translated by Moshe Greenberg. Chicago: University of Chicago Press, 1960.

Kealy, Sean P. *An Interpretation of the Twelve Minor Prophets of the Hebrew Bible: The Emergence of Eschatology as a Major Theme*. Lewiston, NY: Mellen, 2009.

Keil, Carl F. *The Twelve Minor Prophets*. Vol. 2. Translated by James Martin. Edinburgh: T&T Clark, 1878.

Keller, Timothy. *The Reason for God: Belief in an Age of Skepticism*. New York: Dutton, 2008.

Kessler, Ranier. "Nahum-Habakuk als Zweiprophetenschrift: Ein Skizze." Pages 137–45 in *Gotteserdung: Beitrage zur Hermeneutik und Exegese der Hebraischen Bibel*. Edited by Ranier Kessler. BWANT 170. Stuttgart: Kohlhammer, 2006.

Klink, Edward W., III, and Darian R. Lockett. *Understanding Biblical Theology: A Comparison of Theory and Practice*. Grand Rapids: Zondervan, 2012.

Ko, Grace. *Theodicy in Habakkuk*. PBM. Milton Keynes: Paternoster, 2014.

König, Adrio. *The Eclipse of Christ in Eschatology: Toward a Christ-Centered Approach*. Grand Rapids: Eerdmans, 1989.

————. *New and Greater Things: Re-Evaluating the Biblical Message on Creation*. StOri 1. Pretoria: University of South Africa, 1988.

Kraus, Wolfgang. "Hab. 2:3–4 in the Hebrew Tradition and in the Septuagint, with Its Reception in the New Testament." Pages 97–118 in *Septuagint and Reception: Essays Prepared for the Association for the Study of the Septuagint in South Africa*. Edited by Johann Cook. VTSup 127. Leiden: Brill, 2009.

Krey, Philip D. W., and Lesley Smith, eds. *Nicholas of Lyra: The Senses of Scripture*. SCHT 90. Leiden: Brill, 2000.

Laetsch, Theodore. *The Minor Prophets*. St. Louis: Concordia, 1956.

Laird, Martin. *Into the Silent Land: A Guide to the Christian Practice of Contemplation*. Oxford: Oxford University Press, 2006.

Laytner, Anson. *Arguing with God: A Jewish Tradition*. Lanham, MD: Rowman and Littlefield, 1990.

Lecureaux, Jason. "The Thematic Unity of the Book of the Twelve: The Call to Return and the Nature of the Minor Prophets." PhD diss., University of Gloucestershire, 2010.

Lee, Bae Gil. "A Developing Messianic Understanding of Habakkuk 2:3–5 in the New Testament in the Context of Early Jewish Writings." PhD diss., Southwestern Baptist Theological Seminary, 1997.

Lescow, Theodore. "Die Komposition der Bucher Nahum und Habakkuk." *BN* 77 (1995): 59–85.

Levenson, Jon D. *Resurrection and the Restoration of Israel: The Ultimate Victory of the God of Life*. New Haven: Yale University Press, 2006.

Lewis, Alan E. *Between Cross and Resurrection: A Theology of Holy Saturday.* Grand Rapids: Eerdmans, 2001.

Lewis, C. S. *Letters to Malcolm: Chiefly on Prayer.* London: Bles, 1964.

Liere, Frans van. "Andrew of Saint-Victor and His Franciscan Critics." Pages 291–310 in *The Multiple Meaning of Scripture: The Role of Exegesis in Early-Christian and Medieval Culture.* Edited by Ineke van't Spijker. Leiden: Brill, 2009.

Lipschits, Oded. *The Fall and Rise of Jerusalem: Judah under Babylonian Rule.* Winona Lake, IN: Eisenbrauns, 2005.

Luther, Martin. *Lectures on Romans.* Edited by Wilhelm Pauck. LCC. Louisville: Westminster John Knox, 2006.

———. *Luther's Works, Volume 19: Lectures on the Minor Prophets II.* Edited by Hilton C. Oswald. St. Louis: Concordia, 1974.

Lutheran World Federation and the Roman Catholic Church. *Joint Declaration on the Doctrine of Justification.* Grand Rapids: Eerdmans, 1999. Accessible online at the Lutheran World Federation and Vatican web sites.

Magrassi, Mariano. *Praying the Bible: An Introduction to Lectio Divina.* Collegeville, MN: Liturgical Press, 1998.

Mandolfo, Carleen. *God in the Dock: Dialogic Tension in the Psalms of Lament.* JSOTSup 357. London: Sheffield Academic, 2002.

Mann, Thomas W. *The Book of the Torah: The Narrative Integrity of the Pentateuch.* Atlanta: John Knox, 1988.

McCann, J. Clinton, Jr. *A Theological Introduction to the Book of Psalms: The Psalms as Torah.* Nashville: Abingdon, 1993.

McCarthy, Carmel. *The Tiqqune Sopherim and Other Theological Corrections in the Masoretic Text of the Old Testament.* OBO 36. Fribourg: Presses Universitaires; Göttingen: Vandenhoeck & Ruprecht, 1981.

McConville, J. Gordon. *Deuteronomy.* ApOTC 5. Leicester: Apollos, 2002.

———. "The Judgment of God in the Old Testament." *ExAud* 20 (2004): 25–42.

———. *Law and Theology in Deuteronomy.* JSOTSup 33. Sheffield: JSOT Press, 1984.

McKeown, James. *Genesis.* THOTC. Grand Rapids: Eerdmans, 2008.

Meier, Samuel A. *Themes and Transformations in Old Testament Prophecy.* Downers Grove, IL: InterVarsity Press, 2009.

Milikowsky, Chaim. "Seder Olam." Pages 231–37 in *The Literature of the Sages: Second Part.* Edited by S. Safrai et al. CRINT 3b. Assen: Van Gorcum, 2006.

Miller, J. Maxwell, and John H. Hayes. *A History of Ancient Israel and Judah.* London: SCM, 1986.

Miller, Patrick D. "Prayer as Persuasion: The Rhetoric and Intention of Prayer." *Word & World* 13 (1993): 356–62.

Mintz, Alan. *Hurban: Responses to Catastrophe in Hebrew Literature.* Syracuse, NY: Syracuse University Press, 1996.

Moltmann, Jürgen. *The Crucified God: The Cross of Christ as the Foundation and Criticism of Christian Theology.* Translated by R. A. Wilson and J. Bowden. Minneapolis: Fortress, 1993.

Moor, Janny de. "In the Beginning Was Fish: Fish in the Ancient Near East." Pages 84–93 in *Fish: Food from the Waters; Proceedings of the Oxford Symposium on Food and Cookery 1997.* Edited by Harlan Walker. Totnes: Prospect, 1998.

Morrow, William S. *Protest against God: The Eclipse of a Biblical Tradition.* HBM 4. Sheffield: Sheffield Phoenix, 2006.

Mowinckel, Sigmund. *The Psalms in Israel's Worship.* Translated by D. R. Ap-Thomas. 2 vols. Nashville: Abingdon, 1962.

Mulroney, James A. E. "Revisiting Hab. 2:4 and Its Place in the New Testament Eschatological Vision." *STR* 6 (2015): 3–28.

Newbigin, Lesslie. *Signs amid the Rubble: The Purposes of God in Human History.* Introduction by Geoffrey Wainwright. Grand Rapids: Eerdmans, 2003.

Nogalski, James D. *The Book of the Twelve: Micah–Malachi.* SHBC. Macon, GA: Smyth & Helwys, 2011.

———. *Literary Precursors to the Book of the Twelve.* BZAW 217. Berlin: de Gruyter, 1993.

———. *Redactional Processes in the Book of the Twelve.* BZAW 218. Berlin: de Gruyter, 1993.

Nouwen, Henri J. M. *The Inner Voice of Love: A Journey through Anguish to Freedom.* New York: Doubleday, 1996.

Ntamushobora, Faustin. *From Trials to Triumphs: The Voice of Habakkuk to the Suffering African Christian.* Eugene, OR: Wipf & Stock, 2009.

Olson, Dennis T. "Sacred Time: The Sabbath and Christian Worship." Pages 2–34 in *Touching the Altar: The Old Testament for Christian Worship.* Edited by Carol M. Bechtel. Grand Rapids: Eerdmans, 2008.

O'Neal, G. Michael. *Interpreting Habakkuk as Scripture: An Application of the Canonical Approach of Brevard S. Childs.* StBibLit 9. New York: Lang, 2007.

Origen. *Prayer/Exhortation to Martyrdom.* Translated and annotated by John J. O'Meara. ACW 19. New York: Newman Press, 1954.

Pardee, Dennis. "*yph* 'Witness' in Hebrew and Ugaritic." *VT* 28 (1978): 204–13.

Patterson, Richard. "Habakkuk." Pages 395–444 in *Minor Prophets: Hosea–Malachi.* Edited by Philip Comfort. Cornerstone Biblical Commentary 10. Carol Stream, IL: Tyndale, 2008.

———. "A Literary Look at Nahum, Habakkuk, and Zephaniah." *GTJ* 11 (1991): 17–27.

———. *Nahum Habakkuk Zephaniah: An Exegetical Commentary.* Richardson, TX: Biblical Studies Press, 2003.

Peck, M. Scott. *People of the Lie: The Hope for Healing Human Evil.* New York: Simon & Schuster, 1983.

Perlitt, Lothar. *Die Propheten Nahum, Habakuk, Zephanja.* ATD 25/1. Göttingen: Vandenhoeck & Ruprecht, 2004.

Peterson, David G. *The Acts of the Apostles.* PNTCS. Grand Rapids: Eerdmans, 2009.

Peterson, David L. "A Book of the Twelve?" Pages 1–10 in *Reading and Hearing the Book of the Twelve.* Edited by James D. Nogalski and Marvin A. Sweeney. SymS 15. Atlanta: Society of Biblical Literature, 2000.

Peterson, Eugene H. *Christ Plays in Ten Thousand Places: A Conversation in Spiritual Theology.* Grand Rapids: Eerdmans, 2005.

———. *Eat This Book: A Conversation in the Art of Spiritual Reading.* Grand Rapids: Eerdmans, 2006.

———. *Reversed Thunder: The Revelation of John and the Praying Imagination.* San Francisco: Harper San Francisco, 1991.

Plantinga, Cornelius, Jr. *Not the Way It's Supposed to Be: A Breviary of Sin.* Grand Rapids: Eerdmans, 1995.

Polke, Christian. "God, Lament, Contingency: An Essay in Fundamental Theology." Pages 44–58 in *Evoking Lament: A Theological Discussion*. Edited by Eva Harasta and Brian Brock. London: T&T Clark, 2009.

Poole, Matthew. *Annotations upon the Holy Bible*. 4th ed. Vol. 2. London: Poultrey, 1700.

Prinsloo, Gert T. M. "Life for the Righteous, Doom for the Wicked: Reading Habakkuk from a Wisdom Perspective." *SK* 23 (2000): 621–40.

Pusey, Edward B. *The Minor Prophets: With a Commentary Explanatory and Practical and Introductions to the Several Books*. Oxford: Parker, 1860.

Quarles, Charles L. "From Faith to Faith: A Fresh Examination of the Prepositional Series in Romans 1:17." *NovT* 45 (2003): 1–21.

Rad, Gerhard von. *The Message of the Prophets*. London: SCM, 1969.

Rae, Murray. "Theological Interpretation and Historical Criticism." Pages 94–109 in *A Manifesto for Theological Interpretation*. Edited by Craig G. Bartholomew and Heath A. Thomas. Grand Rapids: Baker Academic, 2016.

Rahner, Karl. "Scripture and Theology." Pages 89–97 in *Theological Investigations: Volume 6*. Baltimore: Helicon, 1969.

Redditt, Paul. *Introduction to the Prophets*. Grand Rapids: Eerdmans, 2008.

Redditt, Paul L., and Aaron Schart, eds. *Thematic Threads in the Book of the Twelve*. BZAW 325. Berlin: de Gruyter, 2003.

Rendtorff, Rolf. "Alas for the Day! The 'Day of the LORD' in the Book of the Twelve." Pages 186–97 in *God in the Fray: A Tribute to Walter Brueggemann*. Edited by Tod Linafelt and Timothy K. Beal. Minneapolis: Fortress, 1998.

Roberts, J. J. M. *Nahum, Habakkuk, and Zephaniah*. OTL. Louisville: Westminster John Knox, 1991.

Robertson, O. Palmer. *The Books of Nahum, Habakkuk, and Zephaniah*. NICOT. Grand Rapids: Eerdmans, 1990.

Rudolph, William. *Micah, Nahum, Habakuk, Zephanja*. KAT 13/3. Gütersloh: Mohn, 1975.

Sailhamer, John H. *Introduction to Old Testament Theology: A Canonical Approach*. Grand Rapids: Zondervan, 1995.

Satz, Ronald. N. *American Indian Policy in the Jacksonian Era*. Norman: University of Oklahoma Press, 2002.

Sawyer, John F. A. *Prophecy and Prophets of the Old Testament*. OBS. Oxford: Oxford University Press, 1987.

Schart, Aaron. *Die Entstehung des Zwölfprophetenbuchs: Neubearbeitungen von Amos im Rahmen schriftenübergreifender Redaktionsprozesse*. BZAW 260. Berlin: de Gruyter, 1998.

Schwartz, Regina M. *The Curse of Cain: The Violent Legacy of Monotheism*. Chicago: University of Chicago Press, 1998.

Seitz, Christopher R. *The Character of Christian Scripture: The Significance of a Two-Testament Bible*. STI. Grand Rapids: Baker Academic, 2011.

———. *Prophecy and Hermeneutics: Toward a New Introduction to the Prophets*. STI. Grand Rapids: Baker Academic, 2007.

Sertillanges, Antonin-Dalmace. *The Intellectual Life: Its Spirit, Conditions, Methods*. Translated by Mary Perkins Ryan. Washington, DC: Catholic University of America Press, 1998.

Seybold, Klaus. *Nahum Habakuk Zephanja*. ZBK 24/2. Zurich: TVZ, 1991.

Shakespeare, William. "Hamlet, Prince of Denmark." In *The Complete Works of Shakespeare*. Edited by David Bevington. 4th ed. New York: HarperCollins, 1992.

Shaw, Bernard. *John Bull's Other Island and Major Barbara*. New York: Brentano's, 1911.

Shepherd, Michael B. "Compositional Analysis of the Twelve." *ZAW* 120 (2008): 184–93.

Skehan, Patrick W., and Alexander A. di Lella. *The Wisdom of Ben Sira*. AB 39. New York: Doubleday, 1987.

Smith, George Adam. *The Book of the Twelve Prophets, Commonly Called the Minor*. Vol. 2. New York: Armstrong and Son, 1902.

Smith, James K. A. *Desiring the Kingdom: Worship, Worldview, and Cultural Formation*. Cultural Liturgies 1. Grand Rapids: Baker Academic, 2009.

Spykman, Gordon J. *Reformational Theology: A New Paradigm for Doing Dogmatics*. Grand Rapids: Eerdmans, 1992.

Steiner, George. *Grammars of Creation: Originating in the Gifford Lectures of 1990*. London: Faber and Faber, 2001.

Stewart-Sykes, Alistair, ed. *On the Lord's Prayer: Tertullian, Cyprian, and Origen*. PPS 29. Crestwood, NY: St. Vladamir's Seminary Press, 2004.

Stiver, Dan R. *Life Together in the Way of Jesus Christ: An Introduction to Christian Theology*. Waco, TX: Baylor University Press, 2009.

Strawn, Brent A. "With a Strong Hand and an Outstretched Arm: On the Meaning(s) of the Exodus Tradition(s)." Pages 103–16 in *Iconographic Exegesis of the Hebrew Bible/Old Testament: An Introduction to Its Method and Practice*. Edited by Izaak J. de Hulster, Brent A. Strawn, and Ryan P. Bonfiglio. Gottingen: Vandenhoeck & Ruprecht, 2015.

Stuhlmacher, Peter. *Paul's Letter to the Romans: A Commentary*. Louisville: Westminster John Knox, 1994.

Stumme, Wayne, ed. *The Gospel of Justification in Christ: Where Does the Church Stand Today?* Grand Rapids: Eerdmans, 2006.

Suderman, W. Derek. "Are Individual Complaint Psalms Really Prayers? Recognizing Social Address as Characteristic of Individual Complaints." Pages 153–70 in *The Bible as a Human Witness to Divine Revelation: Hearing the Word of God through Historically Dissimilar Traditions*. Edited by Randall Heskett and Brian Irwin. LHBOTS 469. London: T&T Clark, 2010.

Sulavik, Andrew T. *Guillelmi de Luxi Postilla super Baruch, Postilla super Ionam*. CCCM 219. Turnhout: Brepols, 2006.

Sweeney, Marvin A. "Structure, Genre, and Intent in the Book of Habakkuk." *VT* 41 (1991): 63–83.

———. *The Twelve Prophets*. 2 vols. Berit Olam. Collegeville, MN: Liturgical Press, 2000.

Swenson, Kristin M. *Living through Pain: Psalms and the Search for Wholeness*. Waco, TX: Baylor University Press, 2005.

Theodore of Mopsuestia. *Commentary on the Twelve Prophets*. Edited by Robert C. Hill. FC 108. Washington, DC: Catholic University of America Press, 2004.

Theodoret of Cyrus. *Commentaries on the Prophets*. Translated and introduction by Robert Charles Hill. Commentary on the Twelve Prophets 3. Brookline, MA: Holy Cross Orthodox Press, 2006.

Theophylact of Bulgaria. *Expositio in prophetam Habacuc*. PG 126:819–906.

Tholuck, Friedrich August Gottreu. "On the Hypothesis of the Egyptian or Indian Origin of the Name Jehovah." *Biblical Repository* 4 (1834): 89–108.

Thomas, Heath A. "Divine Violence, Pain, and Prayer in Lamentations." Pages 91–111 in *Wrestling with the Violence of God: Soundings in the Old Testament*. Edited by M. Daniel Carroll R. and J. Blair Wilgus. BBRS 10. Winona Lake, IN: Eisenbrauns, 2015.

———. *Faith amid the Ruins: The Book of Habakkuk*. Bellingham, WA: Lexham Press, 2016.

———. "Hearing the Minor Prophets: The Book of the Twelve and God's Address." Pages 356–79 In *Hearing the Old Testament: Listening for God's Address*. Edited by Craig G. Bartholomew and David H. Beldman Grand Rapids: Eerdmans, 2012.

———. "'I Will Hope in Him': Theology and Hope in Lamentations." Pages 203–21 in *A God of Faithfulness: Essays in Honour of J. Gordon McConville on His 60th Birthday*. Edited by Jamie A. Grant, Alison Lo, and Gordon J. Wenham. LHBOTS 538. London: T&T Clark, 2011.

———. "Life and Death in Deuteronomy." Pages 177–93 in *Interpreting Deuteronomy: Issues and Approaches*. Edited by David G. Firth and Philip S. Johnston. Nottingham: Apollos, 2012.

———. *Poetry and Theology in the Book of Lamentations: The Aesthetics of an Open Text*. HBM 47. Sheffield: Sheffield Phoenix, 2013.

———. "Relating Prayer and Pain: Psychological Analysis and Lamentations Research." *TynBul* 61 (2010): 183–208.

———. "Zion." Pages 907–14 in *Dictionary of the Old Testament: Prophets*. Edited by J. Gordon McConville and Mark J. Boda. Downers Grove, IL: InterVarsity Press, 2012.

Thompson, Michael E. W. "Prayer, Oracle, and Theophany: The Book of Habakkuk." *TynBul* 44 (1993): 33–53.

Torrey, Charles C. "The Prophecy of Habakkuk." Pages 565–82 in *Jewish Studies in Memory of George A. Kohut*. Edited by Salo W. Baron and Alexander Marx. New York: Alexander Kohut Memorial Foundation, 1935.

Toulmin, Stephen. *Cosmopolis: The Hidden Agenda of Modernity*. Chicago: University of Chicago Press, 1992.

Troxel, Ronald L. *Prophetic Literature: From Oracles to Books*. Chichester: Wiley-Blackwell, 2012.

Tuell, Steven. *Reading Nahum–Malachi: A Literary and Theological Commentary*. Macon, GA: Smyth & Helwys, 2016.

Vanderhooft, David S. "Babylonian Strategies of Imperial Control in the West: Royal Practice and Rhetoric." Pages 235–62 in *Judah and the Judeans in the Neo-Babylonian Period*. Edited by Oded Lipschits and Joseph Blenkinsopp. Winona Lake, IN: Eisenbrauns, 2003.

———. *The Neo-Babylonian Empire and Babylon in the Latter Prophets*. HSM 59. Atlanta: Scholars Press, 1999.

———. "The תוכחת, 'Disputation' of Habakkuk as a Contrarian Argument in the Book of the Twelve." Paper presented at the Annual Meeting of the Society of Biblical Literature. Atlanta, Georgia, 20 November 2010.

Wal, A. J. O van der. "*Lo' namut* in Habakkuk I 12: A Suggestion." *VT* 38 (1988): 480–83.

Watson, Francis. *Paul and the Hermeneutics of Faith*. London: T&T Clark, 2004.

———. *Text and Truth: Redefining Biblical Theology*. Grand Rapids: Eerdmans, 1997.

Watts, Rikki E. "For I Am Not Ashamed of the Gospel: Romans 1:16–17 and Habakkuk 2:4." Pages 3–25 in *Romans and the People of God: Essays in Honor of Gordon D. Fee on the*

*Occasion of His 65th Birthday.* Edited by Sven K. Soderlund and N. T. Wright. Grand Rapids: Eerdmans, 1999.

Weis, Richard D. "A Definition of the Genre *Massa'* in the Hebrew Bible." PhD diss., Emory University, 1986.

Weiss, Dov. *Pious Irreverence: Confronting God in Rabbinic Judaism.* Divinations. Philadelphia: University of Pennsylvania Press, 2017.

Westermann, Claus. *Basic Forms of Prophetic Speech.* Translated by Hugh C. White. Cambridge: Lutterworth, 1991.

———. *Praise and Lament in the Psalms.* Translated by Keith R. Crim and Richard N. Soulen. Atlanta: John Knox, 1981.

Widmer, Michael. *Standing in the Breach: An Old Testament Theology and Spirituality of Intercessory Prayer.* Siphrut 13. Winona Lake, IN: Eisenbrauns, 2015.

Williams, Michael D. *Far as the Curse Is Found: The Covenant Story of Redemption.* Phillipsburg, NJ: P&R Publishing, 2005.

———. "Systematic Theology as a Biblical Discipline." Pages 167–96 in *All for Jesus: A Celebration of the 50th Anniversary of Covenant Theological Seminary.* Edited by Robert A. Peterson and Sean Michael Lucas. Fearn: Mentor, 2006.

Witherington, Ben, III. *The Collective Witness.* Vol. 2 of *The Indelible Image: The Theological and Ethical Thought World of the New Testament.* Downers Grove, IL: InterVarsity Press, 2010.

Wolterstorff, Nicholas. *Until Justice and Peace Embrace.* Grand Rapids: Eerdmans, 1983.

Wright, N. T. *Jesus and the Victory of God.* COQG 2. London: SPCK, 1996.

———. *The New Testament and the People of God.* COQG 1. Minneapolis: Fortress, 1992.

Wünsche August, ed. *Midrasch Tehillim: Oder haggadische Erlkärung der Psalmen.* Vol. 1. Trier: Mayer, 1892.

Wüthrich, Matthias. *Gott und das Nichtige: Eine Untersuchung zur Rede vom Nichtigen ausgehend von §50 der Kirchlichen Dogmatik Karl Barths.* Zurich: TVZ, 2006.

———. "Lament for Naught? An Inquiry into the Suppression of Lament in Systematic Theology: On the Example of Karl Barth." Pages 60–76 in *Evoking Lament: A Theological Discussion.* Edited by Eva Harasta and Brian Brock. London: T&T Clark, 2009.

Zuckerman, Paul. *Faith No More: Why People Reject Religion.* Oxford: Oxford University Press, 2012.

# Author Index

# Subject Index

# Scripture Index

**1 Kings**

| | |
|---|---|
| 5:4 | 183 |
| 5:5 | 183 |
| 8:56 | 183 |
| 18 | 7 |

**2 Kings**

| | |
|---|---|
| 4:16 | 12 |
| 21:1–16 | 27 |
| 21:23–24 | 83 |
| 22–23 | 25 |
| 23:37–24:6 | 25 |
| 24:4 | 65 |

**1 Chronicles**

| | |
|---|---|
| 22:9–10 | 183 |
| 22:18–19 | 183 |
| 23:25–26 | 183 |

**2 Chronicles**

| | |
|---|---|
| 7:6 | 12 |
| 8:14 | 12 |
| 35:2 | 12 |

**Ezra**

| | |
|---|---|
| 9:4 | 151 |

**Nehemiah**

| | |
|---|---|
| 3:26 | 113 |
| 13:30 | 12 |

**Job**

| | |
|---|---|
| 2:9 | 72 |
| 3 | 86 |
| 5:6 | 66 |
| 9:21–24 | 86 |
| 9:28–31 | 61 |
| 10:2 | 68 |
| 10:2–22 | 61 |
| 13:6 | 102 |
| 13:17–28 | 61 |
| 13:24 | 68, 196 |
| 14:1–22 | 61 |
| 16:2 | 211 |
| 17:4 | 61 |
| 19:1 | 64 |
| 19:7 | 64 |

| | |
|---|---|
| 23:4 | 102 |
| 24:8 | 12 |
| 30:20 | 196 |
| 30:20–21 | 68 |
| 30:20–31:40 | 61 |
| 31:14 | 100 |
| 31:35 | 196 |
| 38–40 | 86 |
| 38–41 | 61 |
| 42:7–8 | 211 |

**Psalms**

| | |
|---|---|
| 4 | 143 |
| 6 | 143 |
| 7 | 143 |
| 7:1 | 12 |
| 7:6 | 67, 83 |
| 7:9 | 28 |
| 11:4 | 36, 133 |
| 13:1 | 196 |
| 13:3 | 196 |
| 15 | 112 |
| 17:1 | 67 |
| 18:33 | 36, 152 |
| 22 | 61, 160 |
| 22:1 | 67, 206 |
| 27:4 | 196 |
| 27:7 | 196 |
| 27:12 | 106 |
| 37 | 28 |
| 37:4 | 151 |
| 38:15 | 102 |
| 44 | 61, 197 |
| 44:23 | 68 |
| 44:24 | 196 |
| 46:10 | 138 |
| 48:1 | 189 |
| 54 | 143 |
| 55:2 | 196 |
| 69:16–17 | 196 |
| 72 | 26 |
| 73:16 | 66 |
| 74 | 61, 68 |
| 75:8 | 123 |
| 75:10 | 123 |
| 78 | 149 |
| 78:1 | 82 |

| | |
|---|---|
| 78:22 | 80 |
| 78:32 | 80 |
| 78:39 | 89 |
| 78:48 | 146 |
| 85:10 | 173, 186 |
| 85:10–12 | 173 |
| 86:1 | 196 |
| 88 | 61, 197 |
| 88:14 | 196 |
| 90 | 39 |
| 94:2 | 68 |
| 96:9 | 151 |
| 99:1 | 151 |
| 99:1–5 | 189 |
| 102:2 | 196 |
| 106 | 149 |
| 114 | 149 |
| 114:7 | 151 |
| 119:45 | 196 |
| 139 | 192 |
| 143:7 | 196 |

**Proverbs**

| | |
|---|---|
| 1:8 | 79 |
| 3:1 | 82 |
| 3:12 | 88 |
| 3:19–20 | 175 |
| 4:2 | 82 |
| 6:20 | 82 |
| 6:23 | 82 |
| 7:2 | 82 |
| 8 | 82 |
| 10–15 | 28 |
| 12:17 | 106 |
| 13:14 | 82 |
| 14:5 | 106 |
| 14:25 | 106 |
| 14:27 | 82 |
| 18:10 | 108 |
| 19:5 | 106 |
| 19:9 | 106 |
| 21:24 | 123 |
| 28:18 | 104 |

**Ecclesiastes**

| | |
|---|---|
| 5:1 | 102 |
| 7:20 | 93 |